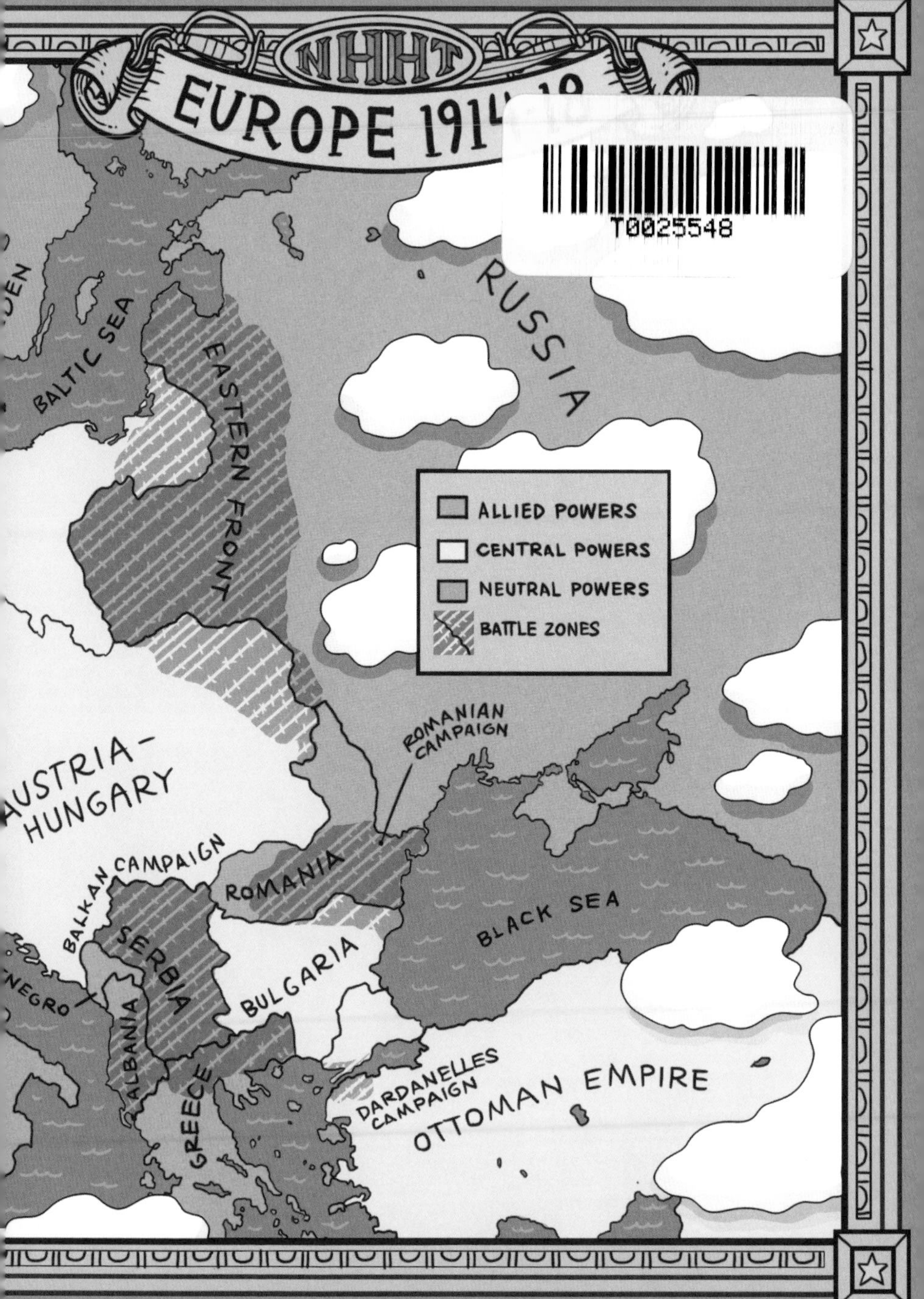
NHHT
EUROPE 1914
RUSSIA
BALTIC SEA
EASTERN FRONT
ALLIED POWERS
CENTRAL POWERS
NEUTRAL POWERS
BATTLE ZONES
ROMANIAN CAMPAIGN
AUSTRIA-HUNGARY
BALKAN CAMPAIGN
ROMANIA
BLACK SEA
SERBIA
BULGARIA
ALBANIA
GREECE
DARDANELLES CAMPAIGN
OTTOMAN EMPIRE

CATALOGING—IN—PUBLICATION DATA HAS BEEN APPLIED FOR AND MAY BE
OBTAINED FROM THE LIBRARY OF CONGRESS.

ISBN 978-1-4197-4952-0

TEXT AND ILLUSTRATIONS © 2023 NATHAN HALE
BOOK DESIGN BY NATHAN HALE AND CHARICE SILVERMAN

PRINTED AND BOUND IN U.S.A.
10 9 8 7 6 5 4 3 2

AMULET BOOKS ARE AVAILABLE AT SPECIAL DISCOUNTS WHEN PURCHASED
IN QUANTITY FOR PREMIUMS AND PROMOTIONS AS WELL AS FUNDRAISING
OR EDUCATIONAL USE. SPECIAL EDITIONS CAN ALSO BE CREATED TO
SPECIFICATION. FOR DETAILS, CONTACT SPECIALSALES@ABRAMSBOOKS.COM
OR THE ADDRESS BELOW.

AMULET BOOKS® IS A REGISTERED TRADEMARK OF HARRY N. ABRAMS, INC.

ABRAMS The Art of Books
195 Broadway, New York, NY 10007
abramsbooks.com

DEDICATED TO THE MEMORY OF
MY ENGLISH MASTIFF, PEPPER

NO ANIMALS WERE HARMED
IN THE CREATION OF THIS BOOK

NHHT

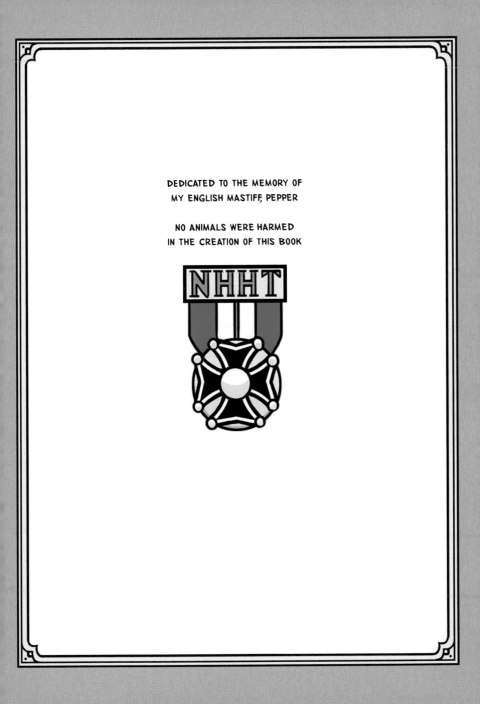

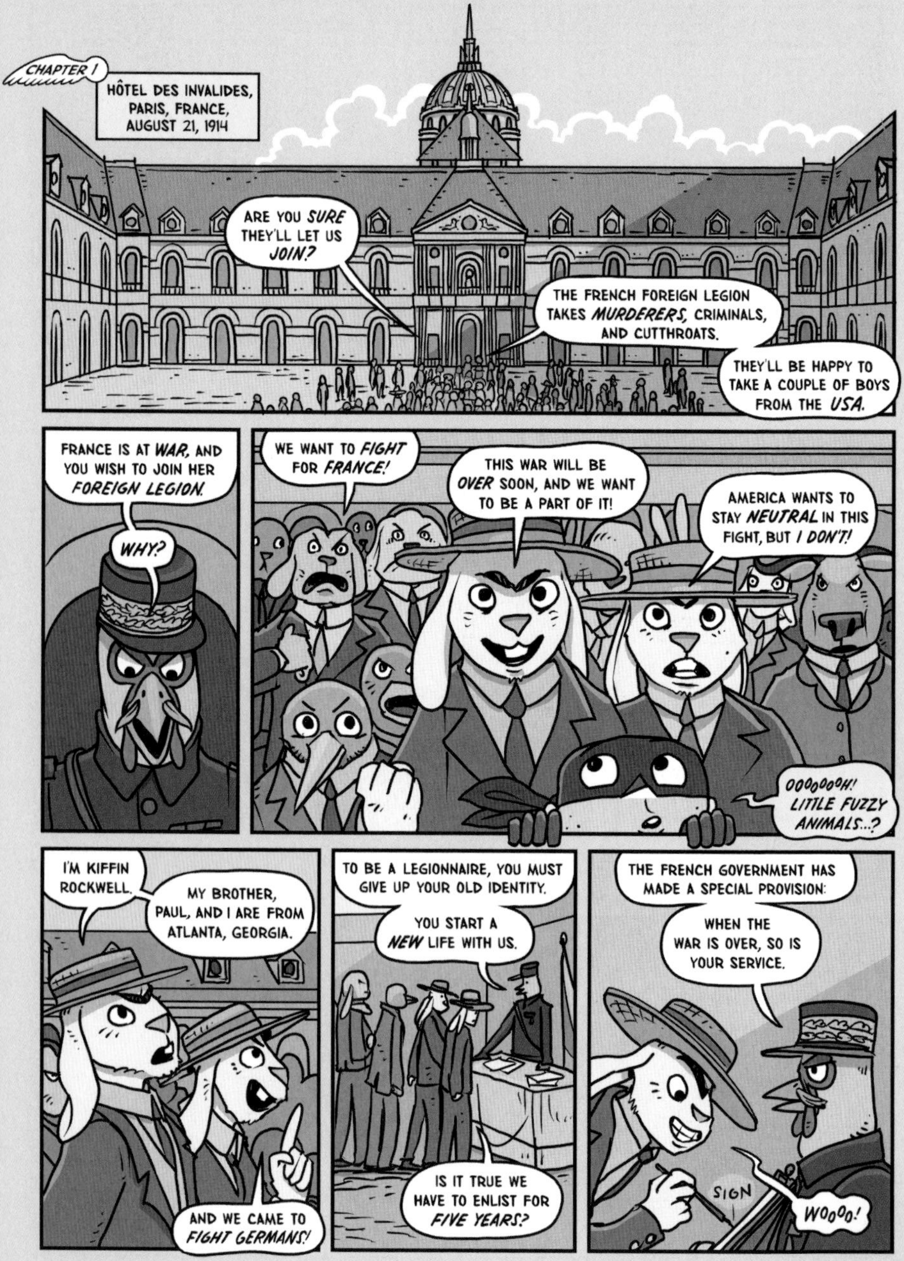

CHAPTER 1
HÔTEL DES INVALIDES, PARIS, FRANCE, AUGUST 21, 1914
ARE YOU *SURE* THEY'LL LET US *JOIN?*
THE FRENCH FOREIGN LEGION TAKES *MURDERERS,* CRIMINALS, AND CUTTHROATS.
THEY'LL BE HAPPY TO TAKE A COUPLE OF BOYS FROM THE *USA.*
FRANCE IS AT *WAR,* AND YOU WISH TO JOIN HER *FOREIGN LEGION.*
WHY?
WE WANT TO *FIGHT* FOR *FRANCE!*
THIS WAR WILL BE *OVER* SOON, AND WE WANT TO BE A PART OF IT!
AMERICA WANTS TO STAY *NEUTRAL* IN THIS FIGHT, BUT *I DON'T!*
OOOOOOOH! LITTLE FUZZY ANIMALS...?
I'M KIFFIN ROCKWELL.
MY BROTHER, PAUL, AND I ARE FROM ATLANTA, GEORGIA.
AND WE CAME TO *FIGHT GERMANS!*
TO BE A LEGIONNAIRE, YOU MUST GIVE UP YOUR OLD IDENTITY.
YOU START A *NEW* LIFE WITH US.
IS IT TRUE WE HAVE TO ENLIST FOR *FIVE YEARS?*
THE FRENCH GOVERNMENT HAS MADE A SPECIAL PROVISION:
WHEN THE WAR IS OVER, SO IS YOUR SERVICE.
SIGN
WOOOO!

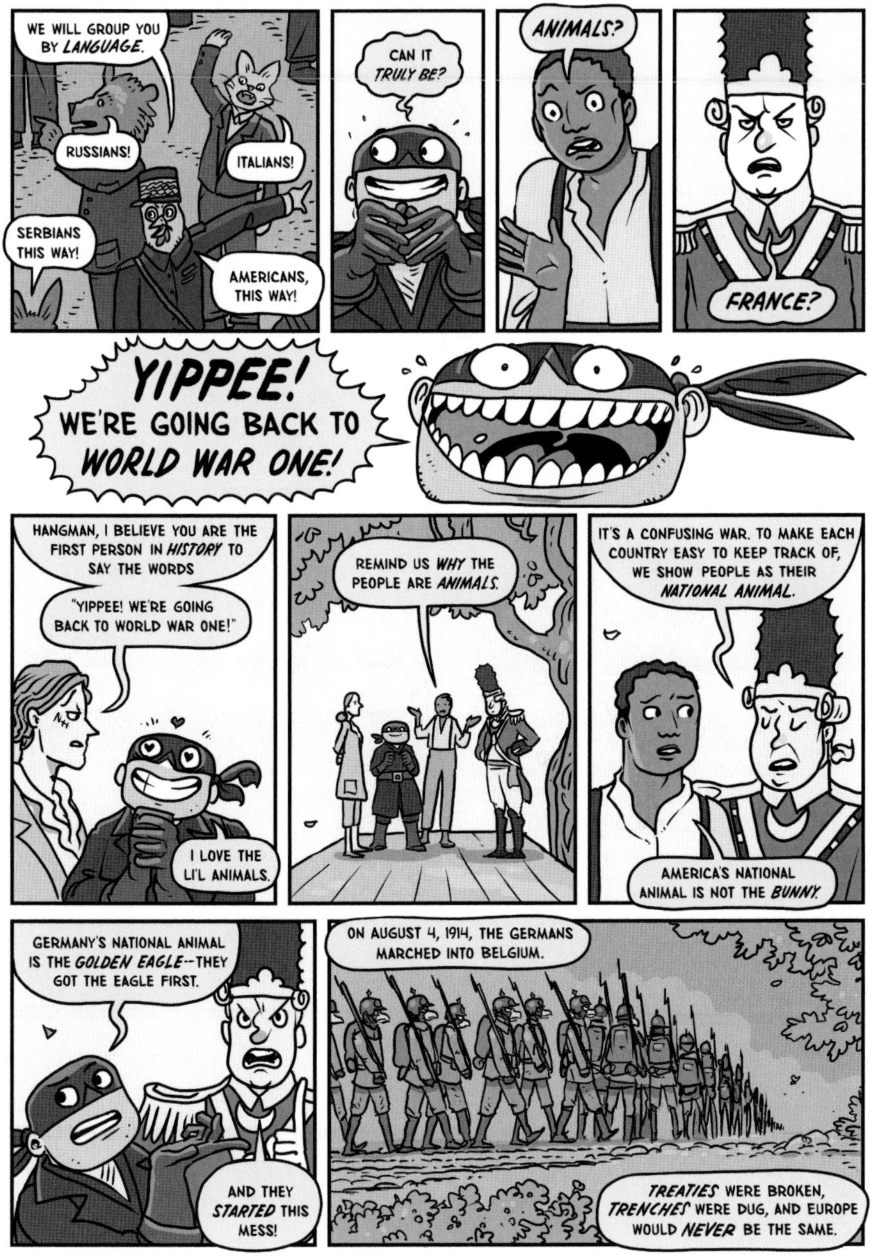
WE WILL GROUP YOU BY *LANGUAGE*.
RUSSIANS!
ITALIANS!
SERBIANS THIS WAY!
AMERICANS, THIS WAY!
CAN IT *TRULY BE?*
ANIMALS?
FRANCE?
YIPPEE! WE'RE GOING BACK TO *WORLD WAR ONE!*
HANGMAN, I BELIEVE YOU ARE THE FIRST PERSON IN *HISTORY* TO SAY THE WORDS
"YIPPEE! WE'RE GOING BACK TO WORLD WAR ONE!"
I LOVE THE LI'L ANIMALS.
REMIND US *WHY* THE PEOPLE ARE *ANIMALS*.
IT'S A CONFUSING WAR. TO MAKE EACH COUNTRY EASY TO KEEP TRACK OF, WE SHOW PEOPLE AS THEIR *NATIONAL ANIMAL*.
AMERICA'S NATIONAL ANIMAL IS NOT THE *BUNNY*.
GERMANY'S NATIONAL ANIMAL IS THE *GOLDEN EAGLE*--THEY GOT THE EAGLE FIRST.
AND THEY *STARTED* THIS MESS!
ON AUGUST 4, 1914, THE GERMANS MARCHED INTO BELGIUM.
TREATIES WERE BROKEN, *TRENCHES* WERE DUG, AND EUROPE WOULD *NEVER* BE THE SAME.

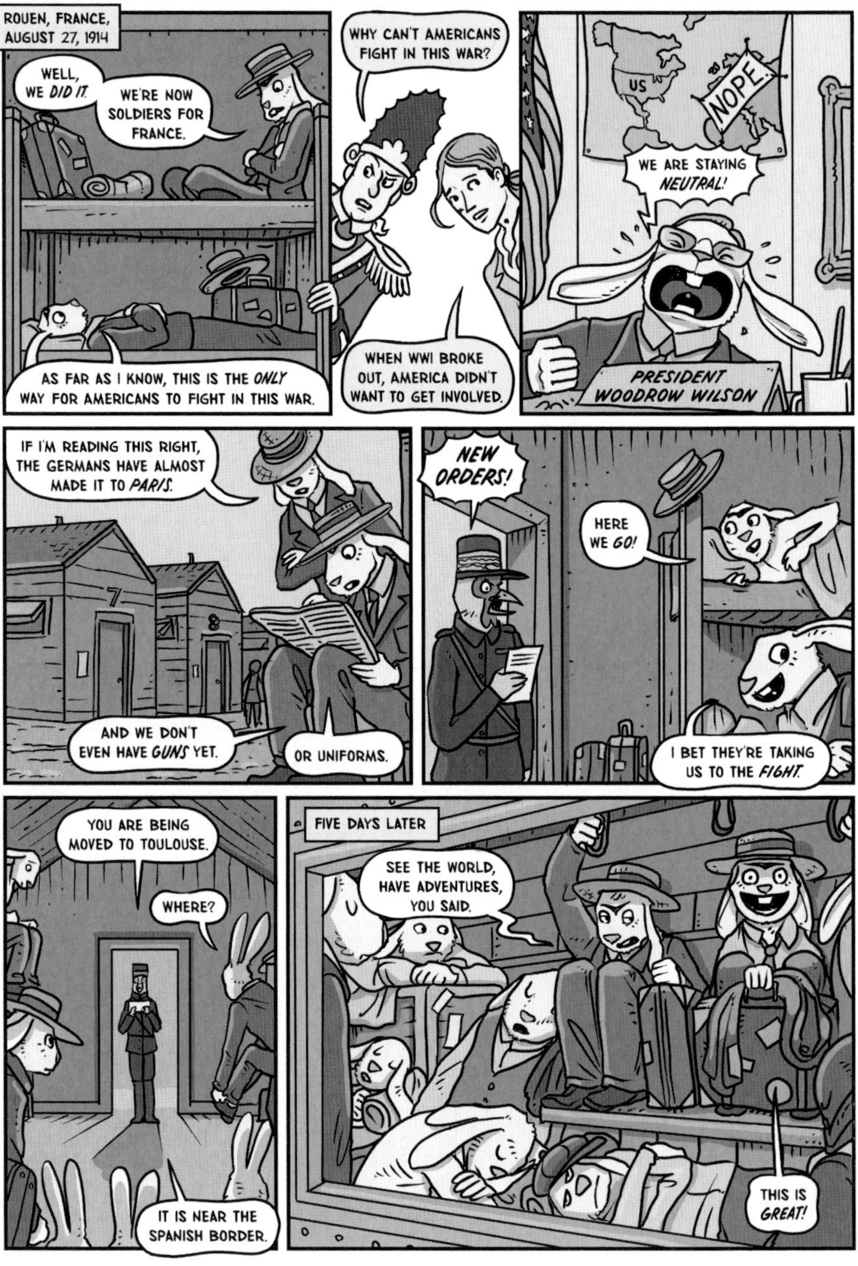
ROUEN, FRANCE, AUGUST 27, 1914
WELL, WE *DID IT.*
WE'RE NOW SOLDIERS FOR FRANCE.
AS FAR AS I KNOW, THIS IS THE *ONLY* WAY FOR AMERICANS TO FIGHT IN THIS WAR.
WHY CAN'T AMERICANS FIGHT IN THIS WAR?
WHEN WWI BROKE OUT, AMERICA DIDN'T WANT TO GET INVOLVED.
US
NOPE.
WE ARE STAYING *NEUTRAL!*
PRESIDENT WOODROW WILSON
IF I'M READING THIS RIGHT, THE GERMANS HAVE ALMOST MADE IT TO *PARIS.*
7
AND WE DON'T EVEN HAVE *GUNS* YET.
OR UNIFORMS.
NEW ORDERS!
HERE WE *GO!*
I BET THEY'RE TAKING US TO THE *FIGHT.*
YOU ARE BEING MOVED TO TOULOUSE.
WHERE?
IT IS NEAR THE SPANISH BORDER.
FIVE DAYS LATER
SEE THE WORLD, HAVE ADVENTURES, YOU SAID.
THIS IS *GREAT!*

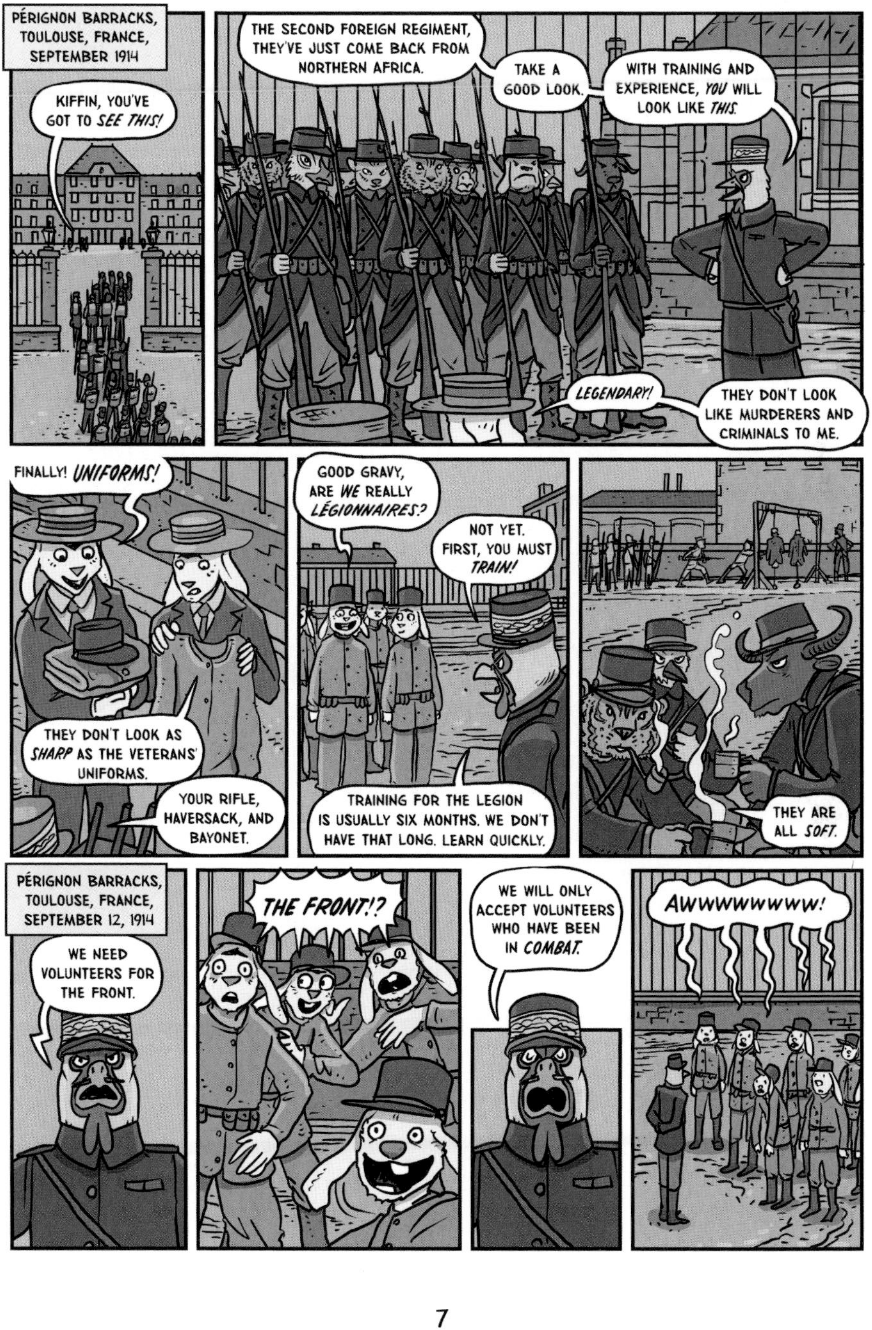
PÉRIGNON BARRACKS, TOULOUSE, FRANCE, SEPTEMBER 1914
KIFFIN, YOU'VE GOT TO *SEE THIS!*
THE SECOND FOREIGN REGIMENT, THEY'VE JUST COME BACK FROM NORTHERN AFRICA.
TAKE A GOOD LOOK.
WITH TRAINING AND EXPERIENCE, *YOU* WILL LOOK LIKE *THIS*.
LEGENDARY!
THEY DON'T LOOK LIKE MURDERERS AND CRIMINALS TO ME.
FINALLY! *UNIFORMS!*
THEY DON'T LOOK AS *SHARP* AS THE VETERANS' UNIFORMS.
YOUR RIFLE, HAVERSACK, AND BAYONET.
GOOD GRAVY, ARE *WE* REALLY *LÉGIONNAIRES*?
NOT YET. FIRST, YOU MUST *TRAIN!*
TRAINING FOR THE LEGION IS USUALLY SIX MONTHS. WE DON'T HAVE THAT LONG. LEARN QUICKLY.
THEY ARE ALL *SOFT*.
PÉRIGNON BARRACKS, TOULOUSE, FRANCE, SEPTEMBER 12, 1914
WE NEED VOLUNTEERS FOR THE FRONT.
THE FRONT!?
WE WILL ONLY ACCEPT VOLUNTEERS WHO HAVE BEEN IN *COMBAT*.
AWWWWWWWW!

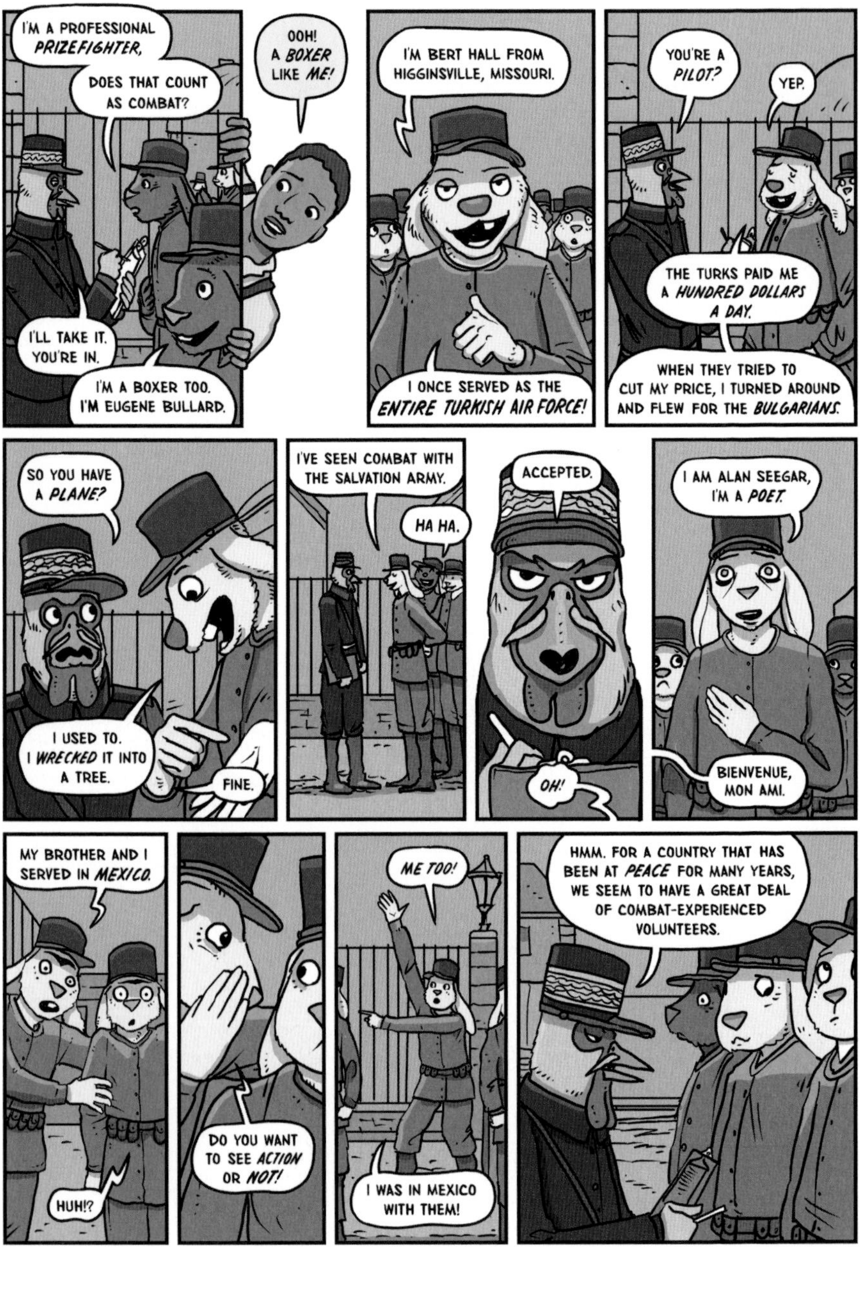
I'M A PROFESSIONAL *PRIZEFIGHTER*.
DOES THAT COUNT AS COMBAT?
OOH! A *BOXER* LIKE *ME!*
I'LL TAKE IT. YOU'RE IN.
I'M A BOXER TOO. I'M EUGENE BULLARD.
I'M BERT HALL FROM HIGGINSVILLE, MISSOURI.
I ONCE SERVED AS THE *ENTIRE TURKISH AIR FORCE!*
YOU'RE A *PILOT?*
YEP.
THE TURKS PAID ME A *HUNDRED DOLLARS A DAY.*
WHEN THEY TRIED TO CUT MY PRICE, I TURNED AROUND AND FLEW FOR THE *BULGARIANS.*
SO YOU HAVE A *PLANE?*
I USED TO. I *WRECKED* IT INTO A TREE.
FINE.
I'VE SEEN COMBAT WITH THE SALVATION ARMY.
HA HA.
ACCEPTED.
OH!
I AM ALAN SEEGAR, I'M A *POET.*
BIENVENUE, MON AMI.
MY BROTHER AND I SERVED IN *MEXICO.*
HUH!?
DO YOU WANT TO SEE *ACTION* OR *NOT!*
ME TOO!
I WAS IN MEXICO WITH THEM!
HMM. FOR A COUNTRY THAT HAS BEEN AT *PEACE* FOR MANY YEARS, WE SEEM TO HAVE A GREAT DEAL OF COMBAT-EXPERIENCED VOLUNTEERS.

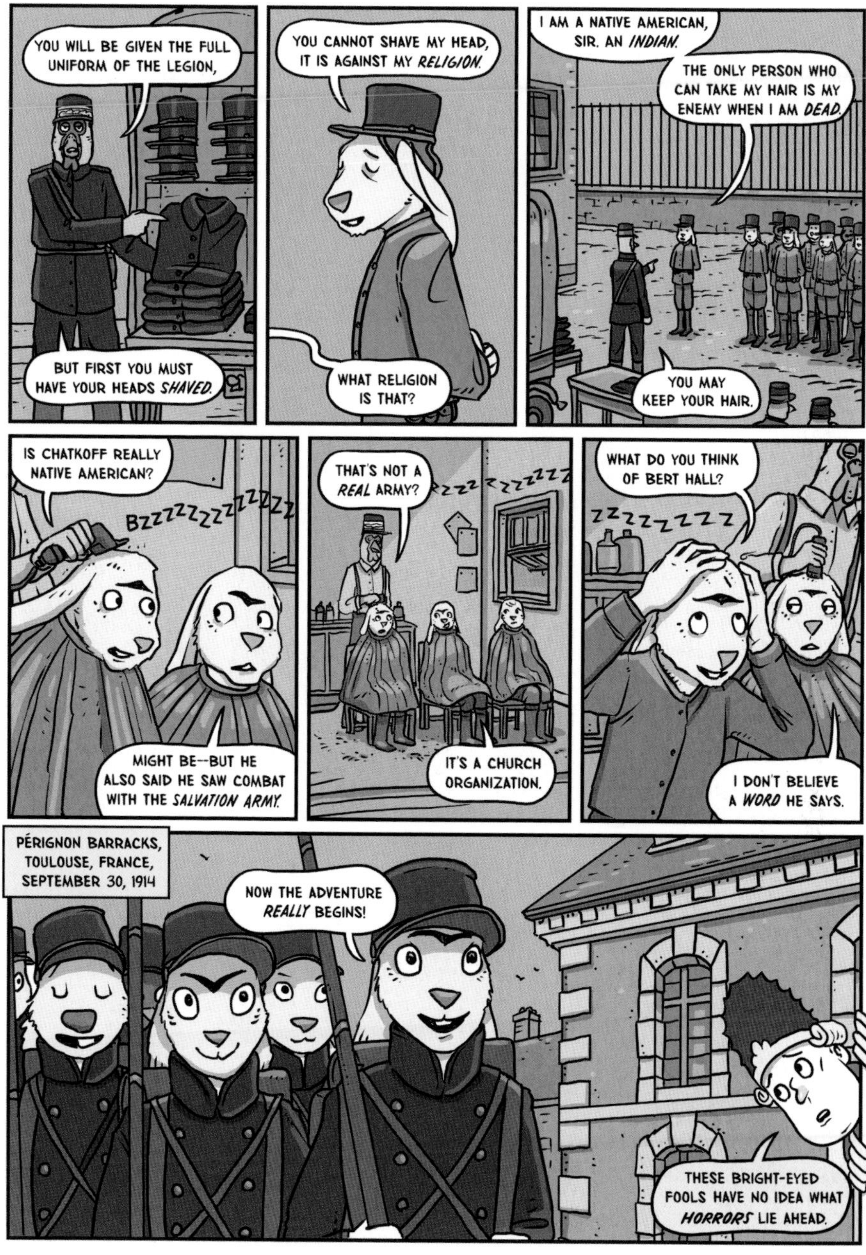
YOU WILL BE GIVEN THE FULL UNIFORM OF THE LEGION,
BUT FIRST YOU MUST HAVE YOUR HEADS SHAVED.
YOU CANNOT SHAVE MY HEAD, IT IS AGAINST MY RELIGION.
WHAT RELIGION IS THAT?
I AM A NATIVE AMERICAN, SIR. AN INDIAN.
THE ONLY PERSON WHO CAN TAKE MY HAIR IS MY ENEMY WHEN I AM DEAD.
YOU MAY KEEP YOUR HAIR.
IS CHATKOFF REALLY NATIVE AMERICAN?
BZZZZZZZZZZZZZ
MIGHT BE--BUT HE ALSO SAID HE SAW COMBAT WITH THE SALVATION ARMY.
THAT'S NOT A REAL ARMY?
ZZZZ ZZZZZZZ
IT'S A CHURCH ORGANIZATION.
WHAT DO YOU THINK OF BERT HALL?
ZZZZZZZZ
I DON'T BELIEVE A WORD HE SAYS.
PÉRIGNON BARRACKS, TOULOUSE, FRANCE, SEPTEMBER 30, 1914
NOW THE ADVENTURE REALLY BEGINS!
THESE BRIGHT-EYED FOOLS HAVE NO IDEA WHAT HORRORS LIE AHEAD.

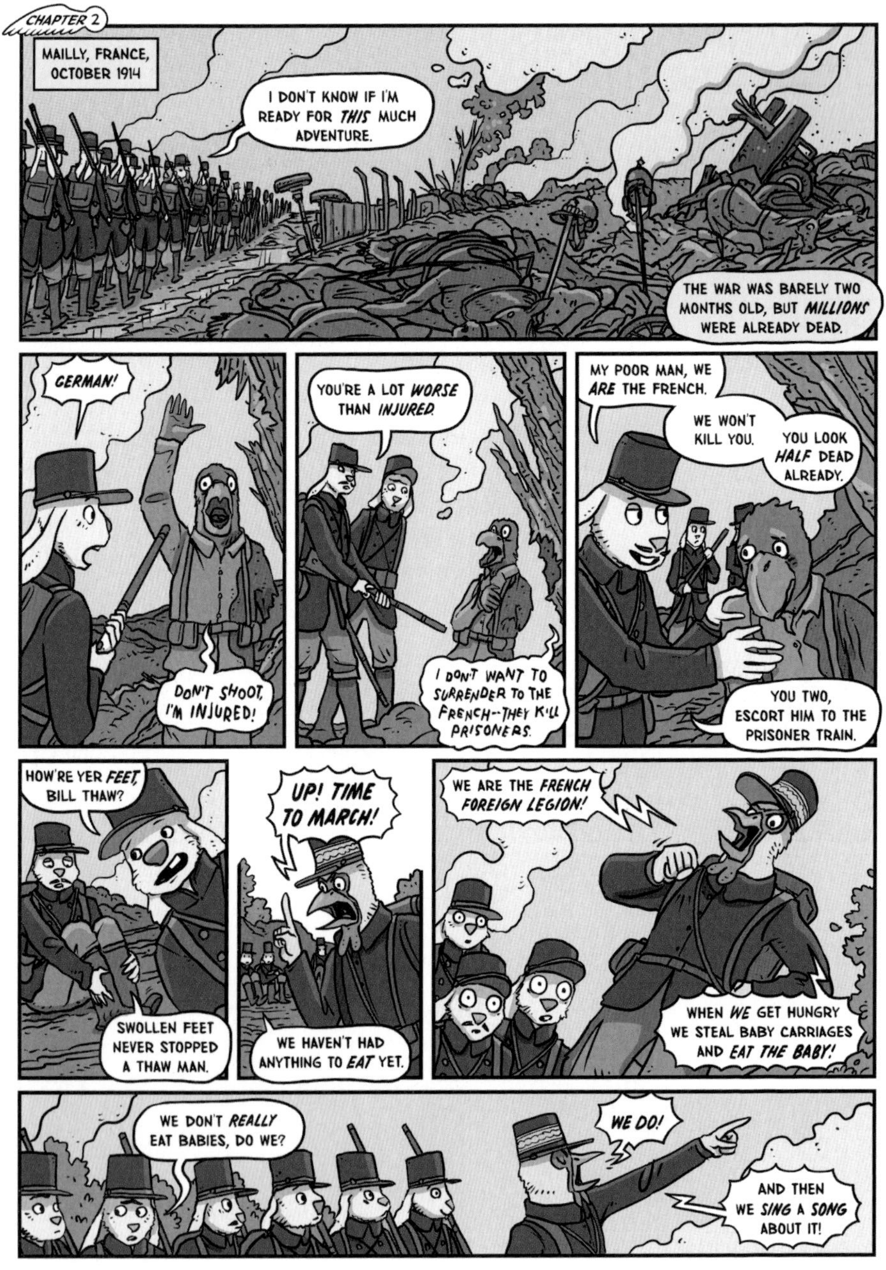
CHAPTER 2
MAILLY, FRANCE, OCTOBER 1914
I DON'T KNOW IF I'M READY FOR THIS MUCH ADVENTURE.
THE WAR WAS BARELY TWO MONTHS OLD, BUT MILLIONS WERE ALREADY DEAD.
GERMAN!
DON'T SHOOT, I'M INJURED!
YOU'RE A LOT WORSE THAN INJURED.
I DON'T WANT TO SURRENDER TO THE FRENCH--THEY KILL PRISONERS.
MY POOR MAN, WE ARE THE FRENCH.
WE WON'T KILL YOU.
YOU LOOK HALF DEAD ALREADY.
YOU TWO, ESCORT HIM TO THE PRISONER TRAIN.
HOW'RE YER FEET, BILL THAW?
SWOLLEN FEET NEVER STOPPED A THAW MAN.
UP! TIME TO MARCH!
WE HAVEN'T HAD ANYTHING TO EAT YET.
WE ARE THE FRENCH FOREIGN LEGION!
WHEN WE GET HUNGRY WE STEAL BABY CARRIAGES AND EAT THE BABY!
WE DON'T REALLY EAT BABIES, DO WE?
WE DO!
AND THEN WE SING A SONG ABOUT IT!

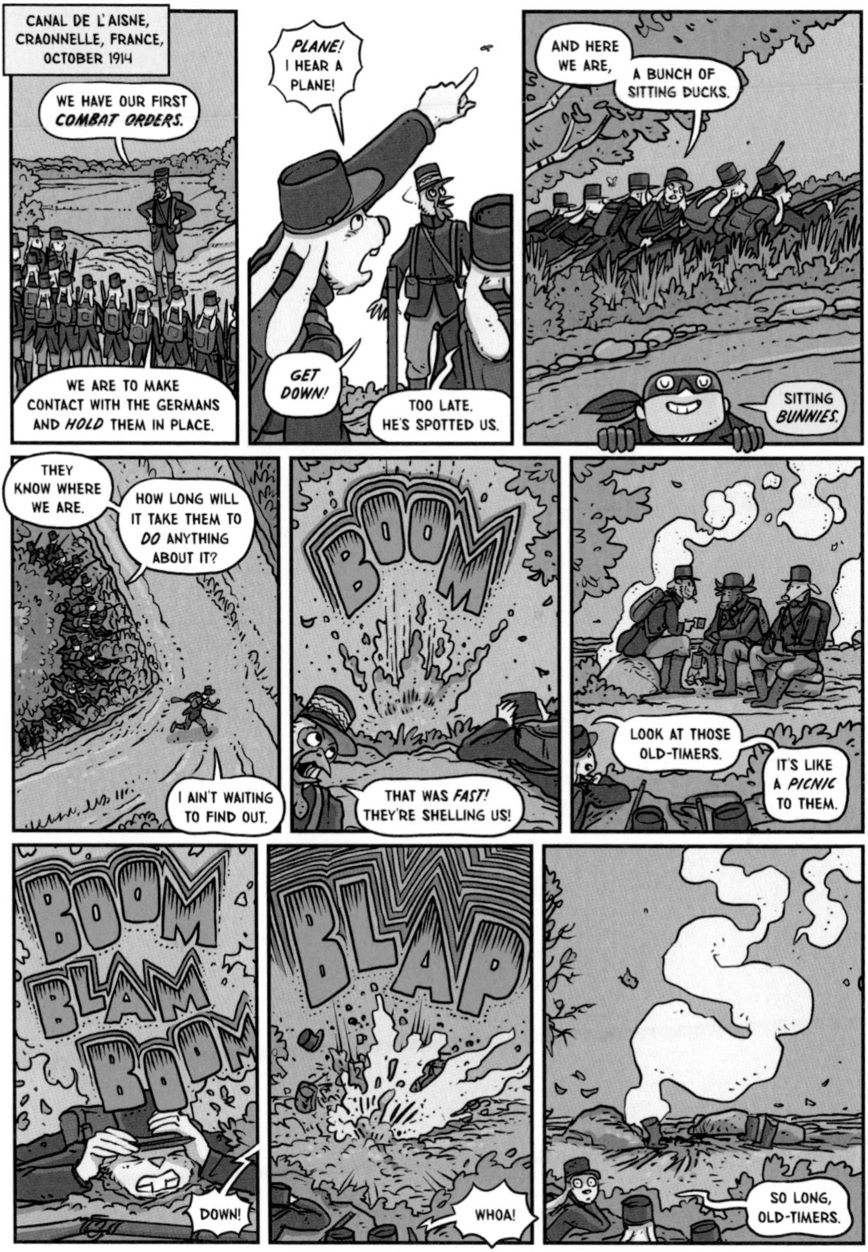

CANAL DE L'AISNE, CRAONNELLE, FRANCE, OCTOBER 1914
WE HAVE OUR FIRST COMBAT ORDERS.
WE ARE TO MAKE CONTACT WITH THE GERMANS AND HOLD THEM IN PLACE.
PLANE! I HEAR A PLANE!
GET DOWN!
TOO LATE. HE'S SPOTTED US.
AND HERE WE ARE,
A BUNCH OF SITTING DUCKS.
SITTING BUNNIES.
THEY KNOW WHERE WE ARE.
HOW LONG WILL IT TAKE THEM TO DO ANYTHING ABOUT IT?
I AIN'T WAITING TO FIND OUT.
BOOM
THAT WAS FAST! THEY'RE SHELLING US!
LOOK AT THOSE OLD-TIMERS.
IT'S LIKE A PICNIC TO THEM.
BOOM BLAM BOOM
DOWN!
BLAP
WHOA!
SO LONG, OLD-TIMERS.

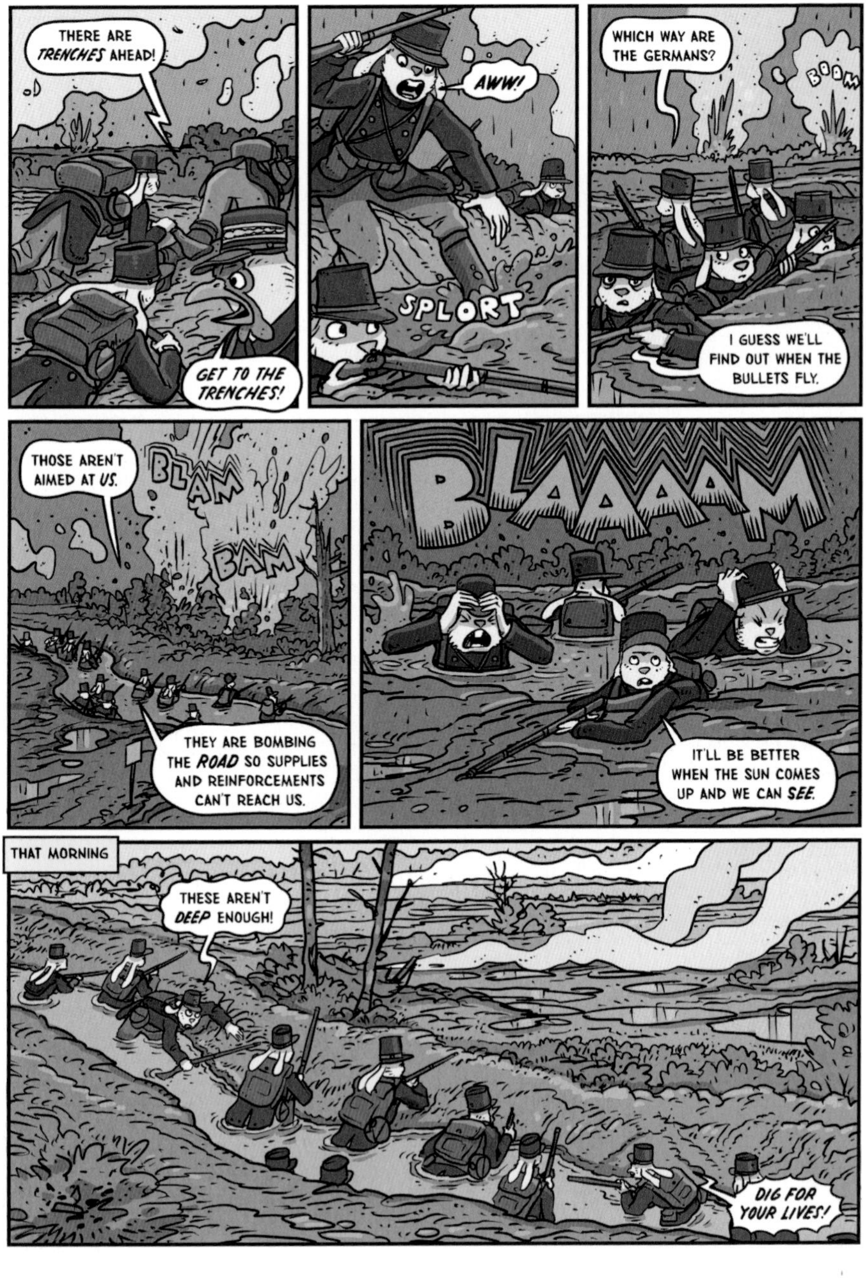
THERE ARE TRENCHES AHEAD!
GET TO THE TRENCHES!
AWW!
SPLORT
WHICH WAY ARE THE GERMANS?
BOOM
I GUESS WE'LL FIND OUT WHEN THE BULLETS FLY.
THOSE AREN'T AIMED AT US.
BLAM
BAM
THEY ARE BOMBING THE ROAD SO SUPPLIES AND REINFORCEMENTS CAN'T REACH US.
BLAAAAM
IT'LL BE BETTER WHEN THE SUN COMES UP AND WE CAN SEE.
THAT MORNING
THESE AREN'T DEEP ENOUGH!
DIG FOR YOUR LIVES!

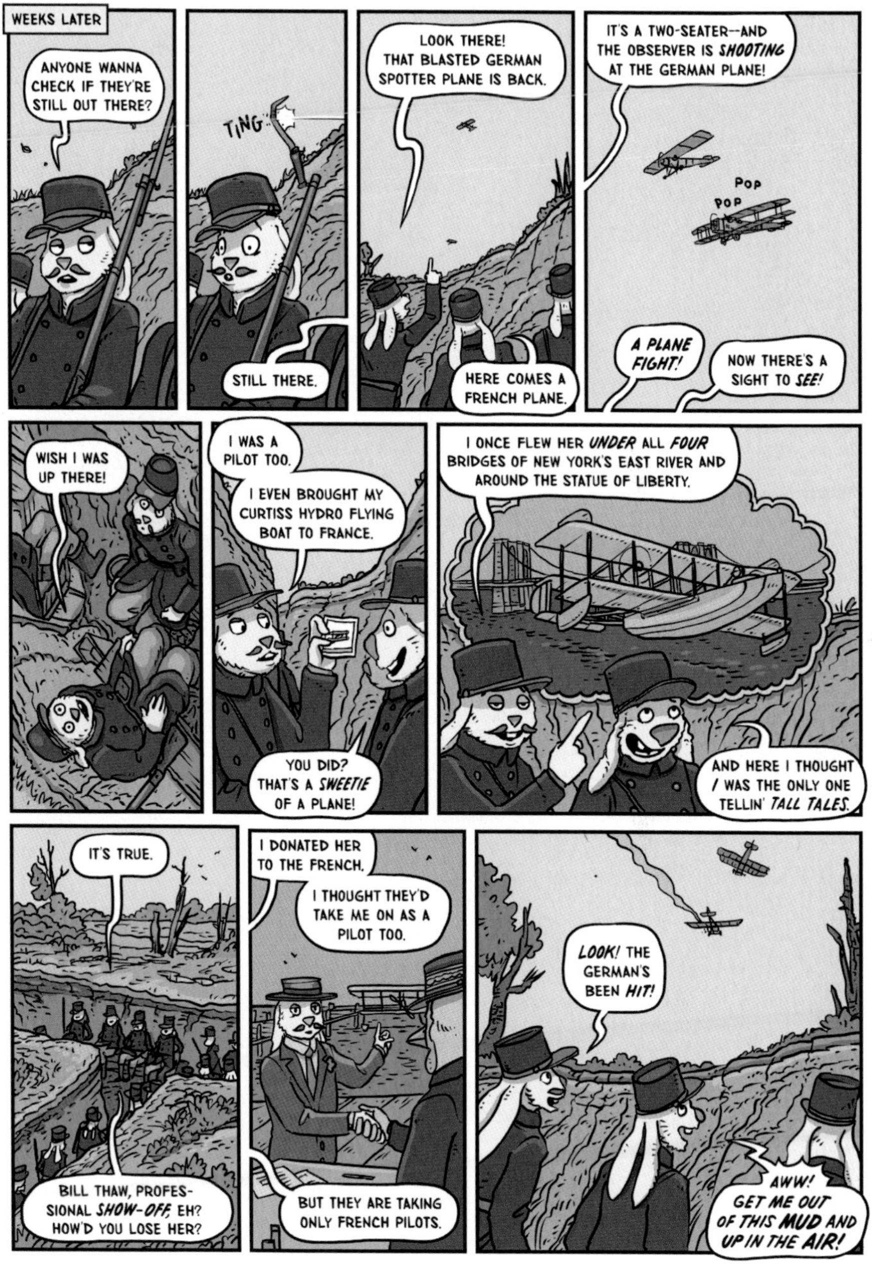
WEEKS LATER
ANYONE WANNA CHECK IF THEY'RE STILL OUT THERE?
TING
STILL THERE.
LOOK THERE! THAT BLASTED GERMAN SPOTTER PLANE IS BACK.
HERE COMES A FRENCH PLANE.
IT'S A TWO-SEATER--AND THE OBSERVER IS SHOOTING AT THE GERMAN PLANE!
POP
POP
A PLANE FIGHT!
NOW THERE'S A SIGHT TO SEE!
WISH I WAS UP THERE!
I WAS A PILOT TOO.
I EVEN BROUGHT MY CURTISS HYDRO FLYING BOAT TO FRANCE.
YOU DID? THAT'S A SWEETIE OF A PLANE!
I ONCE FLEW HER UNDER ALL FOUR BRIDGES OF NEW YORK'S EAST RIVER AND AROUND THE STATUE OF LIBERTY.
AND HERE I THOUGHT I WAS THE ONLY ONE TELLIN' TALL TALES.
IT'S TRUE.
BILL THAW, PROFES-SIONAL SHOW-OFF, EH? HOW'D YOU LOSE HER?
I DONATED HER TO THE FRENCH.
I THOUGHT THEY'D TAKE ME ON AS A PILOT TOO.
BUT THEY ARE TAKING ONLY FRENCH PILOTS.
LOOK! THE GERMAN'S BEEN HIT!
AWW! GET ME OUT OF THIS MUD AND UP IN THE AIR!

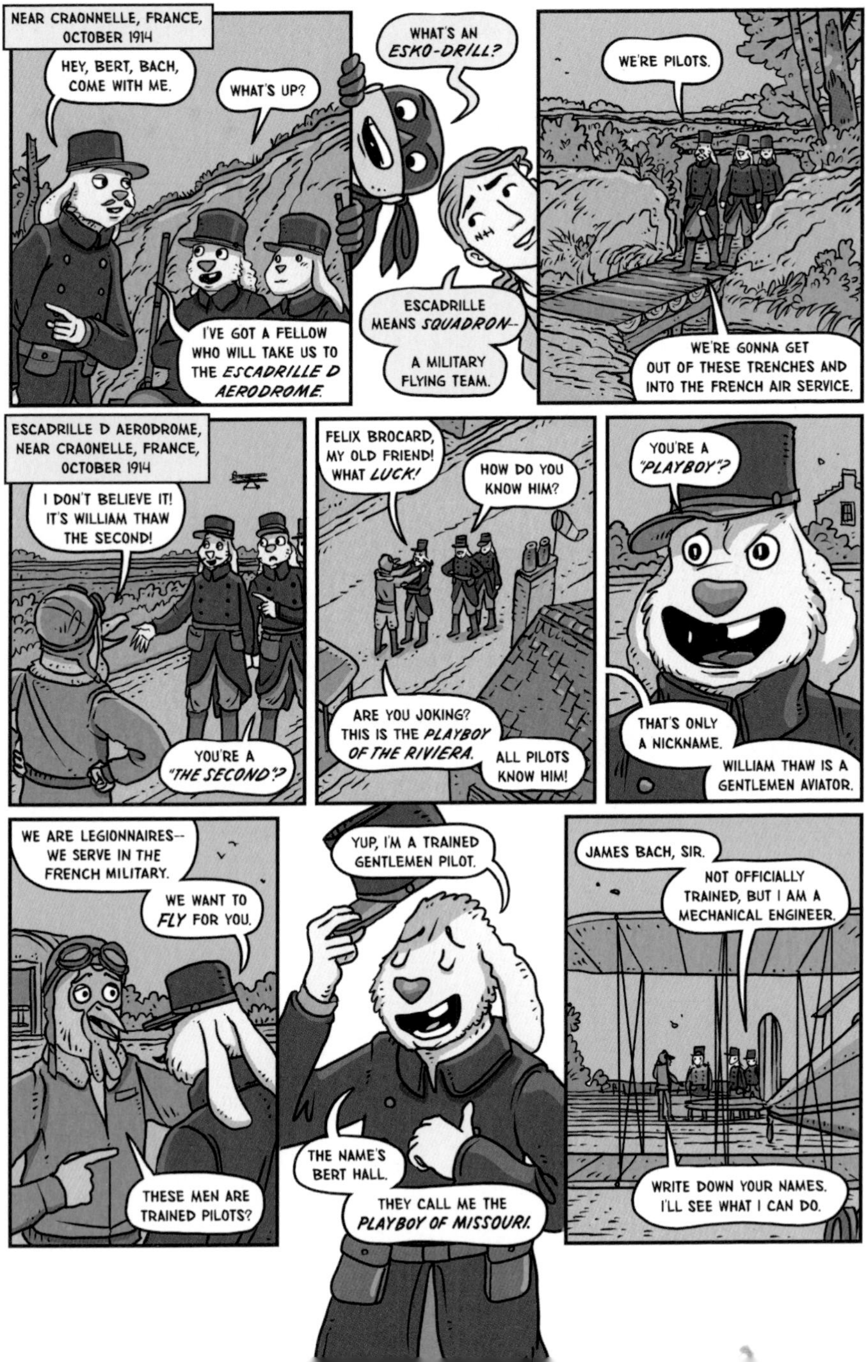
NEAR CRAONNELLE, FRANCE, OCTOBER 1914
HEY, BERT, BACH, COME WITH ME.
WHAT'S UP?
I'VE GOT A FELLOW WHO WILL TAKE US TO THE *ESCADRILLE D AERODROME.*
WHAT'S AN *ESKO-DRILL?*
ESCADRILLE MEANS *SQUADRON*--
A MILITARY FLYING TEAM.
WE'RE PILOTS.
WE'RE GONNA GET OUT OF THESE TRENCHES AND INTO THE FRENCH AIR SERVICE.
ESCADRILLE D AERODROME, NEAR CRAONNELLE, FRANCE, OCTOBER 1914
I DON'T BELIEVE IT! IT'S WILLIAM THAW THE SECOND!
YOU'RE A *"THE SECOND"?*
FELIX BROCARD, MY OLD FRIEND! WHAT *LUCK!*
HOW DO YOU KNOW HIM?
ARE YOU JOKING? THIS IS THE *PLAYBOY OF THE RIVIERA.*
ALL PILOTS KNOW HIM!
YOU'RE A *"PLAYBOY"?*
THAT'S ONLY A NICKNAME.
WILLIAM THAW IS A GENTLEMEN AVIATOR.
WE ARE LEGIONNAIRES-- WE SERVE IN THE FRENCH MILITARY.
WE WANT TO *FLY* FOR YOU.
THESE MEN ARE TRAINED PILOTS?
YUP, I'M A TRAINED GENTLEMEN PILOT.
THE NAME'S BERT HALL.
THEY CALL ME THE *PLAYBOY OF MISSOURI.*
JAMES BACH, SIR.
NOT OFFICIALLY TRAINED, BUT I AM A MECHANICAL ENGINEER.
WRITE DOWN YOUR NAMES. I'LL SEE WHAT I CAN DO.

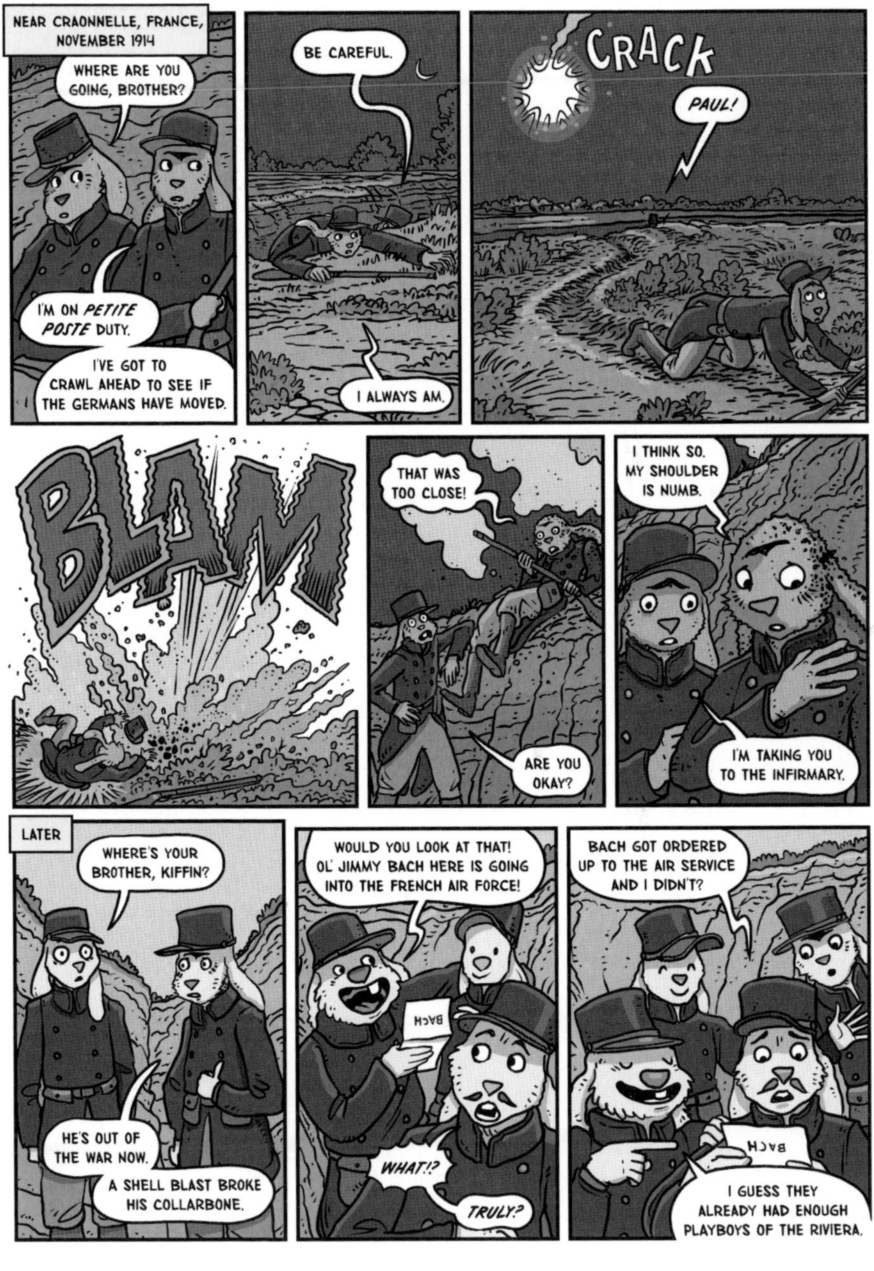
NEAR CRAONNELLE, FRANCE, NOVEMBER 1914
WHERE ARE YOU GOING, BROTHER?
I'M ON *PETITE POSTE* DUTY.
I'VE GOT TO CRAWL AHEAD TO SEE IF THE GERMANS HAVE MOVED.
BE CAREFUL.
I ALWAYS AM.
CRACK
PAUL!
BLAM
THAT WAS TOO CLOSE!
ARE YOU OKAY?
I THINK SO. MY SHOULDER IS NUMB.
I'M TAKING YOU TO THE INFIRMARY.
LATER
WHERE'S YOUR BROTHER, KIFFIN?
HE'S OUT OF THE WAR NOW.
A SHELL BLAST BROKE HIS COLLARBONE.
WOULD YOU LOOK AT THAT! OL' JIMMY BACH HERE IS GOING INTO THE FRENCH AIR FORCE!
WHAT!?
TRULY?
BACH GOT ORDERED UP TO THE AIR SERVICE AND I DIDN'T?
I GUESS THEY ALREADY HAD ENOUGH PLAYBOYS OF THE RIVIERA.

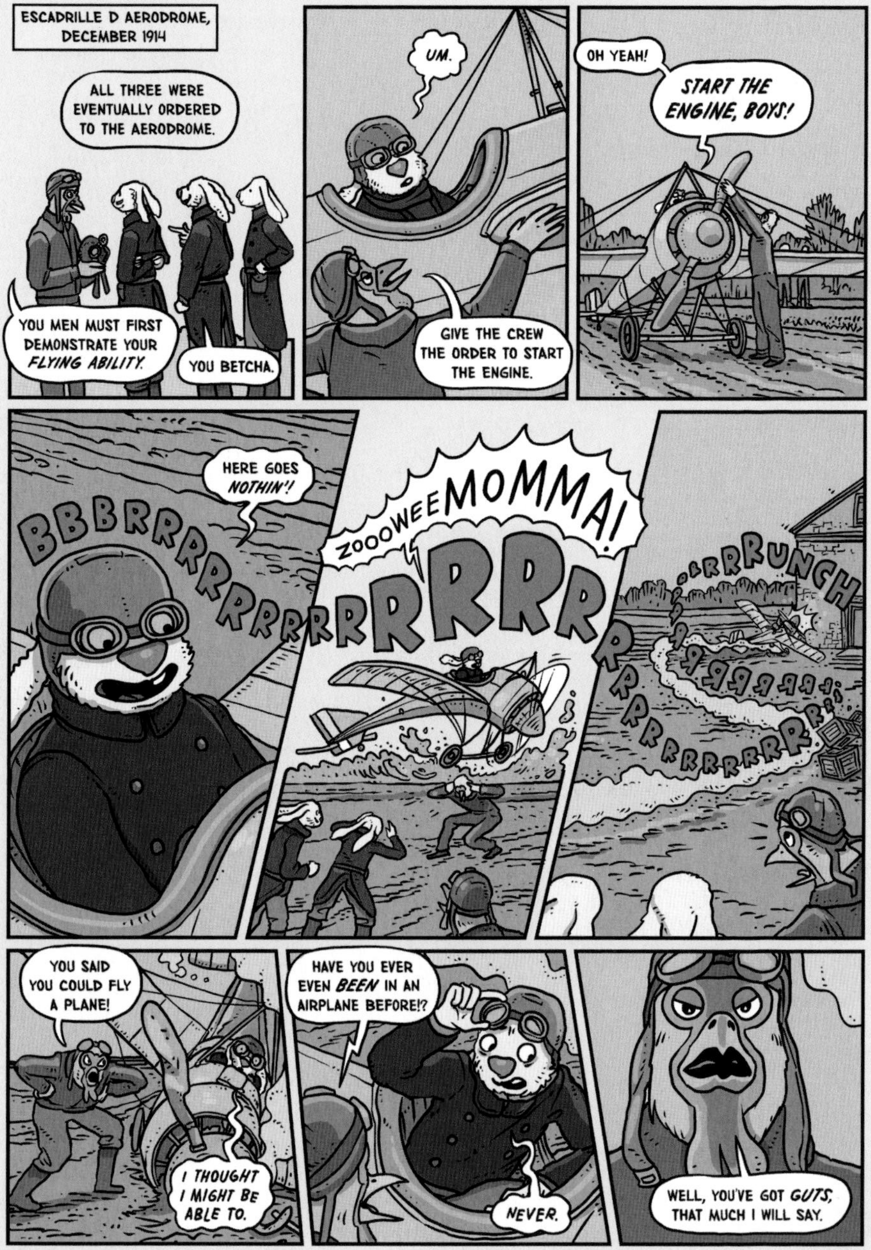
ESCADRILLE D AERODROME, DECEMBER 1914
ALL THREE WERE EVENTUALLY ORDERED TO THE AERODROME.
YOU MEN MUST FIRST DEMONSTRATE YOUR *FLYING ABILITY.*
YOU BETCHA.
UM.
GIVE THE CREW THE ORDER TO START THE ENGINE.
OH YEAH!
START THE ENGINE, BOYS!
HERE GOES *NOTHIN'!*
BBBRRRRRRRRRRRRRRRR
ZOOOWEE MOMMA!
RRRRRRRRRRRRRRRRRRRRR
..RRRRUNCH
YOU SAID YOU COULD FLY A PLANE!
I THOUGHT I MIGHT BE ABLE TO.
HAVE YOU EVER EVEN *BEEN* IN AN AIRPLANE BEFORE!?
NEVER.
WELL, YOU'VE GOT *GUTS,* THAT MUCH I WILL SAY.

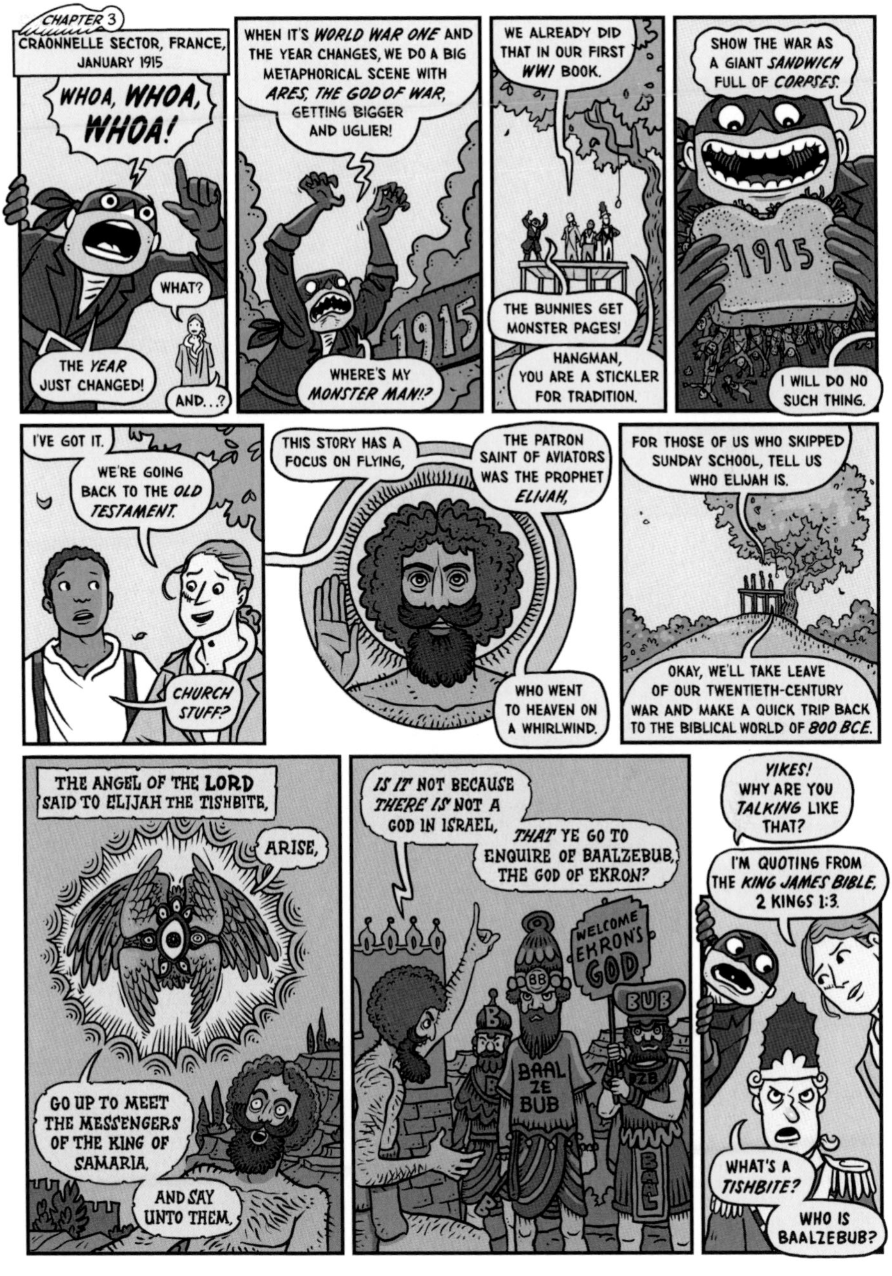
CHAPTER 3
CRAONNELLE SECTOR, FRANCE, JANUARY 1915
WHOA, WHOA, WHOA!
WHAT?
THE YEAR JUST CHANGED!
AND...?
WHEN IT'S WORLD WAR ONE AND THE YEAR CHANGES, WE DO A BIG METAPHORICAL SCENE WITH ARES, THE GOD OF WAR, GETTING BIGGER AND UGLIER!
1915
WHERE'S MY MONSTER MAN!?
WE ALREADY DID THAT IN OUR FIRST WWI BOOK.
THE BUNNIES GET MONSTER PAGES!
HANGMAN, YOU ARE A STICKLER FOR TRADITION.
SHOW THE WAR AS A GIANT SANDWICH FULL OF CORPSES.
1915
I WILL DO NO SUCH THING.
I'VE GOT IT.
WE'RE GOING BACK TO THE OLD TESTAMENT.
CHURCH STUFF?
THIS STORY HAS A FOCUS ON FLYING,
THE PATRON SAINT OF AVIATORS WAS THE PROPHET ELIJAH,
WHO WENT TO HEAVEN ON A WHIRLWIND.
FOR THOSE OF US WHO SKIPPED SUNDAY SCHOOL, TELL US WHO ELIJAH IS.
OKAY, WE'LL TAKE LEAVE OF OUR TWENTIETH-CENTURY WAR AND MAKE A QUICK TRIP BACK TO THE BIBLICAL WORLD OF 800 BCE.
THE ANGEL OF THE LORD SAID TO ELIJAH THE TISHBITE,
ARISE,
GO UP TO MEET THE MESSENGERS OF THE KING OF SAMARIA,
AND SAY UNTO THEM,
IS IT NOT BECAUSE THERE IS NOT A GOD IN ISRAEL,
THAT YE GO TO ENQUIRE OF BAALZEBUB, THE GOD OF EKRON?
WELCOME EKRON'S GOD
BB
B
BUB
BAAL ZE BUB
BZB
BAAL
YIKES! WHY ARE YOU TALKING LIKE THAT?
I'M QUOTING FROM THE KING JAMES BIBLE, 2 KINGS 1:3.
WHAT'S A TISHBITE?
WHO IS BAALZEBUB?

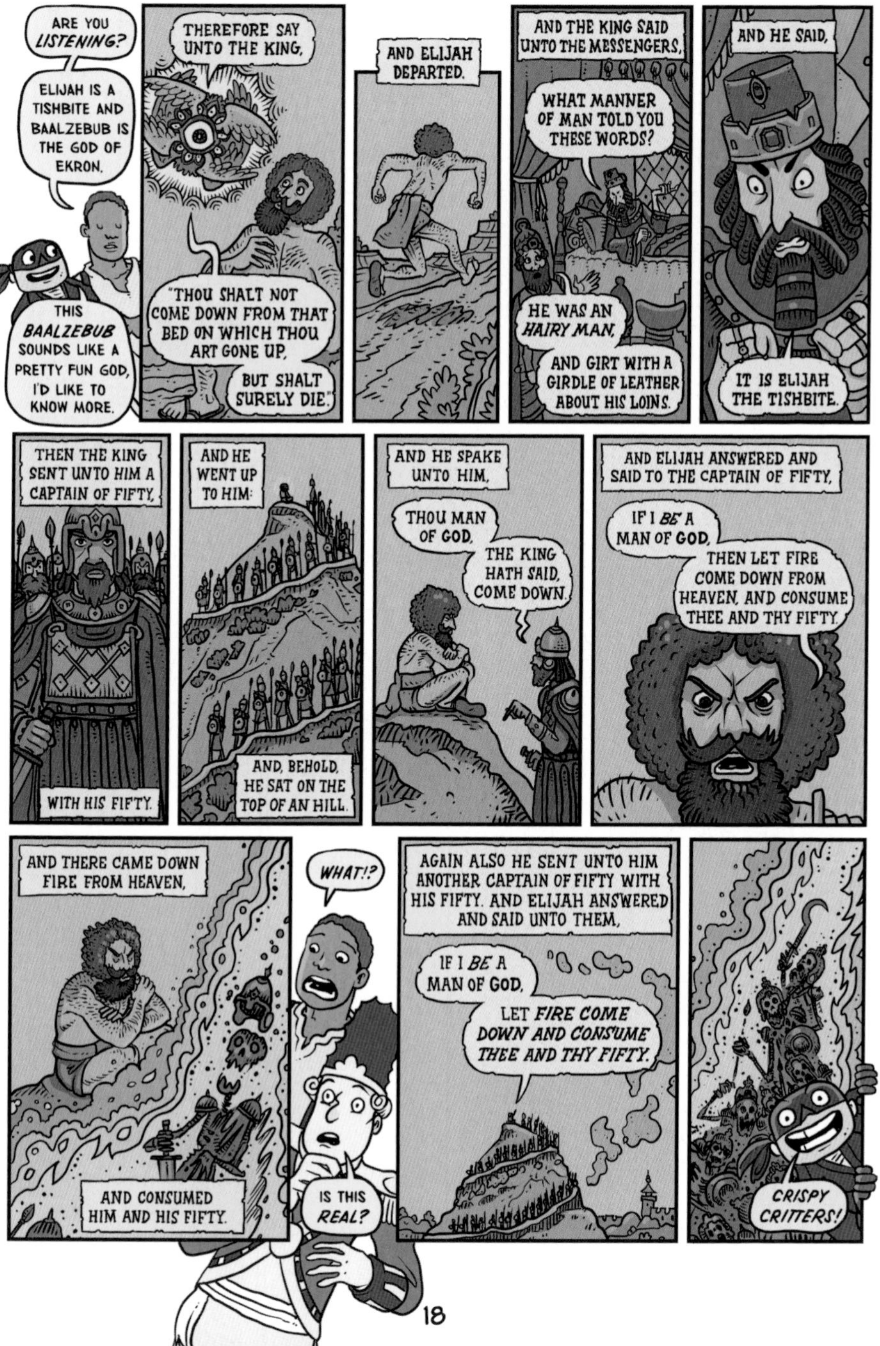

ARE YOU LISTENING?
ELIJAH IS A TISHBITE AND BAALZEBUB IS THE GOD OF EKRON.
THIS BAALZEBUB SOUNDS LIKE A PRETTY FUN GOD, I'D LIKE TO KNOW MORE.
THEREFORE SAY UNTO THE KING,
"THOU SHALT NOT COME DOWN FROM THAT BED ON WHICH THOU ART GONE UP,
BUT SHALT SURELY DIE."
AND ELIJAH DEPARTED.
AND THE KING SAID UNTO THE MESSENGERS,
WHAT MANNER OF MAN TOLD YOU THESE WORDS?
HE WAS AN HAIRY MAN,
AND GIRT WITH A GIRDLE OF LEATHER ABOUT HIS LOINS.
AND HE SAID,
IT IS ELIJAH THE TISHBITE.
THEN THE KING SENT UNTO HIM A CAPTAIN OF FIFTY,
WITH HIS FIFTY.
AND HE WENT UP TO HIM:
AND, BEHOLD, HE SAT ON THE TOP OF AN HILL.
AND HE SPAKE UNTO HIM,
THOU MAN OF GOD,
THE KING HATH SAID, COME DOWN.
AND ELIJAH ANSWERED AND SAID TO THE CAPTAIN OF FIFTY,
IF I BE A MAN OF GOD,
THEN LET FIRE COME DOWN FROM HEAVEN, AND CONSUME THEE AND THY FIFTY.
AND THERE CAME DOWN FIRE FROM HEAVEN,
AND CONSUMED HIM AND HIS FIFTY.
WHAT!?
IS THIS REAL?
AGAIN ALSO HE SENT UNTO HIM ANOTHER CAPTAIN OF FIFTY WITH HIS FIFTY. AND ELIJAH ANSWERED AND SAID UNTO THEM,
IF I BE A MAN OF GOD,
LET FIRE COME DOWN AND CONSUME THEE AND THY FIFTY.
CRISPY CRITTERS!

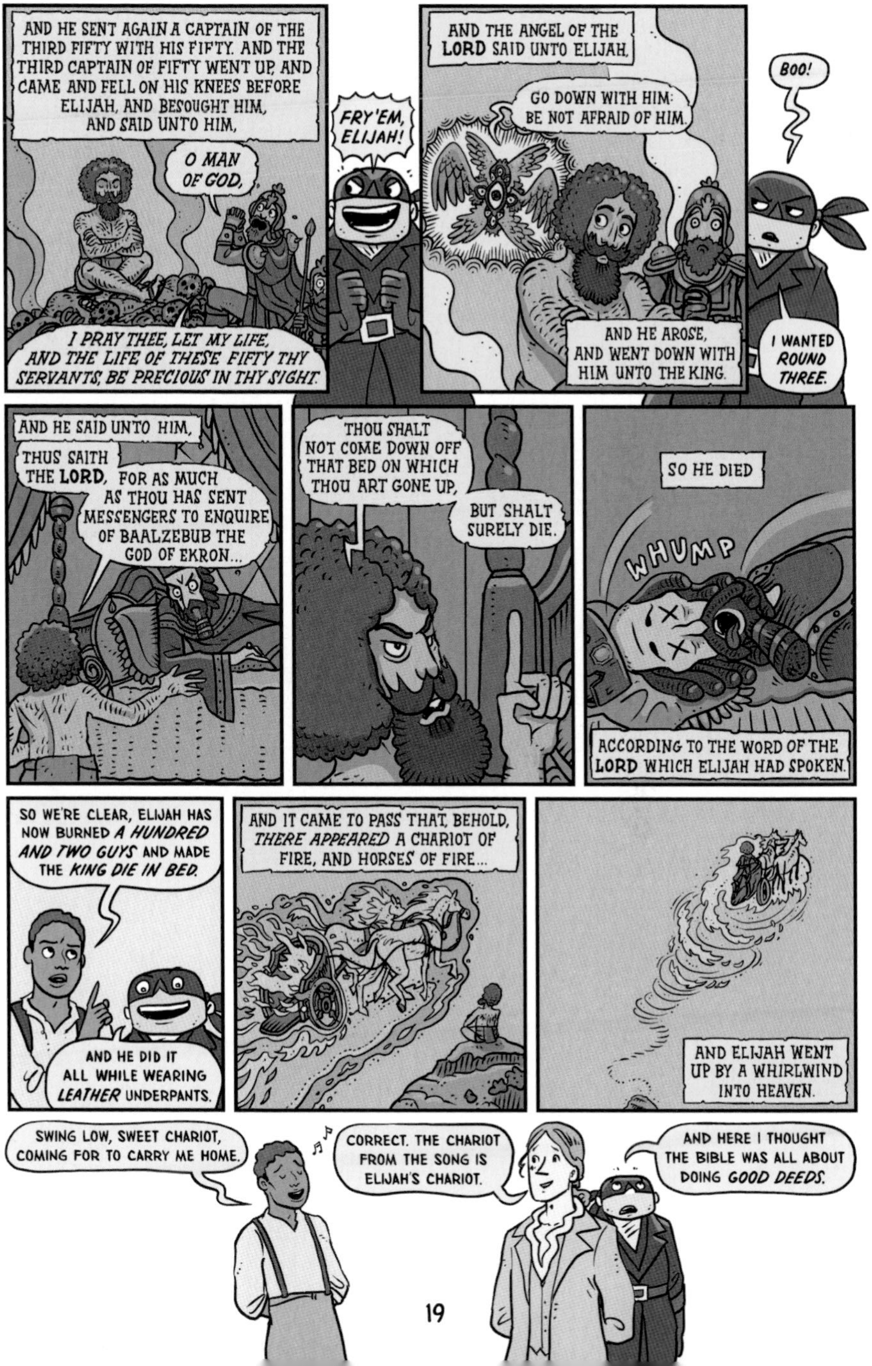
AND HE SENT AGAIN A CAPTAIN OF THE THIRD FIFTY WITH HIS FIFTY. AND THE THIRD CAPTAIN OF FIFTY WENT UP, AND CAME AND FELL ON HIS KNEES BEFORE ELIJAH, AND BESOUGHT HIM, AND SAID UNTO HIM,
O MAN OF GOD,
I PRAY THEE, LET MY LIFE, AND THE LIFE OF THESE FIFTY THY SERVANTS, BE PRECIOUS IN THY SIGHT.
FRY'EM, ELIJAH!
AND THE ANGEL OF THE LORD SAID UNTO ELIJAH,
GO DOWN WITH HIM: BE NOT AFRAID OF HIM.
AND HE AROSE, AND WENT DOWN WITH HIM UNTO THE KING.
BOO!
I WANTED ROUND THREE.
AND HE SAID UNTO HIM,
THUS SAITH THE LORD, FOR AS MUCH AS THOU HAS SENT MESSENGERS TO ENQUIRE OF BAALZEBUB THE GOD OF EKRON...
THOU SHALT NOT COME DOWN OFF THAT BED ON WHICH THOU ART GONE UP,
BUT SHALT SURELY DIE.
SO HE DIED
WHUMP
ACCORDING TO THE WORD OF THE LORD WHICH ELIJAH HAD SPOKEN.
SO WE'RE CLEAR, ELIJAH HAS NOW BURNED A HUNDRED AND TWO GUYS AND MADE THE KING DIE IN BED.
AND HE DID IT ALL WHILE WEARING LEATHER UNDERPANTS.
AND IT CAME TO PASS THAT, BEHOLD, THERE APPEARED A CHARIOT OF FIRE, AND HORSES OF FIRE...
AND ELIJAH WENT UP BY A WHIRLWIND INTO HEAVEN.
SWING LOW, SWEET CHARIOT, COMING FOR TO CARRY ME HOME.
CORRECT. THE CHARIOT FROM THE SONG IS ELIJAH'S CHARIOT.
AND HERE I THOUGHT THE BIBLE WAS ALL ABOUT DOING GOOD DEEDS.

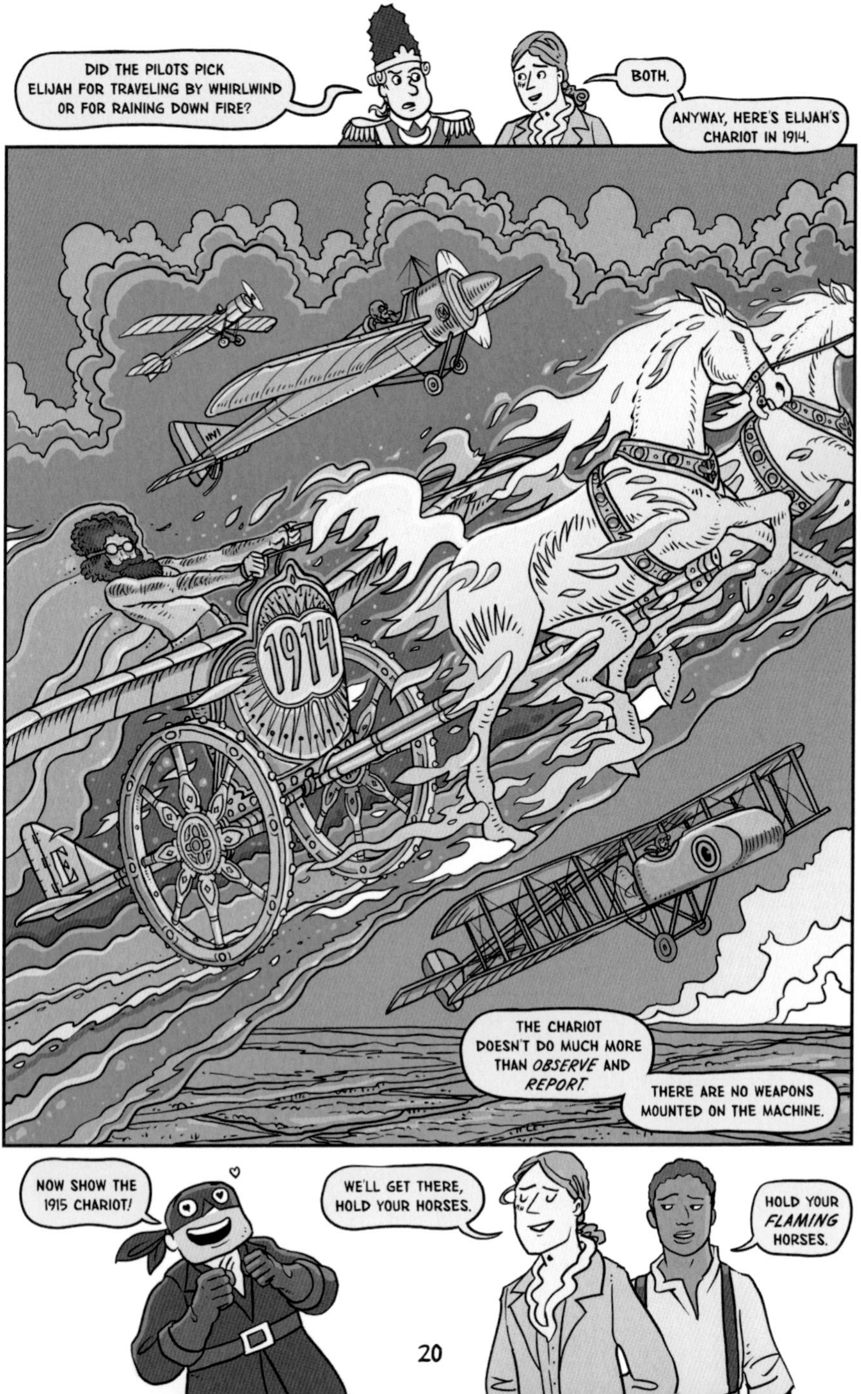
DID THE PILOTS PICK ELIJAH FOR TRAVELING BY WHIRLWIND OR FOR RAINING DOWN FIRE?
BOTH.
ANYWAY, HERE'S ELIJAH'S CHARIOT IN 1914.
1914
1914
THE CHARIOT DOESN'T DO MUCH MORE THAN *OBSERVE* AND *REPORT.*
THERE ARE NO WEAPONS MOUNTED ON THE MACHINE.
NOW SHOW THE 1915 CHARIOT!
WE'LL GET THERE, HOLD YOUR HORSES.
HOLD YOUR *FLAMING* HORSES.

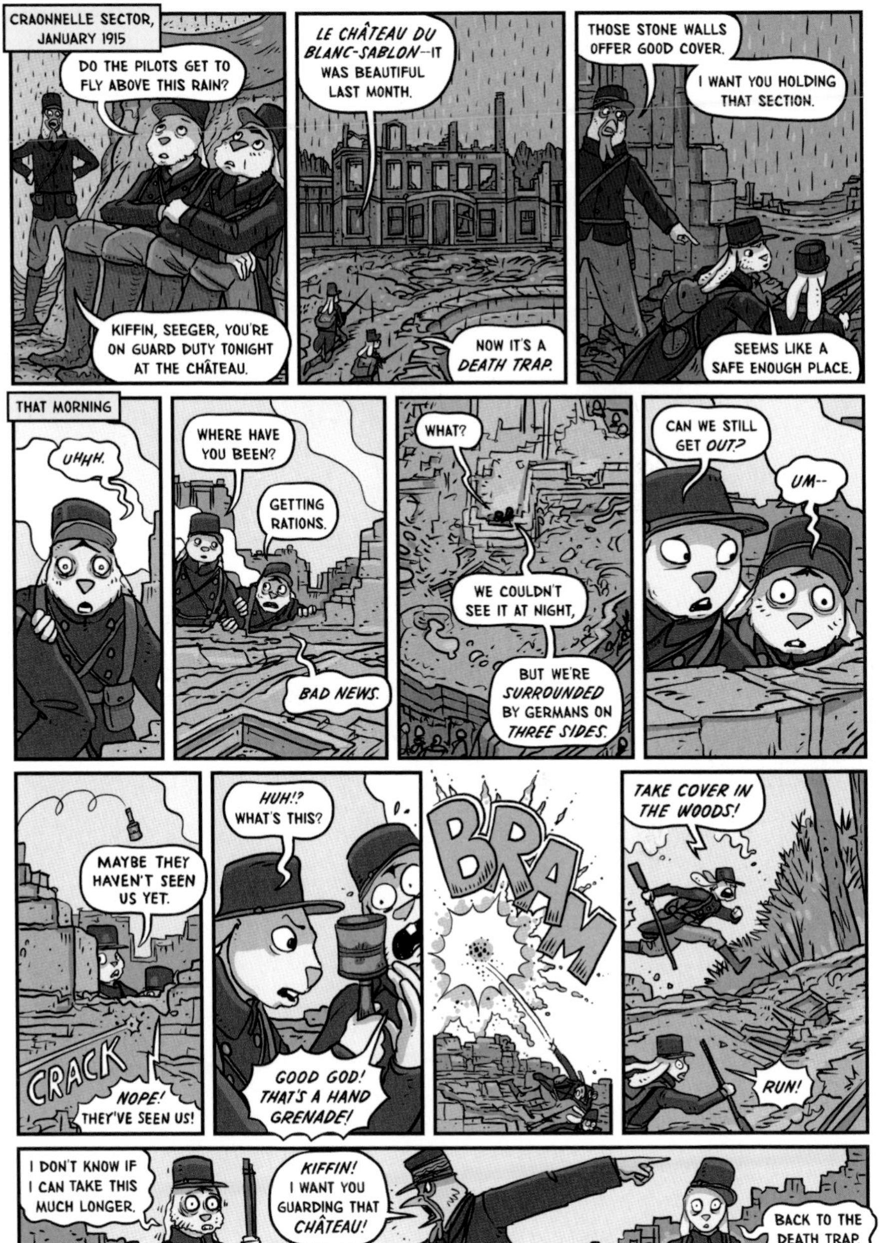
CRAONNELLE SECTOR, JANUARY 1915
DO THE PILOTS GET TO FLY ABOVE THIS RAIN?
KIFFIN, SEEGER, YOU'RE ON GUARD DUTY TONIGHT AT THE CHÂTEAU.
LE CHÂTEAU DU BLANC-SABLON--IT WAS BEAUTIFUL LAST MONTH.
NOW IT'S A DEATH TRAP.
THOSE STONE WALLS OFFER GOOD COVER.
I WANT YOU HOLDING THAT SECTION.
SEEMS LIKE A SAFE ENOUGH PLACE.
THAT MORNING
UHHH.
WHERE HAVE YOU BEEN?
GETTING RATIONS.
BAD NEWS.
WHAT?
WE COULDN'T SEE IT AT NIGHT,
BUT WE'RE SURROUNDED BY GERMANS ON THREE SIDES.
CAN WE STILL GET OUT?
UM--
MAYBE THEY HAVEN'T SEEN US YET.
CRACK
NOPE! THEY'VE SEEN US!
HUH!? WHAT'S THIS?
GOOD GOD! THAT'S A HAND GRENADE!
BRAM
TAKE COVER IN THE WOODS!
RUN!
I DON'T KNOW IF I CAN TAKE THIS MUCH LONGER.
KIFFIN! I WANT YOU GUARDING THAT CHÂTEAU!
BACK TO THE DEATH TRAP.

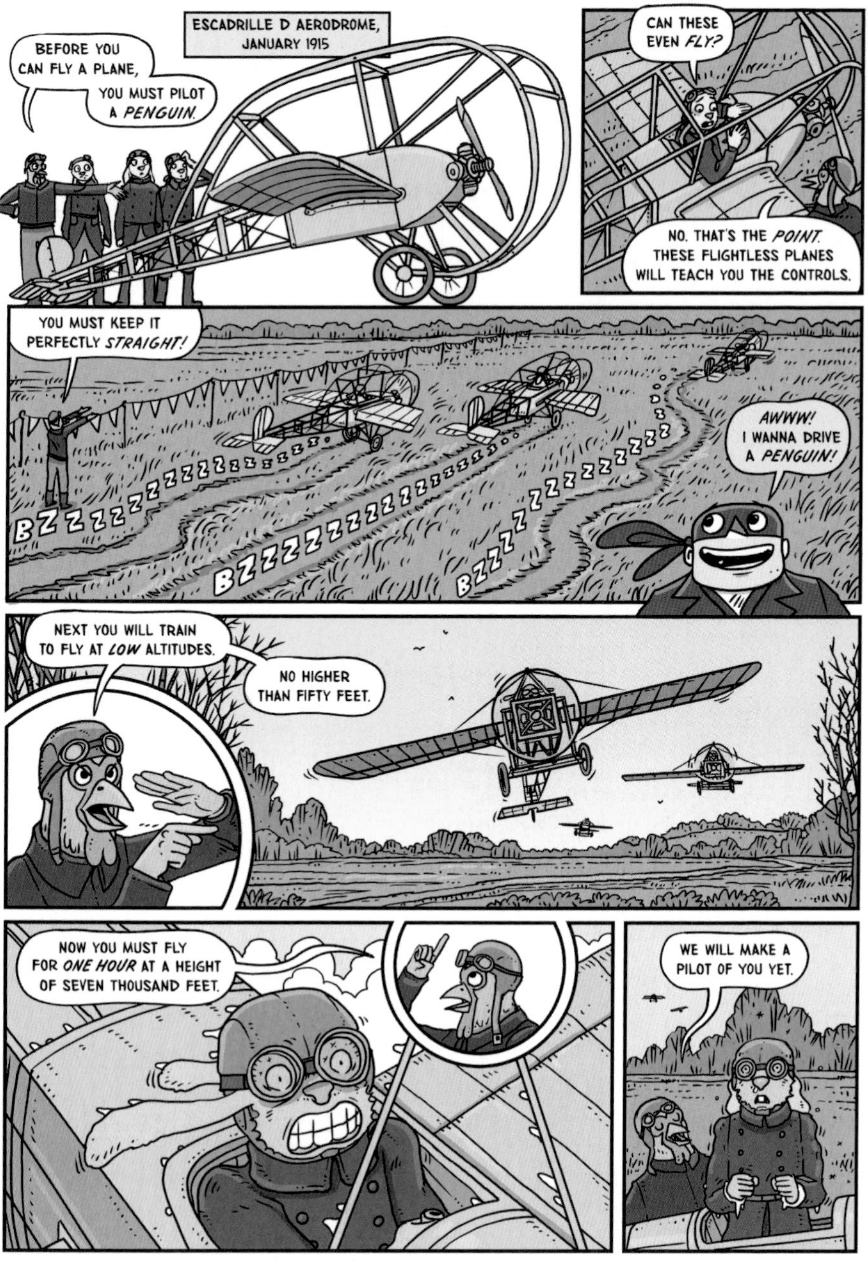
ESCADRILLE D AERODROME, JANUARY 1915
BEFORE YOU CAN FLY A PLANE,
YOU MUST PILOT A *PENGUIN.*
CAN THESE EVEN *FLY?*
NO. THAT'S THE *POINT.* THESE FLIGHTLESS PLANES WILL TEACH YOU THE CONTROLS.
YOU MUST KEEP IT PERFECTLY *STRAIGHT!*
BZZZZZZZZZZZZZZZZ
BZZZZZZZZZZZZZZZZZZ
BZZZZZZZZZZZZZZ
AWWW! I WANNA DRIVE A *PENGUIN!*
NEXT YOU WILL TRAIN TO FLY AT *LOW* ALTITUDES.
NO HIGHER THAN FIFTY FEET.
NOW YOU MUST FLY FOR *ONE HOUR* AT A HEIGHT OF SEVEN THOUSAND FEET.
WE WILL MAKE A PILOT OF YOU YET.

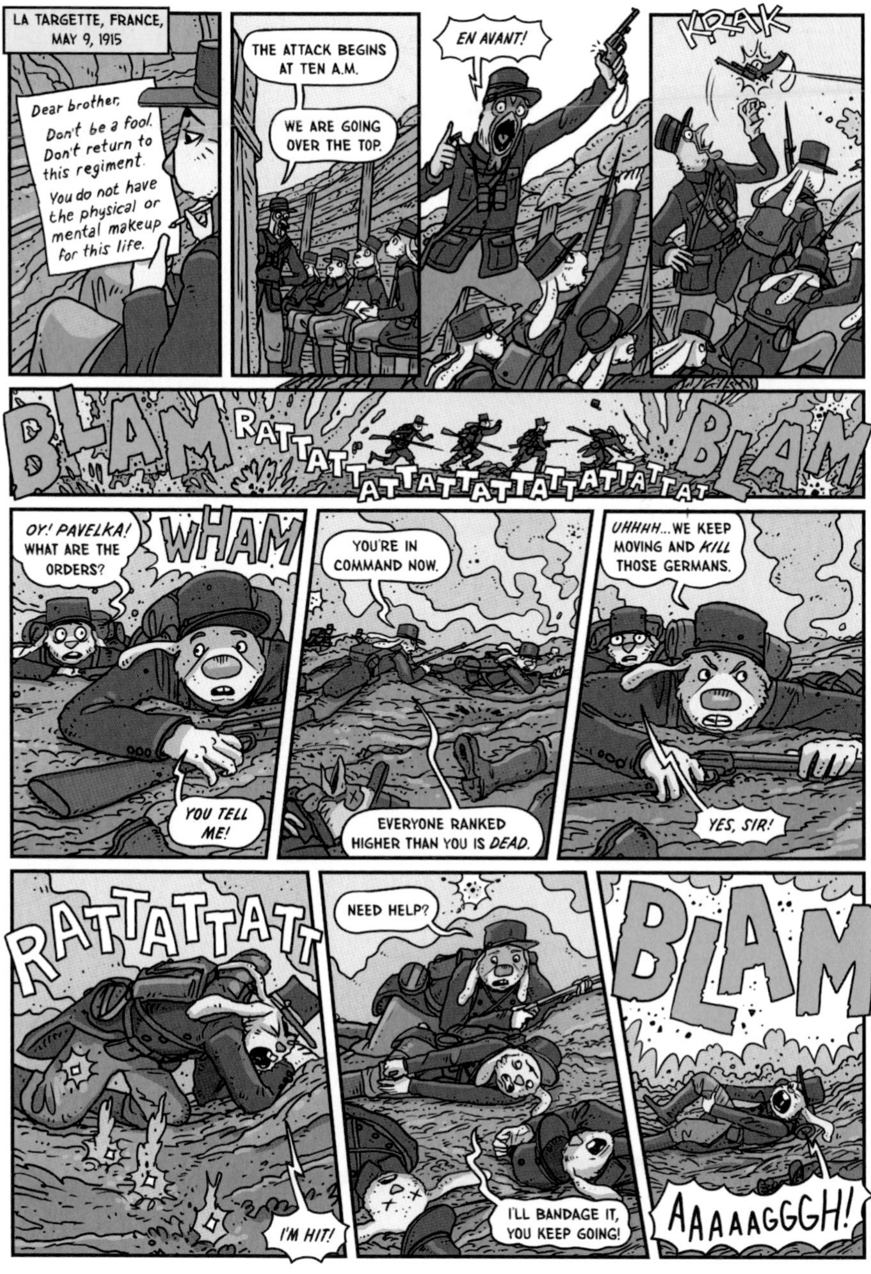

LA TARGETTE, FRANCE, MAY 9, 1915
Dear brother,
Don't be a fool. Don't return to this regiment.
You do not have the physical or mental makeup for this life.
THE ATTACK BEGINS AT TEN A.M.
WE ARE GOING OVER THE TOP.
EN AVANT!
KRAK
BLAM
RATTATTATTATTATTATTATTATTAT
BLAM
OY! PAVELKA! WHAT ARE THE ORDERS?
WHAM
YOU TELL ME!
YOU'RE IN COMMAND NOW.
EVERYONE RANKED HIGHER THAN YOU IS DEAD.
UHHHH...WE KEEP MOVING AND KILL THOSE GERMANS.
YES, SIR!
RATTATTATT
I'M HIT!
NEED HELP?
I'LL BANDAGE IT, YOU KEEP GOING!
BLAM
AAAAAGGGH!

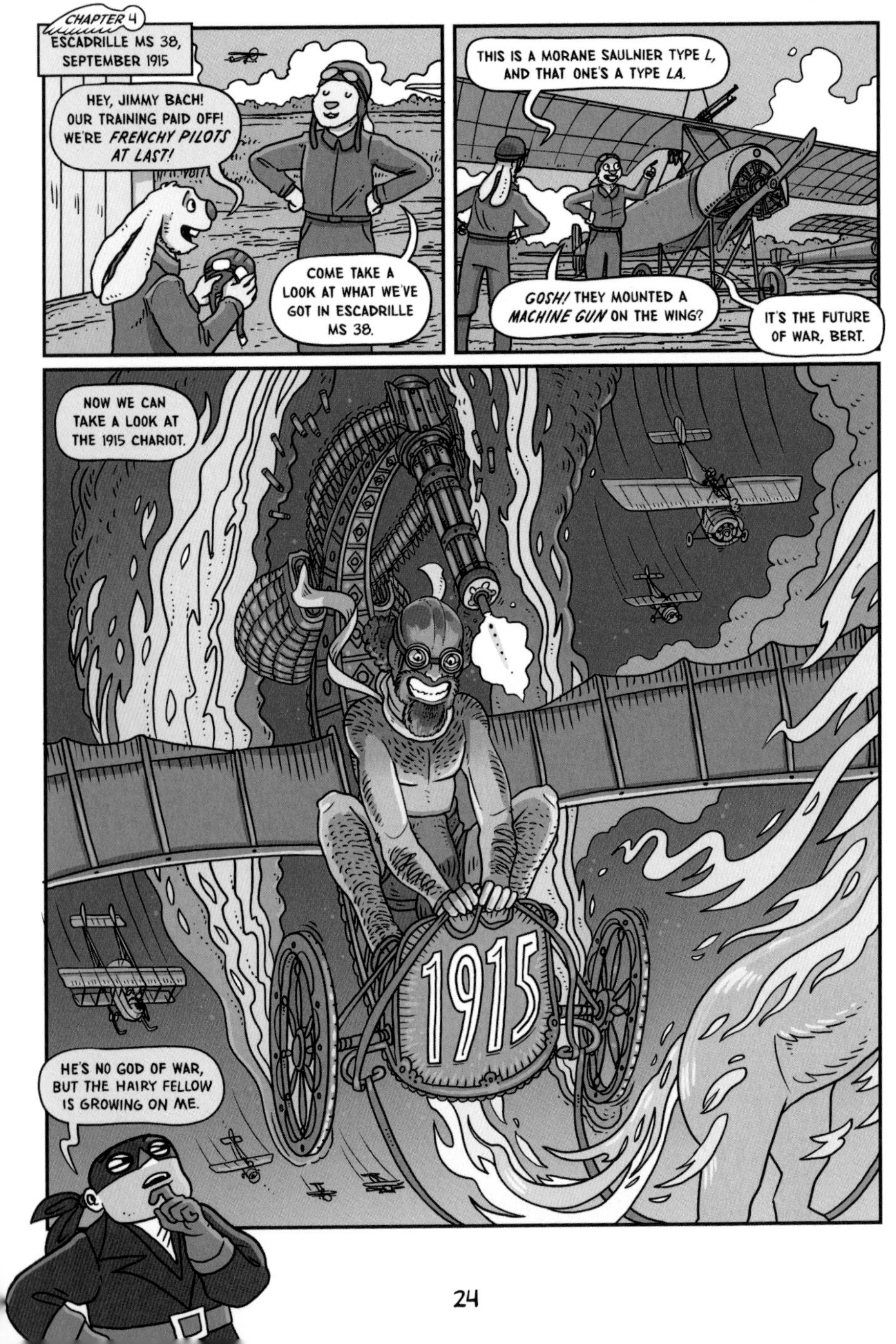
CHAPTER 4
ESCADRILLE MS 38, SEPTEMBER 1915
HEY, JIMMY BACH! OUR TRAINING PAID OFF! WE'RE *FRENCHY PILOTS AT LAST!*
COME TAKE A LOOK AT WHAT WE'VE GOT IN ESCADRILLE MS 38.
THIS IS A MORANE SAULNIER TYPE *L*, AND THAT ONE'S A TYPE *LA*.
GOSH! THEY MOUNTED A *MACHINE GUN* ON THE WING?
IT'S THE FUTURE OF WAR, BERT.
NOW WE CAN TAKE A LOOK AT THE 1915 CHARIOT.
1915
HE'S NO GOD OF WAR, BUT THE HAIRY FELLOW IS GROWING ON ME.

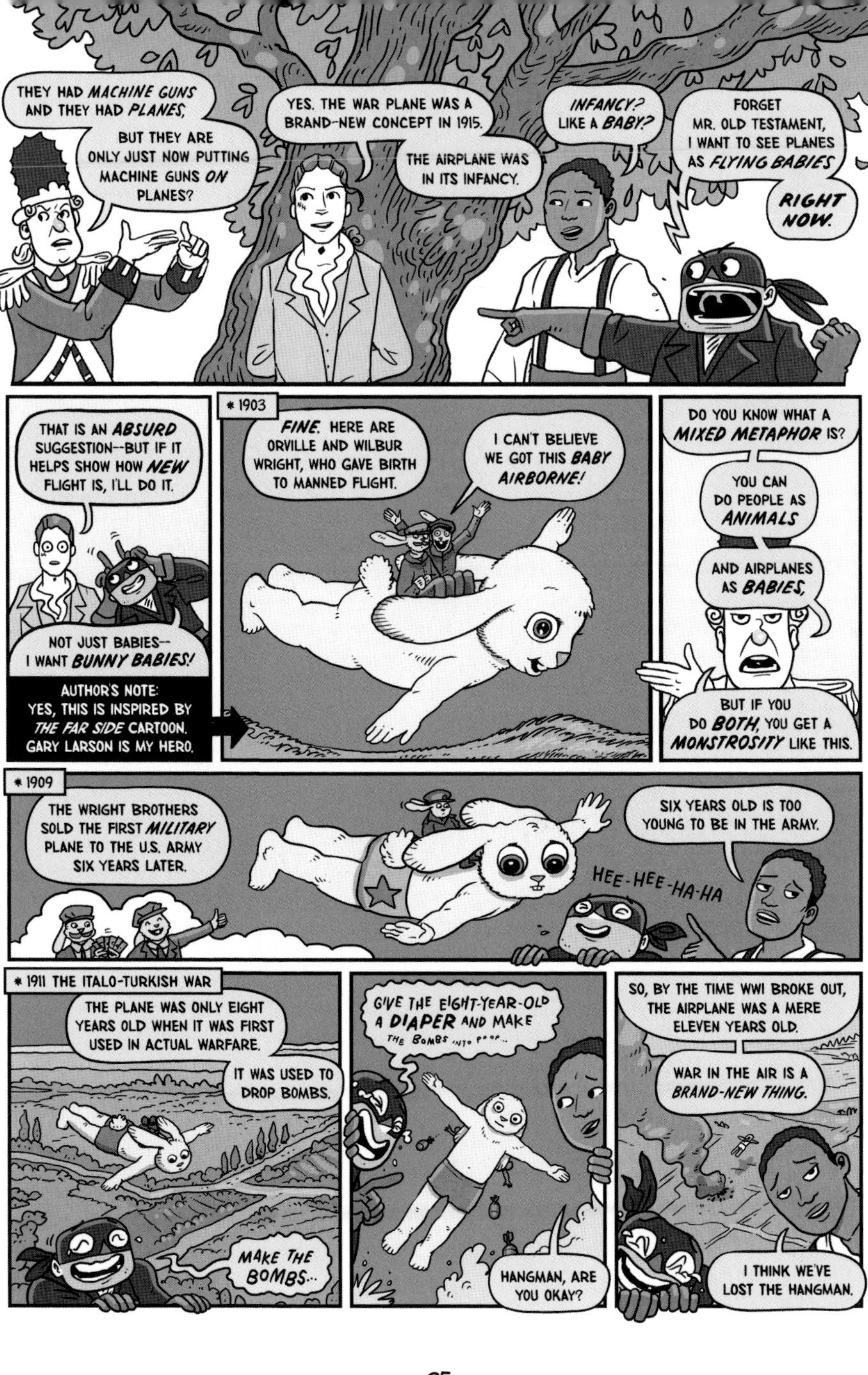
THEY HAD MACHINE GUNS AND THEY HAD PLANES,
BUT THEY ARE ONLY JUST NOW PUTTING MACHINE GUNS ON PLANES?
YES. THE WAR PLANE WAS A BRAND-NEW CONCEPT IN 1915.
THE AIRPLANE WAS IN ITS INFANCY.
INFANCY? LIKE A BABY?
FORGET MR. OLD TESTAMENT, I WANT TO SEE PLANES AS FLYING BABIES
RIGHT NOW.
THAT IS AN ABSURD SUGGESTION--BUT IF IT HELPS SHOW HOW NEW FLIGHT IS, I'LL DO IT.
NOT JUST BABIES-- I WANT BUNNY BABIES!
AUTHOR'S NOTE: YES, THIS IS INSPIRED BY THE FAR SIDE CARTOON. GARY LARSON IS MY HERO.
* 1903
FINE. HERE ARE ORVILLE AND WILBUR WRIGHT, WHO GAVE BIRTH TO MANNED FLIGHT.
I CAN'T BELIEVE WE GOT THIS BABY AIRBORNE!
DO YOU KNOW WHAT A MIXED METAPHOR IS?
YOU CAN DO PEOPLE AS ANIMALS
AND AIRPLANES AS BABIES,
BUT IF YOU DO BOTH, YOU GET A MONSTROSITY LIKE THIS.
* 1909
THE WRIGHT BROTHERS SOLD THE FIRST MILITARY PLANE TO THE U.S. ARMY SIX YEARS LATER.
SIX YEARS OLD IS TOO YOUNG TO BE IN THE ARMY.
HEE-HEE-HA-HA
* 1911 THE ITALO-TURKISH WAR
THE PLANE WAS ONLY EIGHT YEARS OLD WHEN IT WAS FIRST USED IN ACTUAL WARFARE.
IT WAS USED TO DROP BOMBS.
MAKE THE BOMBS...
GIVE THE EIGHT-YEAR-OLD A DIAPER AND MAKE THE BOMBS INTO POOP...
HANGMAN, ARE YOU OKAY?
SO, BY THE TIME WWI BROKE OUT, THE AIRPLANE WAS A MERE ELEVEN YEARS OLD.
WAR IN THE AIR IS A BRAND-NEW THING.
I THINK WE'VE LOST THE HANGMAN.

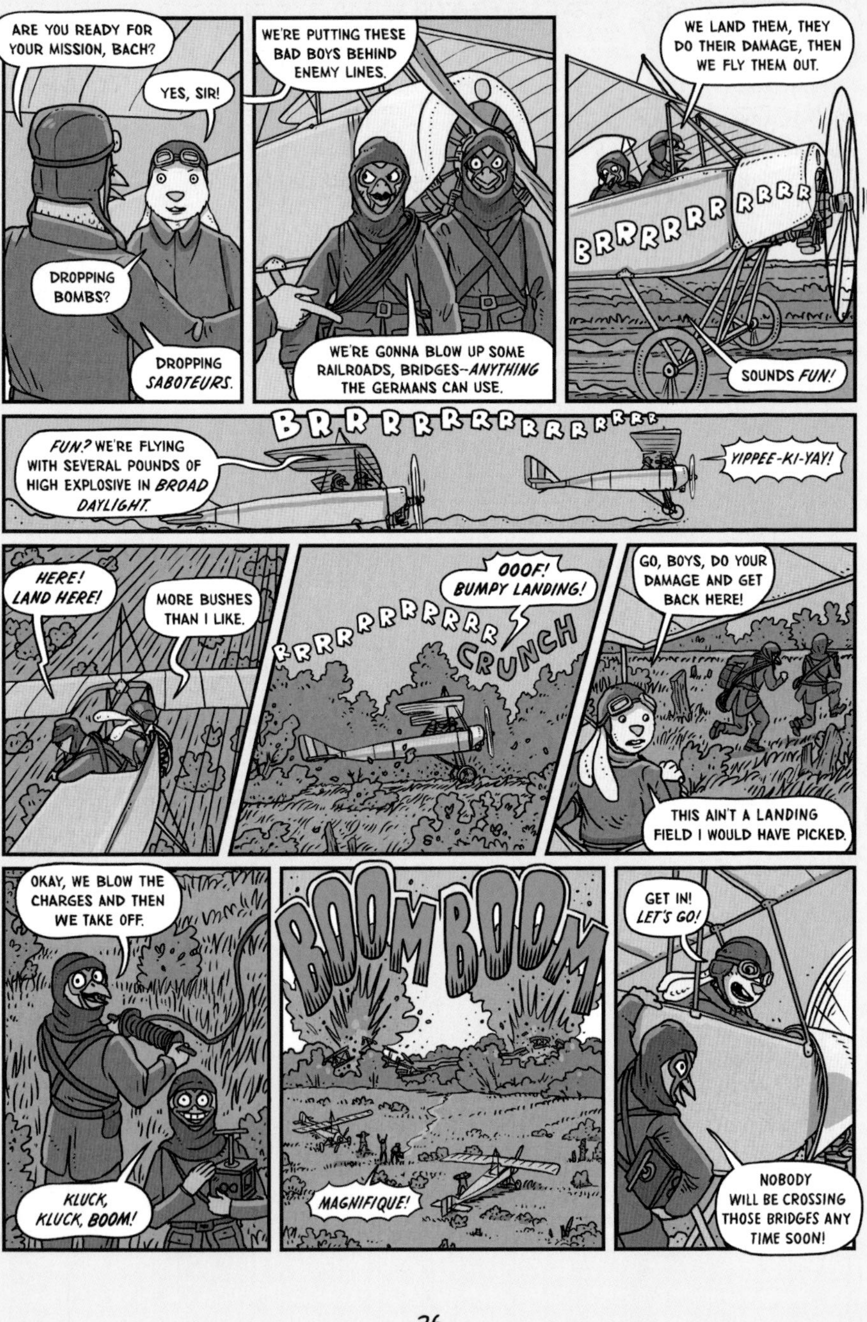

ARE YOU READY FOR YOUR MISSION, BACH?
YES, SIR!
DROPPING BOMBS?
DROPPING *SABOTEURS*.
WE'RE PUTTING THESE BAD BOYS BEHIND ENEMY LINES.
WE'RE GONNA BLOW UP SOME RAILROADS, BRIDGES--*ANYTHING* THE GERMANS CAN USE.
WE LAND THEM, THEY DO THEIR DAMAGE, THEN WE FLY THEM OUT.
BRRRRRRRRRRRR
SOUNDS *FUN!*
BRRRRRRRRRRRRRR
FUN? WE'RE FLYING WITH SEVERAL POUNDS OF HIGH EXPLOSIVE IN *BROAD DAYLIGHT.*
YIPPEE-KI-YAY!
HERE! LAND HERE!
MORE BUSHES THAN I LIKE.
OOOF! BUMPY LANDING!
RRRRRRRRRRRR
CRUNCH
GO, BOYS, DO YOUR DAMAGE AND GET BACK HERE!
THIS AIN'T A LANDING FIELD I WOULD HAVE PICKED.
OKAY, WE BLOW THE CHARGES AND THEN WE TAKE OFF.
KLUCK, KLUCK, BOOM!
BOOM BOOM
MAGNIFIQUE!
GET IN! *LET'S GO!*
NOBODY WILL BE CROSSING THOSE BRIDGES ANY TIME SOON!

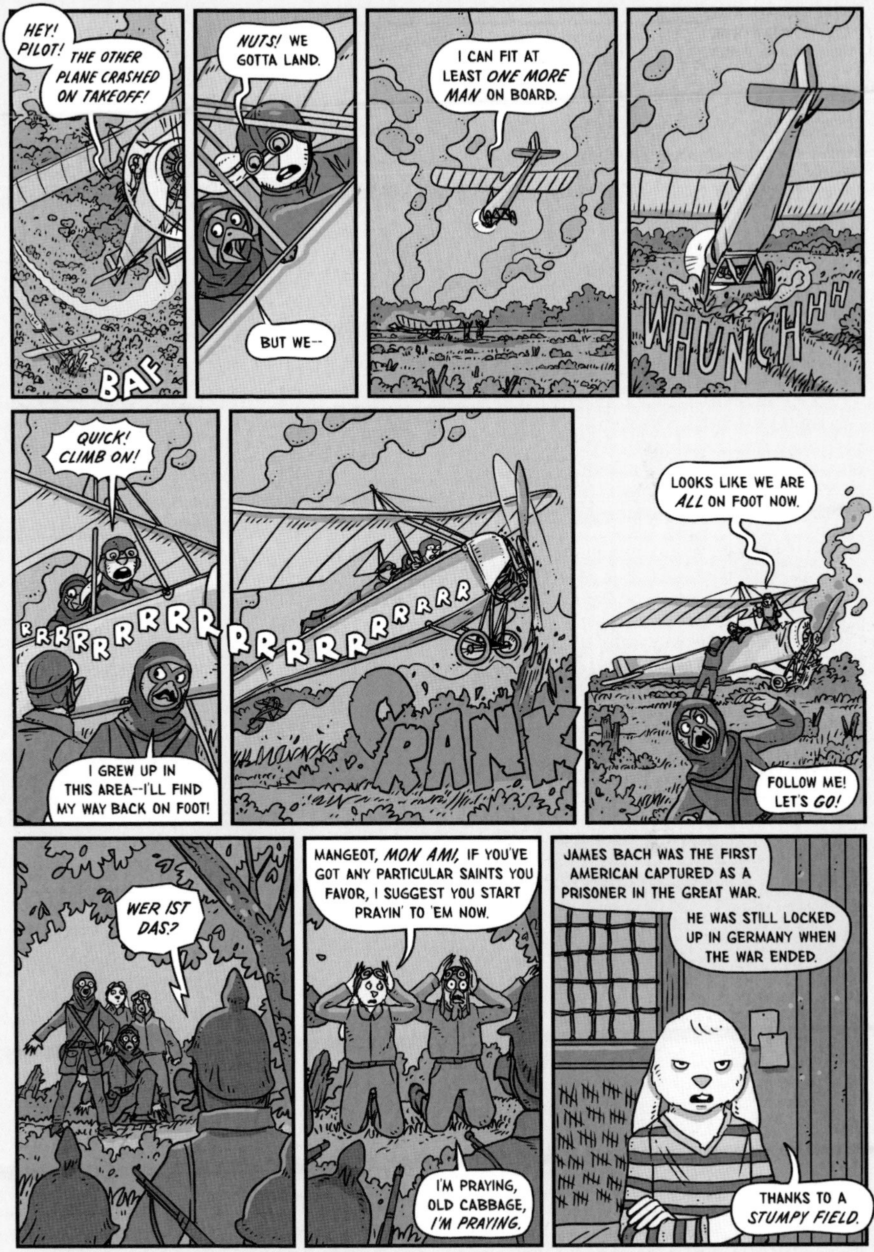
HEY! PILOT!
THE OTHER PLANE CRASHED ON TAKEOFF!
BAF
NUTS! WE GOTTA LAND.
BUT WE--
I CAN FIT AT LEAST ONE MORE MAN ON BOARD.
WHUNCHHH
QUICK! CLIMB ON!
RRRRRRRRR
I GREW UP IN THIS AREA--I'LL FIND MY WAY BACK ON FOOT!
RRRRRRRRRRRR
CRANK
LOOKS LIKE WE ARE ALL ON FOOT NOW.
FOLLOW ME! LET'S GO!
WER IST DAS?
MANGEOT, MON AMI, IF YOU'VE GOT ANY PARTICULAR SAINTS YOU FAVOR, I SUGGEST YOU START PRAYIN' TO 'EM NOW.
I'M PRAYING, OLD CABBAGE, I'M PRAYING.
JAMES BACH WAS THE FIRST AMERICAN CAPTURED AS A PRISONER IN THE GREAT WAR.
HE WAS STILL LOCKED UP IN GERMANY WHEN THE WAR ENDED.
THANKS TO A STUMPY FIELD.

CHAPTER 5 DEATH BALLOONS

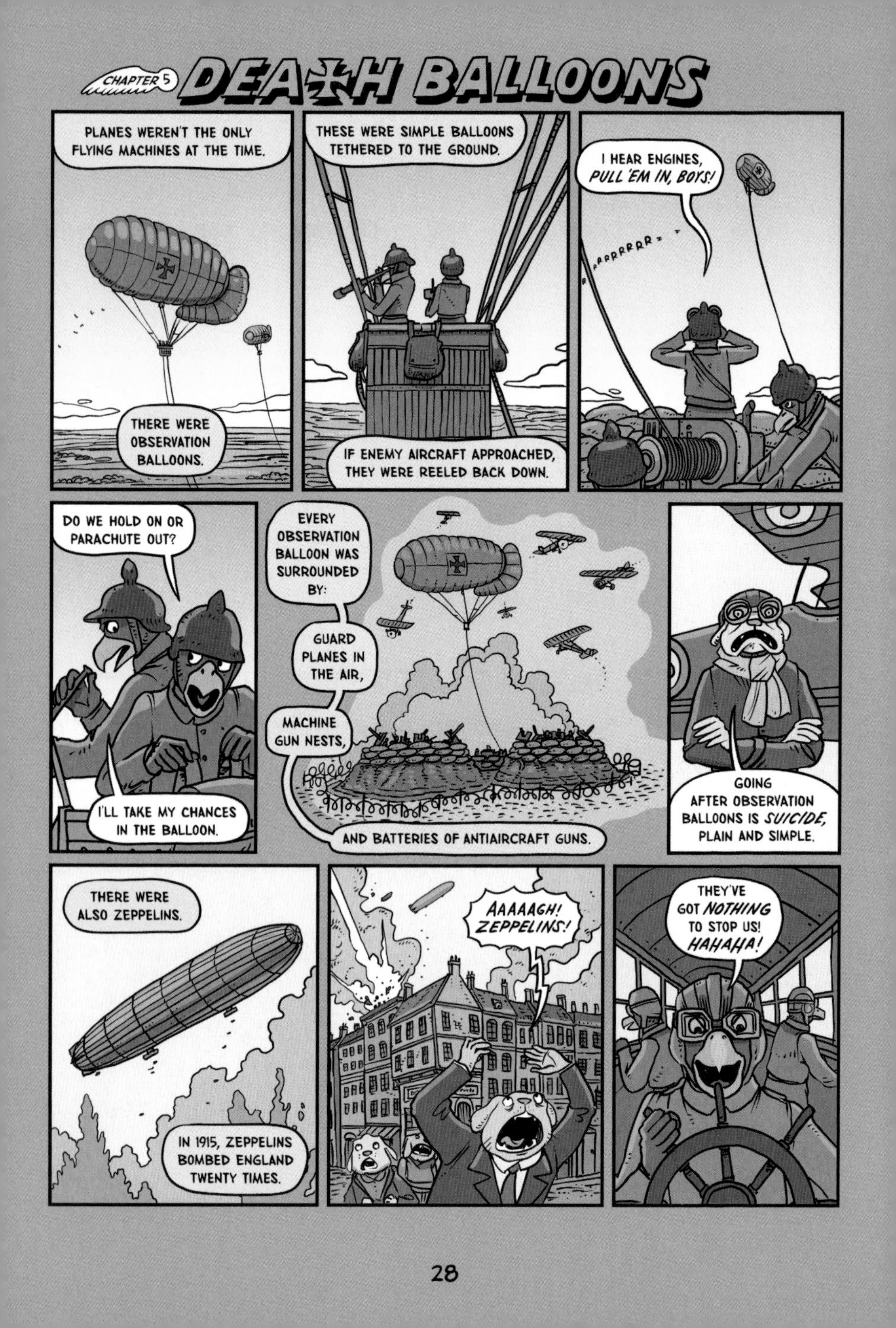

PLANES WEREN'T THE ONLY FLYING MACHINES AT THE TIME.
THERE WERE OBSERVATION BALLOONS.
THESE WERE SIMPLE BALLOONS TETHERED TO THE GROUND.
IF ENEMY AIRCRAFT APPROACHED, THEY WERE REELED BACK DOWN.
I HEAR ENGINES, PULL 'EM IN, BOYS!
RRRRRRRRR
DO WE HOLD ON OR PARACHUTE OUT?
I'LL TAKE MY CHANCES IN THE BALLOON.
EVERY OBSERVATION BALLOON WAS SURROUNDED BY:
GUARD PLANES IN THE AIR,
MACHINE GUN NESTS,
AND BATTERIES OF ANTIAIRCRAFT GUNS.
GOING AFTER OBSERVATION BALLOONS IS SUICIDE, PLAIN AND SIMPLE.
THERE WERE ALSO ZEPPELINS.
IN 1915, ZEPPELINS BOMBED ENGLAND TWENTY TIMES.
AAAAAGH! ZEPPELINS!
THEY'VE GOT NOTHING TO STOP US! HAHAHA!

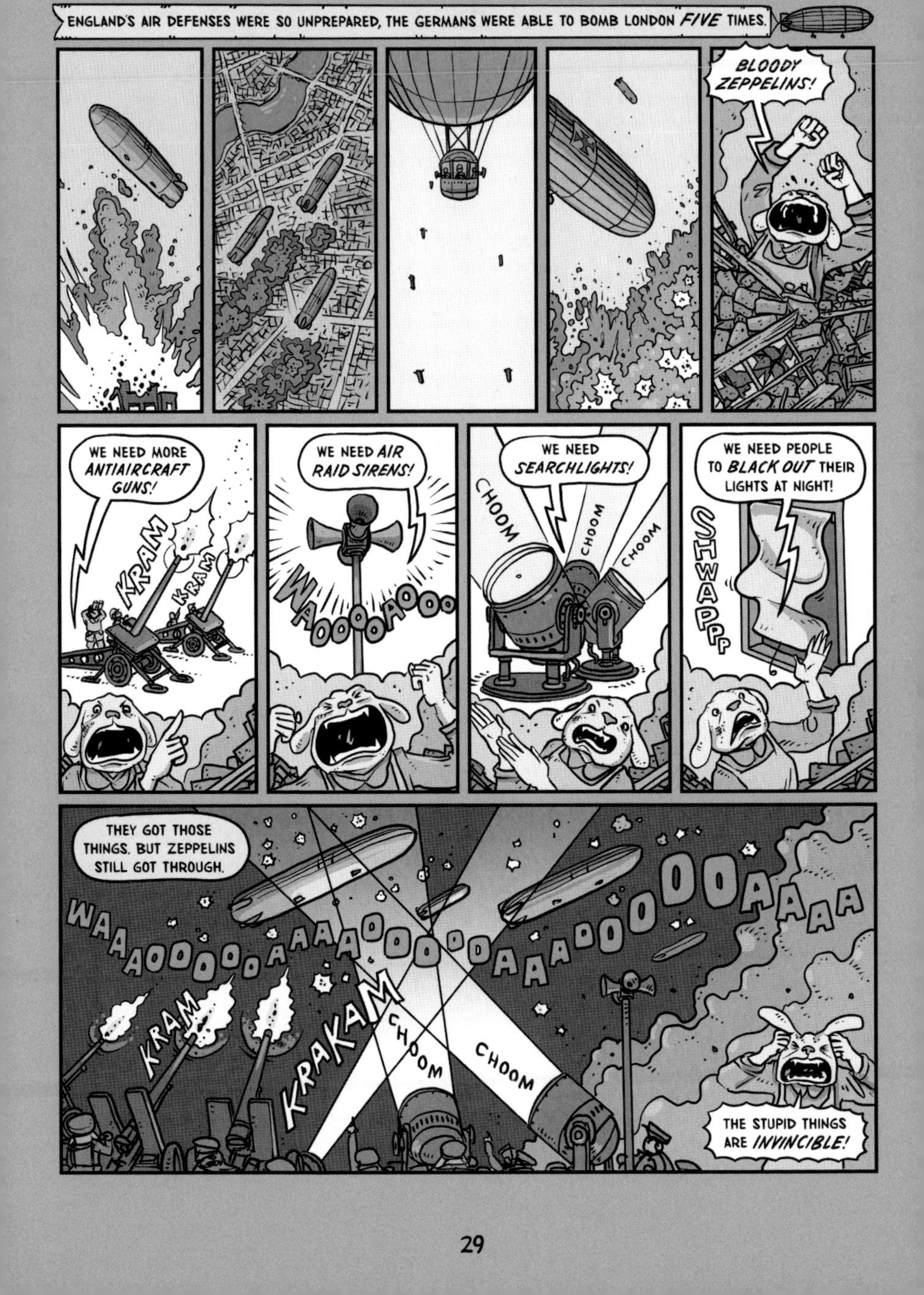

ENGLAND'S AIR DEFENSES WERE SO UNPREPARED, THE GERMANS WERE ABLE TO BOMB LONDON *FIVE* TIMES.
BLOODY ZEPPELINS!
WE NEED MORE *ANTIAIRCRAFT GUNS!*
KRAM
KRAM
WE NEED *AIR RAID SIRENS!*
WAOOOOAOOO
WE NEED *SEARCHLIGHTS!*
CHOOM
CHOOM
CHOOM
WE NEED PEOPLE TO *BLACK OUT* THEIR LIGHTS AT NIGHT!
SHWAPPP
THEY GOT THOSE THINGS. BUT ZEPPELINS STILL GOT THROUGH.
WAAAOOOOOAAAAAOOOOAAAAAOOOOOAAAAA
KRAM
KRAKAM
CHOOM
CHOOM
THE STUPID THINGS ARE *INVINCIBLE!*

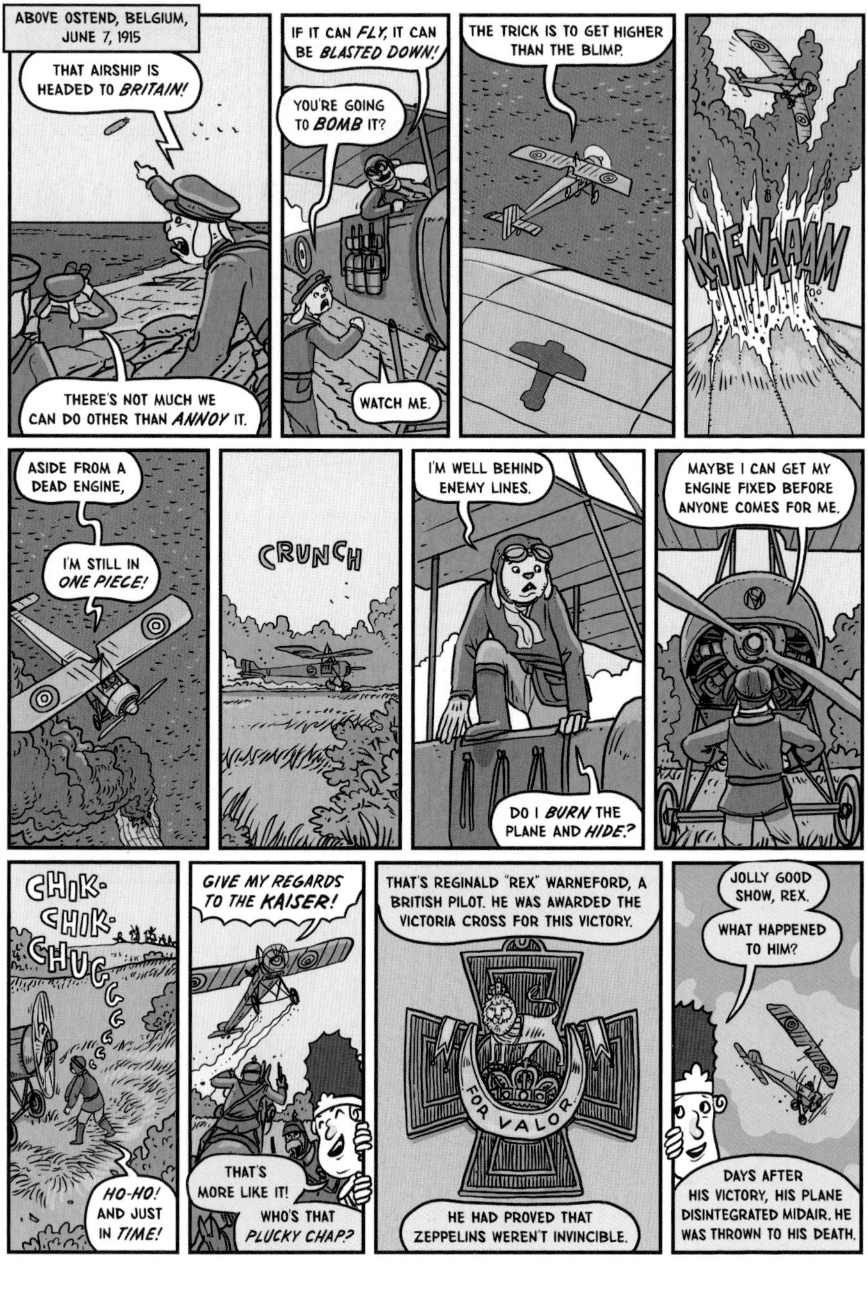
ABOVE OSTEND, BELGIUM, JUNE 7, 1915
THAT AIRSHIP IS HEADED TO BRITAIN!
THERE'S NOT MUCH WE CAN DO OTHER THAN ANNOY IT.
IF IT CAN FLY, IT CAN BE BLASTED DOWN!
YOU'RE GOING TO BOMB IT?
WATCH ME.
THE TRICK IS TO GET HIGHER THAN THE BLIMP.
KAFWAAAM
ASIDE FROM A DEAD ENGINE,
I'M STILL IN ONE PIECE!
CRUNCH
I'M WELL BEHIND ENEMY LINES.
DO I BURN THE PLANE AND HIDE?
MAYBE I CAN GET MY ENGINE FIXED BEFORE ANYONE COMES FOR ME.
CHIK-CHIK-CHUGGGGG
HO-HO! AND JUST IN TIME!
GIVE MY REGARDS TO THE KAISER!
THAT'S MORE LIKE IT!
WHO'S THAT PLUCKY CHAP?
THAT'S REGINALD "REX" WARNEFORD, A BRITISH PILOT. HE WAS AWARDED THE VICTORIA CROSS FOR THIS VICTORY.
FOR VALOR
HE HAD PROVED THAT ZEPPELINS WEREN'T INVINCIBLE.
JOLLY GOOD SHOW, REX.
WHAT HAPPENED TO HIM?
DAYS AFTER HIS VICTORY, HIS PLANE DISINTEGRATED MIDAIR. HE WAS THROWN TO HIS DEATH.

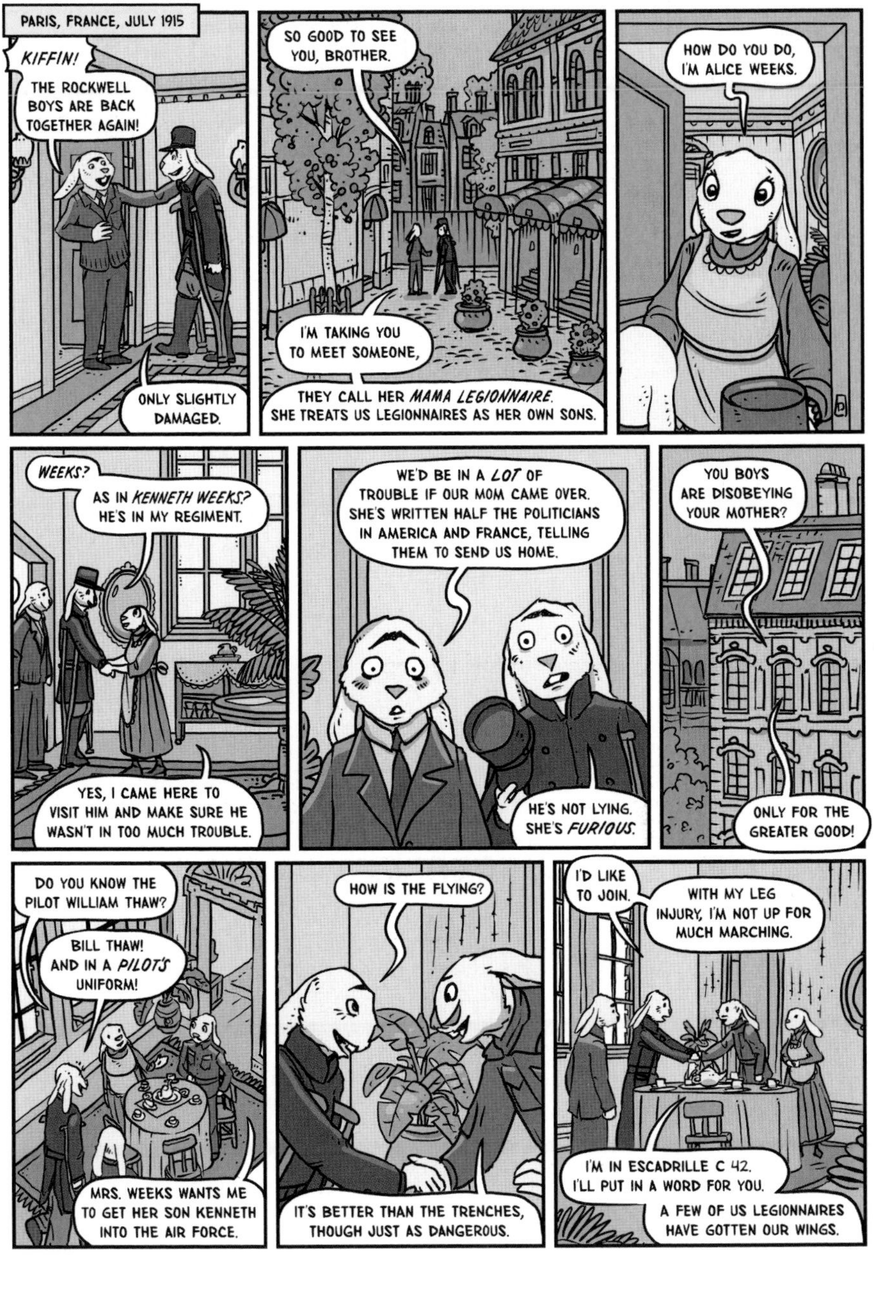
PARIS, FRANCE, JULY 1915
KIFFIN!
THE ROCKWELL BOYS ARE BACK TOGETHER AGAIN!
ONLY SLIGHTLY DAMAGED.
SO GOOD TO SEE YOU, BROTHER.
I'M TAKING YOU TO MEET SOMEONE,
THEY CALL HER MAMA LEGIONNAIRE. SHE TREATS US LEGIONNAIRES AS HER OWN SONS.
HOW DO YOU DO, I'M ALICE WEEKS.
WEEKS?
AS IN KENNETH WEEKS? HE'S IN MY REGIMENT.
YES, I CAME HERE TO VISIT HIM AND MAKE SURE HE WASN'T IN TOO MUCH TROUBLE.
WE'D BE IN A LOT OF TROUBLE IF OUR MOM CAME OVER. SHE'S WRITTEN HALF THE POLITICIANS IN AMERICA AND FRANCE, TELLING THEM TO SEND US HOME.
HE'S NOT LYING. SHE'S FURIOUS.
YOU BOYS ARE DISOBEYING YOUR MOTHER?
ONLY FOR THE GREATER GOOD!
DO YOU KNOW THE PILOT WILLIAM THAW?
BILL THAW! AND IN A PILOT'S UNIFORM!
MRS. WEEKS WANTS ME TO GET HER SON KENNETH INTO THE AIR FORCE.
HOW IS THE FLYING?
IT'S BETTER THAN THE TRENCHES, THOUGH JUST AS DANGEROUS.
I'D LIKE TO JOIN.
WITH MY LEG INJURY, I'M NOT UP FOR MUCH MARCHING.
I'M IN ESCADRILLE C 42. I'LL PUT IN A WORD FOR YOU.
A FEW OF US LEGIONNAIRES HAVE GOTTEN OUR WINGS.

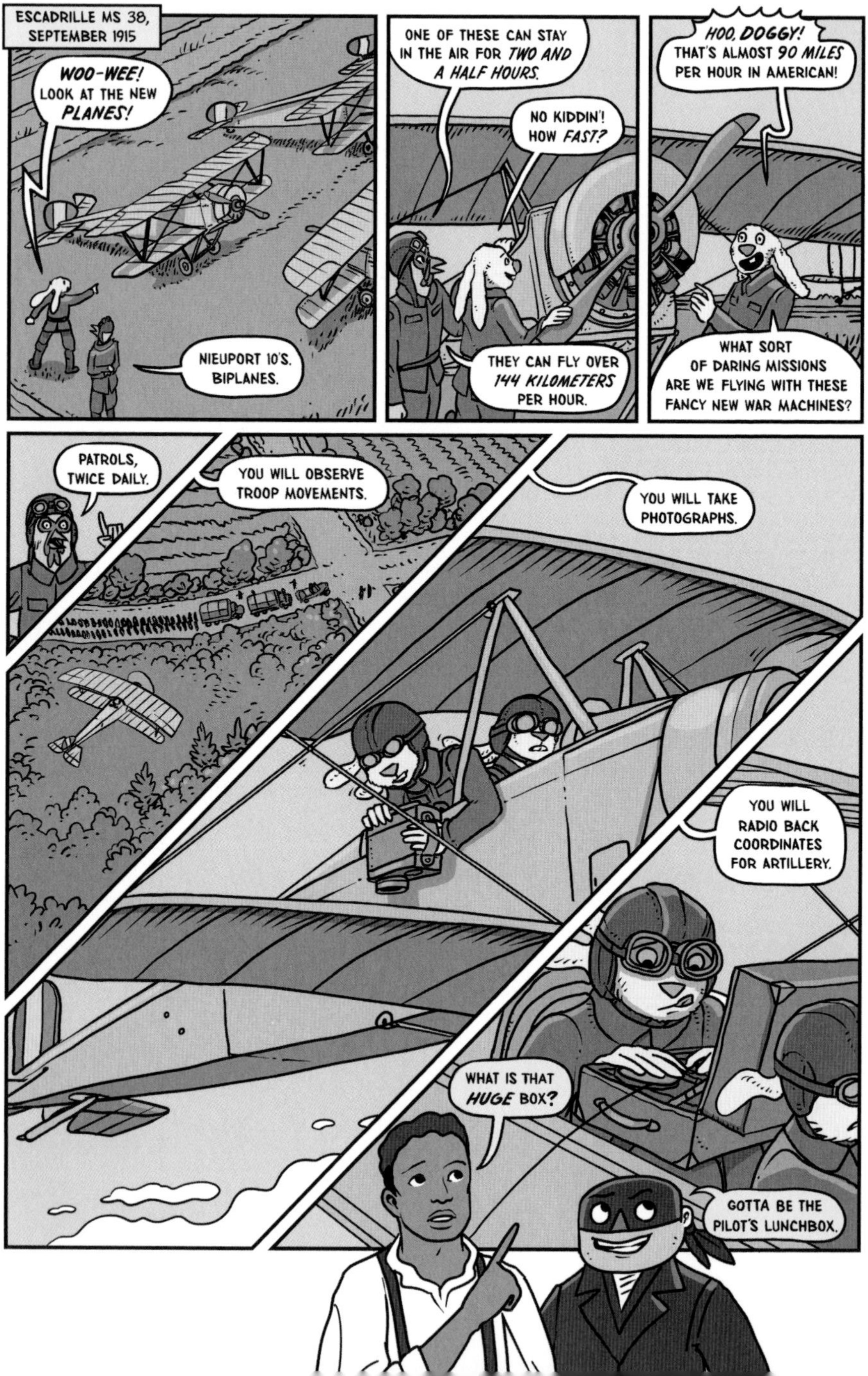
ESCADRILLE MS 38, SEPTEMBER 1915
WOO-WEE! LOOK AT THE NEW PLANES!
NIEUPORT 10'S. BIPLANES.
ONE OF THESE CAN STAY IN THE AIR FOR TWO AND A HALF HOURS.
NO KIDDIN'! HOW FAST?
THEY CAN FLY OVER 144 KILOMETERS PER HOUR.
HOO, DOGGY! THAT'S ALMOST 90 MILES PER HOUR IN AMERICAN!
WHAT SORT OF DARING MISSIONS ARE WE FLYING WITH THESE FANCY NEW WAR MACHINES?
PATROLS, TWICE DAILY.
YOU WILL OBSERVE TROOP MOVEMENTS.
YOU WILL TAKE PHOTOGRAPHS.
YOU WILL RADIO BACK COORDINATES FOR ARTILLERY.
WHAT IS THAT HUGE BOX?
GOTTA BE THE PILOT'S LUNCHBOX.

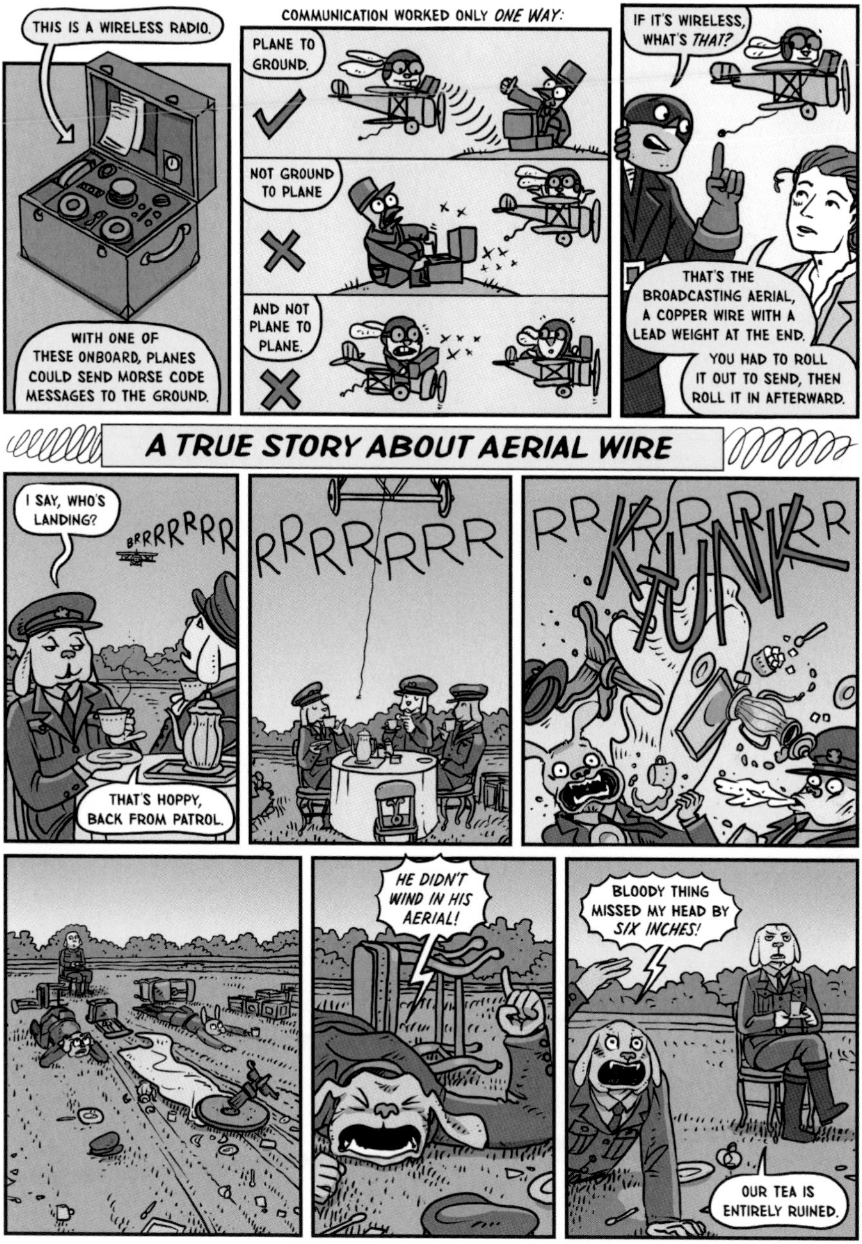
THIS IS A WIRELESS RADIO.
WITH ONE OF THESE ONBOARD, PLANES COULD SEND MORSE CODE MESSAGES TO THE GROUND.
COMMUNICATION WORKED ONLY *ONE WAY*:
PLANE TO GROUND.
NOT GROUND TO PLANE
AND NOT PLANE TO PLANE.
IF IT'S WIRELESS, WHAT'S *THAT?*
THAT'S THE BROADCASTING AERIAL, A COPPER WIRE WITH A LEAD WEIGHT AT THE END.
YOU HAD TO ROLL IT OUT TO SEND, THEN ROLL IT IN AFTERWARD.
A TRUE STORY ABOUT AERIAL WIRE
I SAY, WHO'S LANDING?
BRRRRRRR
THAT'S HOPPY, BACK FROM PATROL.
RRRRRRR
RR KTUNK RRRRRR
HE DIDN'T WIND IN HIS AERIAL!
BLOODY THING MISSED MY HEAD BY *SIX INCHES!*
OUR TEA IS ENTIRELY RUINED.

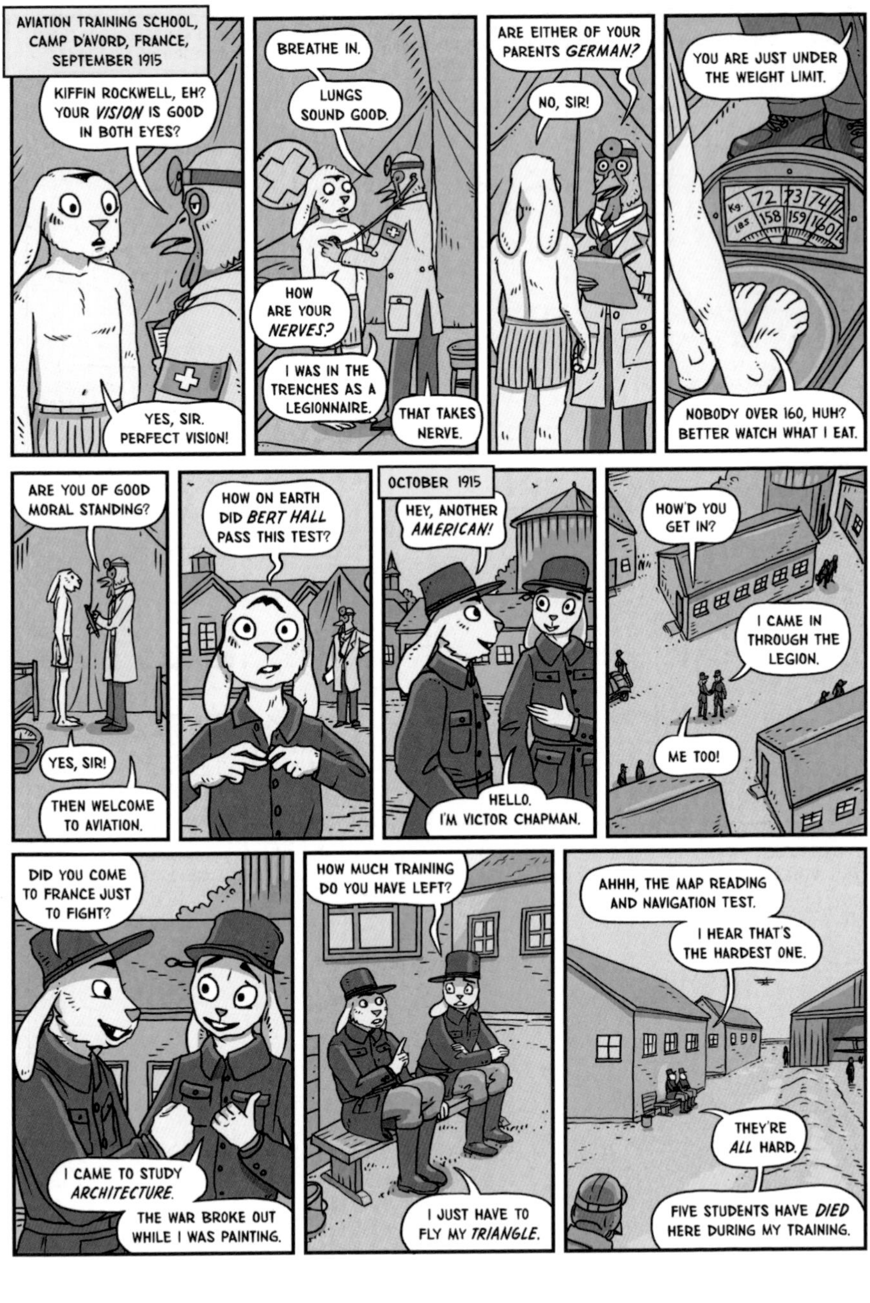
AVIATION TRAINING SCHOOL, CAMP D'AVORD, FRANCE, SEPTEMBER 1915
KIFFIN ROCKWELL, EH? YOUR *VISION* IS GOOD IN BOTH EYES?
YES, SIR. PERFECT VISION!
BREATHE IN.
LUNGS SOUND GOOD.
HOW ARE YOUR *NERVES?*
I WAS IN THE TRENCHES AS A LEGIONNAIRE.
THAT TAKES NERVE.
ARE EITHER OF YOUR PARENTS *GERMAN?*
NO, SIR!
YOU ARE JUST UNDER THE WEIGHT LIMIT.
Kg. 72 73 74
LBS. 158 159 160
NOBODY OVER 160, HUH? BETTER WATCH WHAT I EAT.
ARE YOU OF GOOD MORAL STANDING?
YES, SIR!
THEN WELCOME TO AVIATION.
HOW ON EARTH DID *BERT HALL* PASS THIS TEST?
OCTOBER 1915
HEY, ANOTHER *AMERICAN!*
HELLO. I'M VICTOR CHAPMAN.
HOW'D YOU GET IN?
I CAME IN THROUGH THE LEGION.
ME TOO!
DID YOU COME TO FRANCE JUST TO FIGHT?
I CAME TO STUDY *ARCHITECTURE*.
THE WAR BROKE OUT WHILE I WAS PAINTING.
HOW MUCH TRAINING DO YOU HAVE LEFT?
I JUST HAVE TO FLY MY *TRIANGLE*.
AHHH, THE MAP READING AND NAVIGATION TEST.
I HEAR THAT'S THE HARDEST ONE.
THEY'RE *ALL* HARD.
FIVE STUDENTS HAVE *DIED* HERE DURING MY TRAINING.

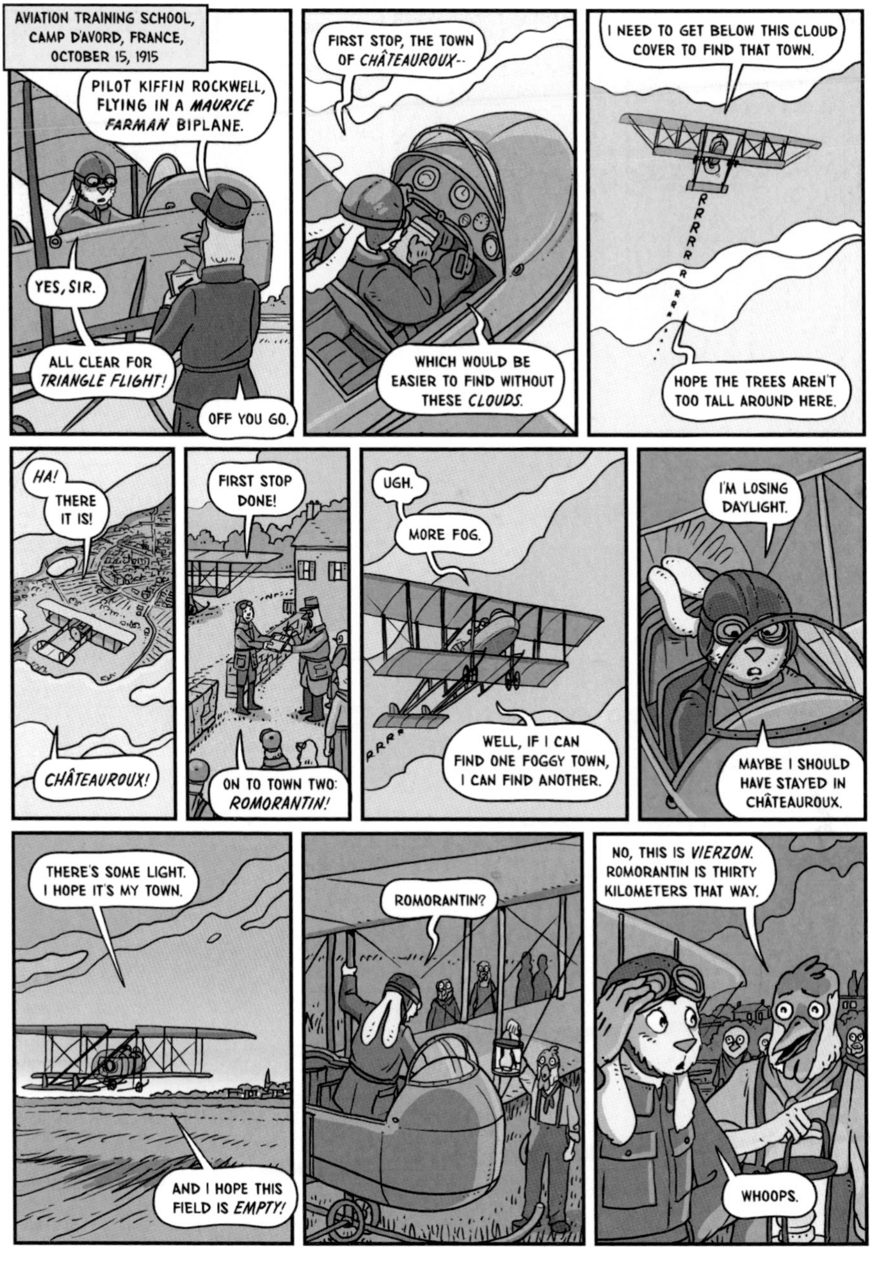
AVIATION TRAINING SCHOOL, CAMP D'AVORD, FRANCE, OCTOBER 15, 1915
PILOT KIFFIN ROCKWELL, FLYING IN A *MAURICE FARMAN* BIPLANE.
YES, SIR.
ALL CLEAR FOR *TRIANGLE FLIGHT!*
OFF YOU GO.
FIRST STOP, THE TOWN OF *CHÂTEAUROUX*--
WHICH WOULD BE EASIER TO FIND WITHOUT THESE *CLOUDS*.
I NEED TO GET BELOW THIS CLOUD COVER TO FIND THAT TOWN.
RRRRRR
HOPE THE TREES AREN'T TOO TALL AROUND HERE.
HA!
THERE IT IS!
CHÂTEAUROUX!
FIRST STOP DONE!
ON TO TOWN TWO: *ROMORANTIN!*
UGH.
MORE FOG.
RRRR
WELL, IF I CAN FIND ONE FOGGY TOWN, I CAN FIND ANOTHER.
I'M LOSING DAYLIGHT.
MAYBE I SHOULD HAVE STAYED IN CHÂTEAUROUX.
THERE'S SOME LIGHT. I HOPE IT'S MY TOWN.
AND I HOPE THIS FIELD IS *EMPTY!*
ROMORANTIN?
NO, THIS IS *VIERZON.* ROMORANTIN IS THIRTY KILOMETERS THAT WAY.
WHOOPS.

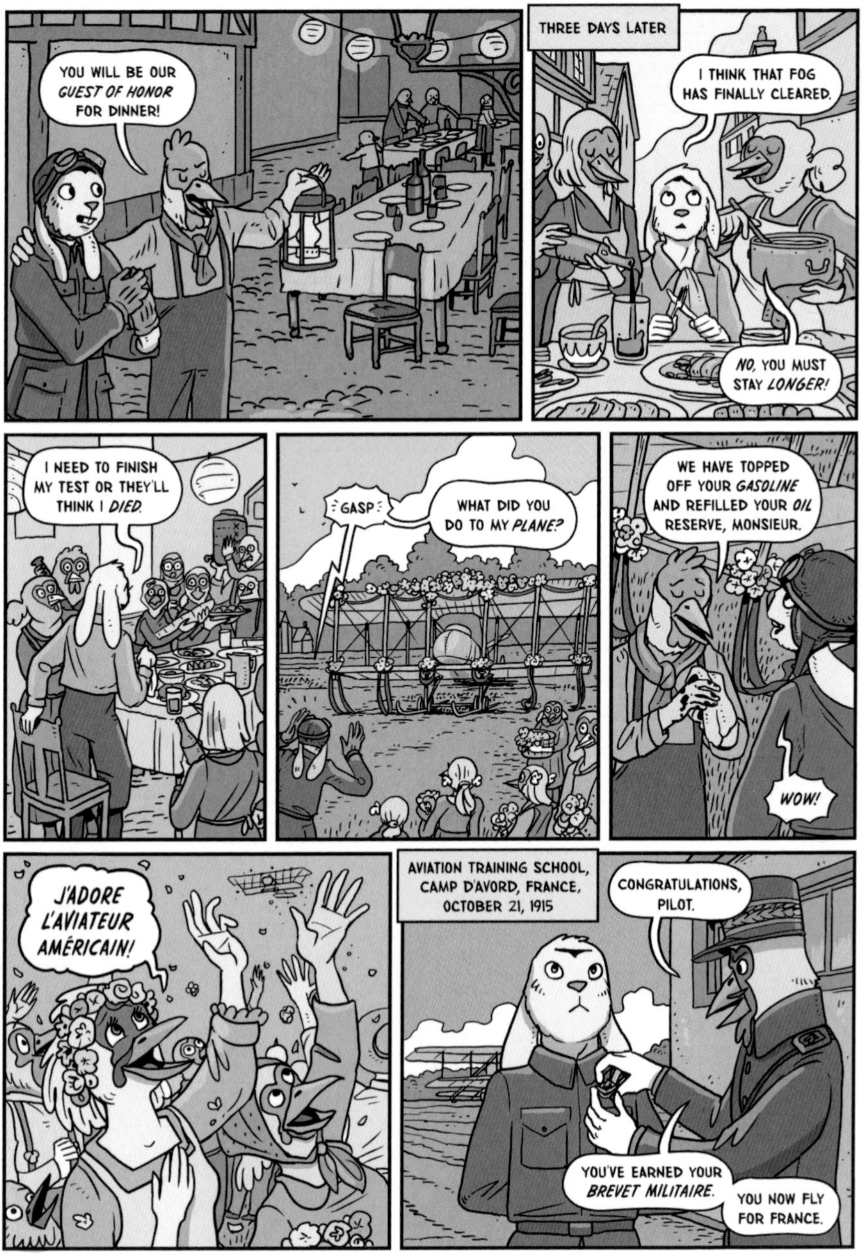
YOU WILL BE OUR *GUEST OF HONOR* FOR DINNER!
THREE DAYS LATER
I THINK THAT FOG HAS FINALLY CLEARED.
NO, YOU MUST STAY *LONGER!*
I NEED TO FINISH MY TEST OR THEY'LL THINK I *DIED.*
GASP
WHAT DID YOU DO TO MY *PLANE?*
WE HAVE TOPPED OFF YOUR *GASOLINE* AND REFILLED YOUR *OIL* RESERVE, MONSIEUR.
WOW!
J'ADORE L'AVIATEUR AMÉRICAIN!
AVIATION TRAINING SCHOOL, CAMP D'AVORD, FRANCE, OCTOBER 21, 1915
CONGRATULATIONS, PILOT.
YOU'VE EARNED YOUR *BREVET MILITAIRE.*
YOU NOW FLY FOR FRANCE.

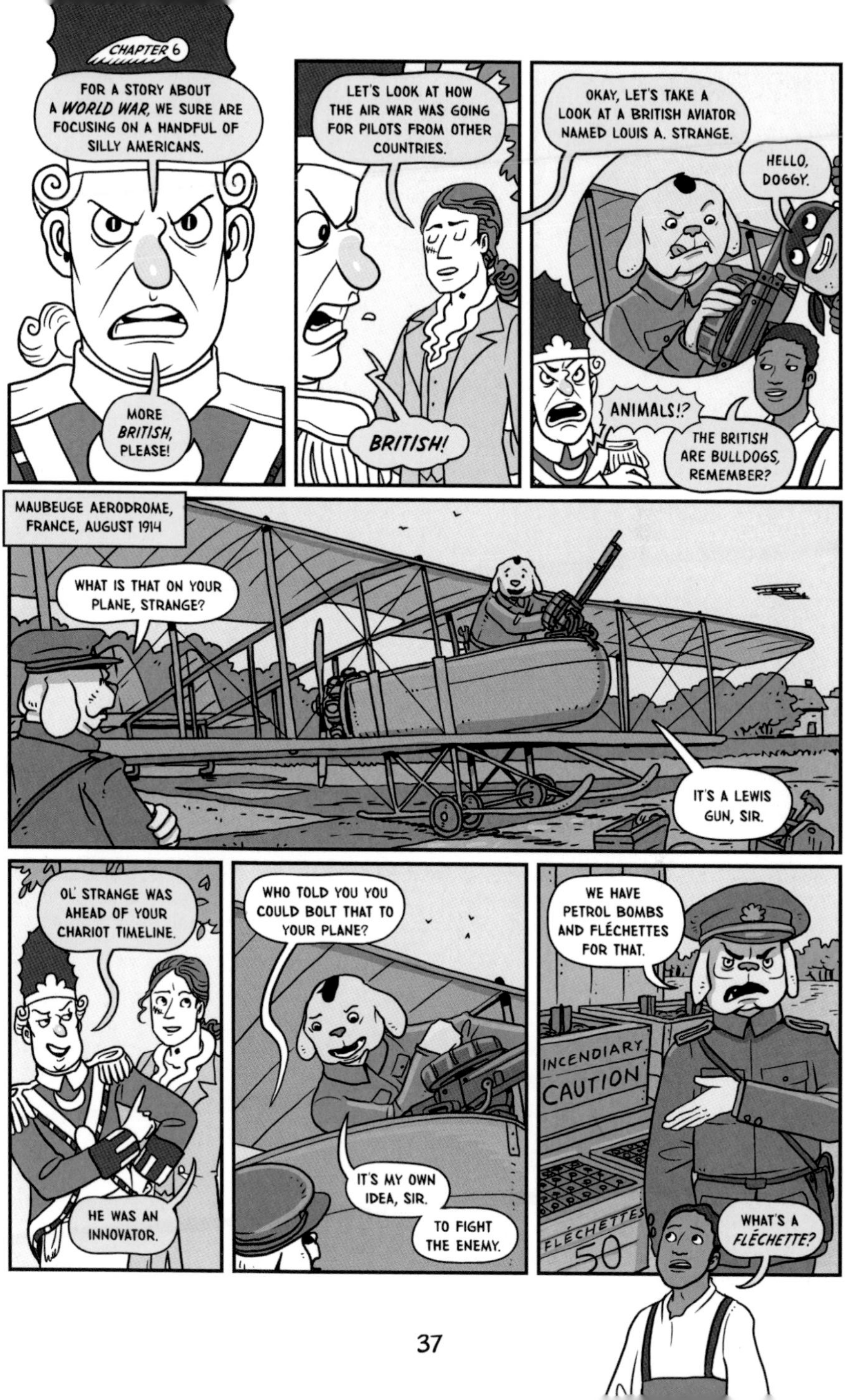
CHAPTER 6
FOR A STORY ABOUT A *WORLD WAR*, WE SURE ARE FOCUSING ON A HANDFUL OF SILLY AMERICANS.
MORE *BRITISH*, PLEASE!
LET'S LOOK AT HOW THE AIR WAR WAS GOING FOR PILOTS FROM OTHER COUNTRIES.
BRITISH!
OKAY, LET'S TAKE A LOOK AT A BRITISH AVIATOR NAMED LOUIS A. STRANGE.
HELLO, DOGGY.
ANIMALS!?
THE BRITISH ARE BULLDOGS, REMEMBER?
MAUBEUGE AERODROME, FRANCE, AUGUST 1914
WHAT IS THAT ON YOUR PLANE, STRANGE?
IT'S A LEWIS GUN, SIR.
OL' STRANGE WAS AHEAD OF YOUR CHARIOT TIMELINE.
HE WAS AN INNOVATOR.
WHO TOLD YOU YOU COULD BOLT THAT TO YOUR PLANE?
IT'S MY OWN IDEA, SIR.
TO FIGHT THE ENEMY.
WE HAVE PETROL BOMBS AND FLÉCHETTES FOR THAT.
INCENDIARY
CAUTION
FLÉCHETTES
50
WHAT'S A *FLÉCHETTE?*

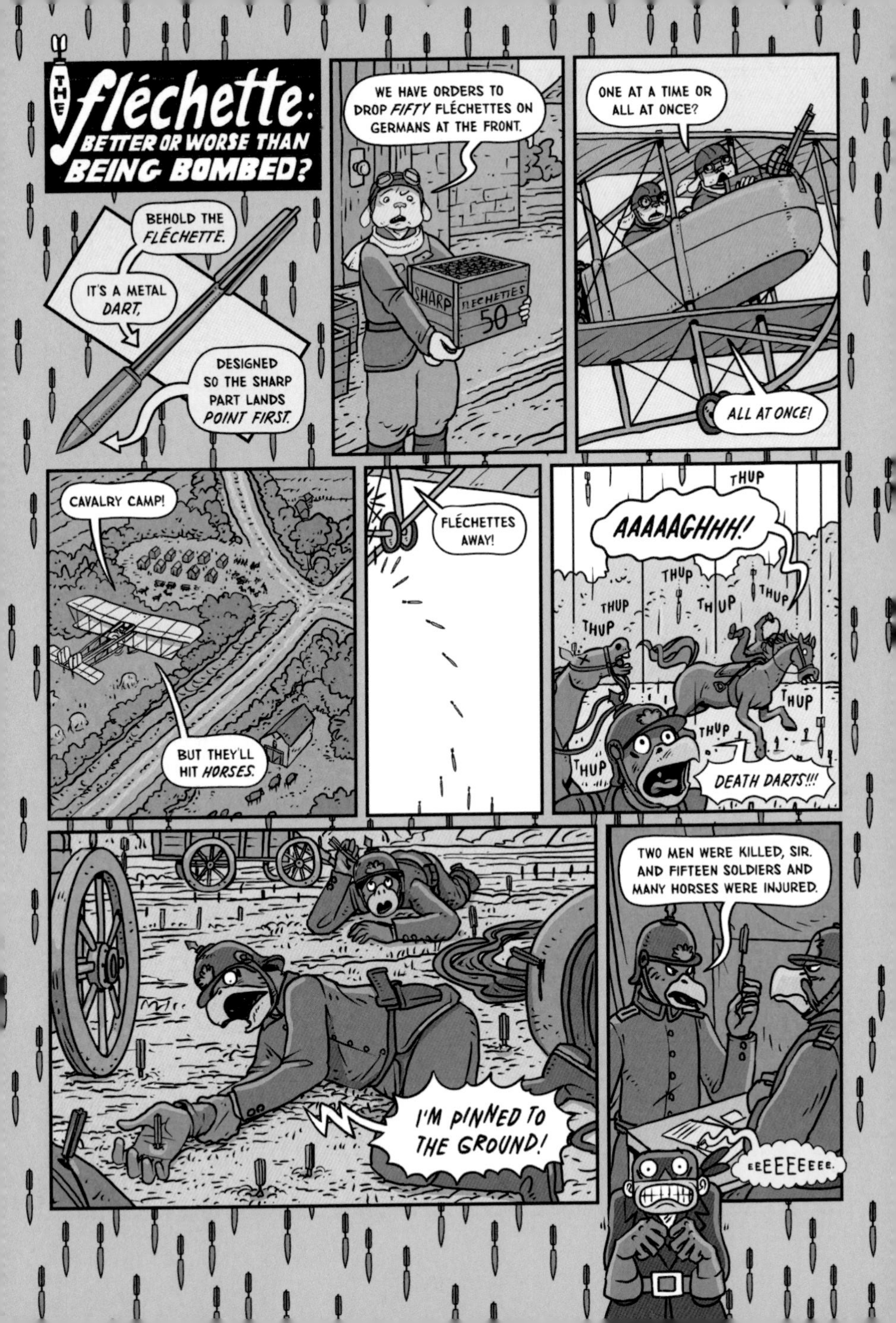
THE flèchette: BETTER OR WORSE THAN BEING BOMBED?
BEHOLD THE FLÉCHETTE.
IT'S A METAL DART,
DESIGNED SO THE SHARP PART LANDS POINT FIRST.
WE HAVE ORDERS TO DROP FIFTY FLÉCHETTES ON GERMANS AT THE FRONT.
SHARP FLECHETTES 50
ONE AT A TIME OR ALL AT ONCE?
ALL AT ONCE!
CAVALRY CAMP!
BUT THEY'LL HIT HORSES.
FLÉCHETTES AWAY!
THUP
AAAAAGHHH!
THUP THUP THUP THUP THUP THUP THUP THUP THUP
DEATH DARTS!!!
I'M PINNED TO THE GROUND!
TWO MEN WERE KILLED, SIR. AND FIFTEEN SOLDIERS AND MANY HORSES WERE INJURED.
EEEEEEEEE.

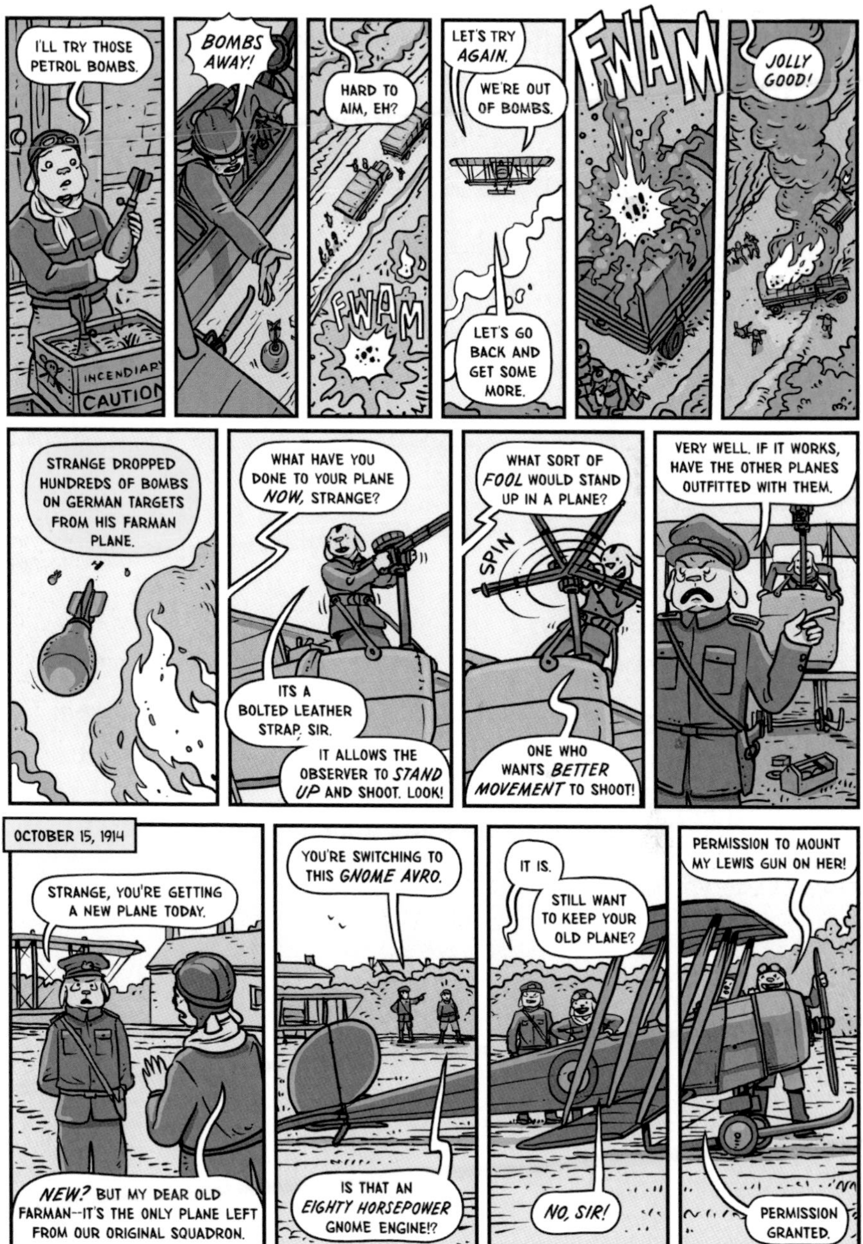
I'LL TRY THOSE PETROL BOMBS.
INCENDIARY
CAUTION
BOMBS AWAY!
HARD TO AIM, EH?
FWAM
LET'S TRY AGAIN.
WE'RE OUT OF BOMBS.
LET'S GO BACK AND GET SOME MORE.
FWAM
JOLLY GOOD!
STRANGE DROPPED HUNDREDS OF BOMBS ON GERMAN TARGETS FROM HIS FARMAN PLANE.
WHAT HAVE YOU DONE TO YOUR PLANE NOW, STRANGE?
ITS A BOLTED LEATHER STRAP, SIR.
IT ALLOWS THE OBSERVER TO STAND UP AND SHOOT. LOOK!
WHAT SORT OF FOOL WOULD STAND UP IN A PLANE?
SPIN
ONE WHO WANTS BETTER MOVEMENT TO SHOOT!
VERY WELL. IF IT WORKS, HAVE THE OTHER PLANES OUTFITTED WITH THEM.
OCTOBER 15, 1914
STRANGE, YOU'RE GETTING A NEW PLANE TODAY.
NEW? BUT MY DEAR OLD FARMAN--IT'S THE ONLY PLANE LEFT FROM OUR ORIGINAL SQUADRON.
YOU'RE SWITCHING TO THIS GNOME AVRO.
IS THAT AN EIGHTY HORSEPOWER GNOME ENGINE!?
IT IS.
STILL WANT TO KEEP YOUR OLD PLANE?
NO, SIR!
PERMISSION TO MOUNT MY LEWIS GUN ON HER!
PERMISSION GRANTED.

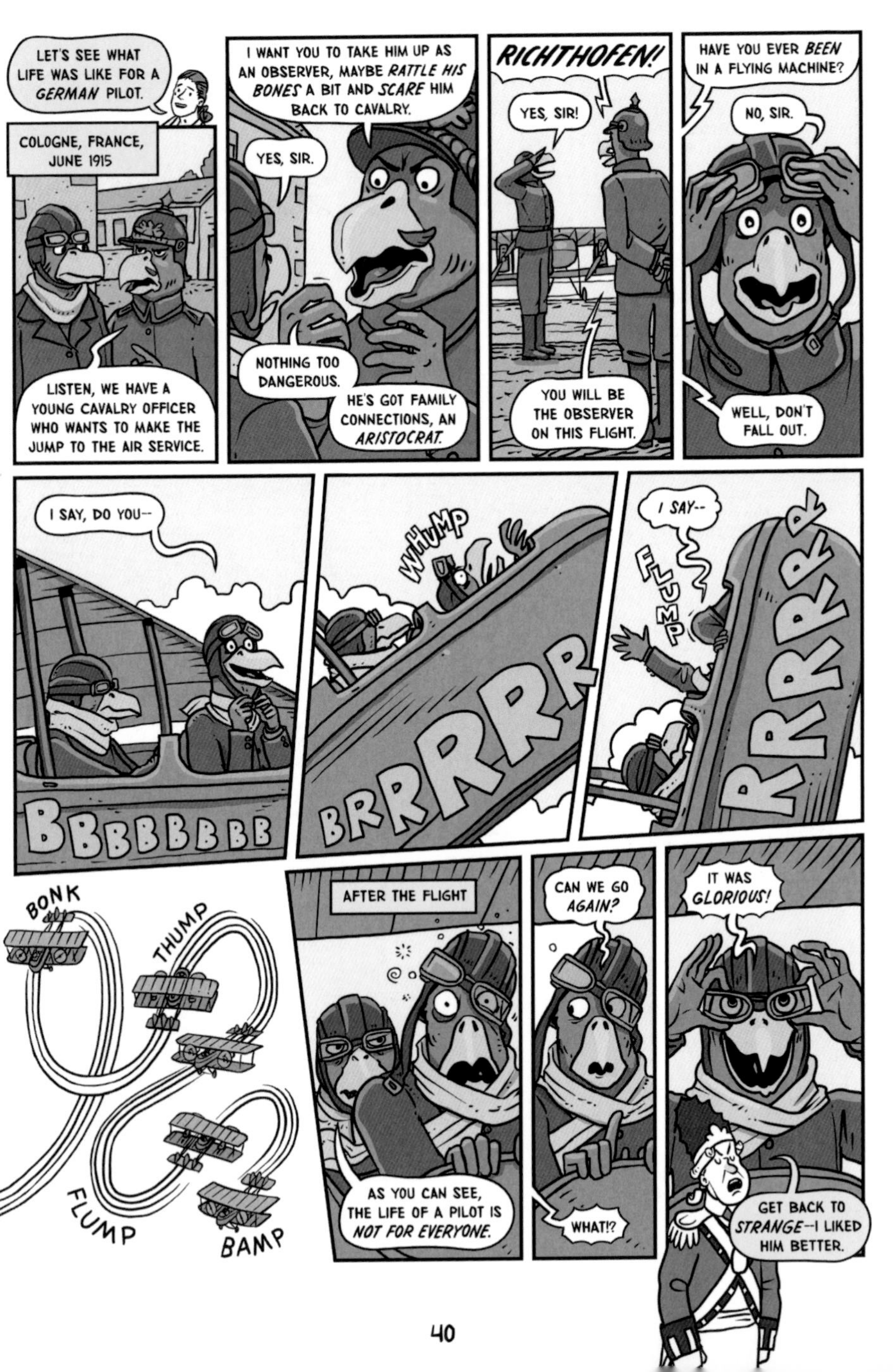
LET'S SEE WHAT LIFE WAS LIKE FOR A *GERMAN* PILOT.
COLOGNE, FRANCE, JUNE 1915
LISTEN, WE HAVE A YOUNG CAVALRY OFFICER WHO WANTS TO MAKE THE JUMP TO THE AIR SERVICE.
I WANT YOU TO TAKE HIM UP AS AN OBSERVER, MAYBE *RATTLE HIS BONES* A BIT AND *SCARE* HIM BACK TO CAVALRY.
YES, SIR.
NOTHING TOO DANGEROUS.
HE'S GOT FAMILY CONNECTIONS, AN *ARISTOCRAT.*
RICHTHOFEN!
YES, SIR!
YOU WILL BE THE OBSERVER ON THIS FLIGHT.
HAVE YOU EVER *BEEN* IN A FLYING MACHINE?
NO, SIR.
WELL, DON'T FALL OUT.
I SAY, DO YOU--
BBBBBBBBB
WHUMP
BRRRRR
I SAY--
FLUMP
RRRRRR
BONK
THUMP
FLUMP
BAMP
AFTER THE FLIGHT
AS YOU CAN SEE, THE LIFE OF A PILOT IS *NOT FOR EVERYONE.*
CAN WE GO *AGAIN?*
WHAT!?
IT WAS *GLORIOUS!*
GET BACK TO *STRANGE*--I LIKED HIM BETTER.

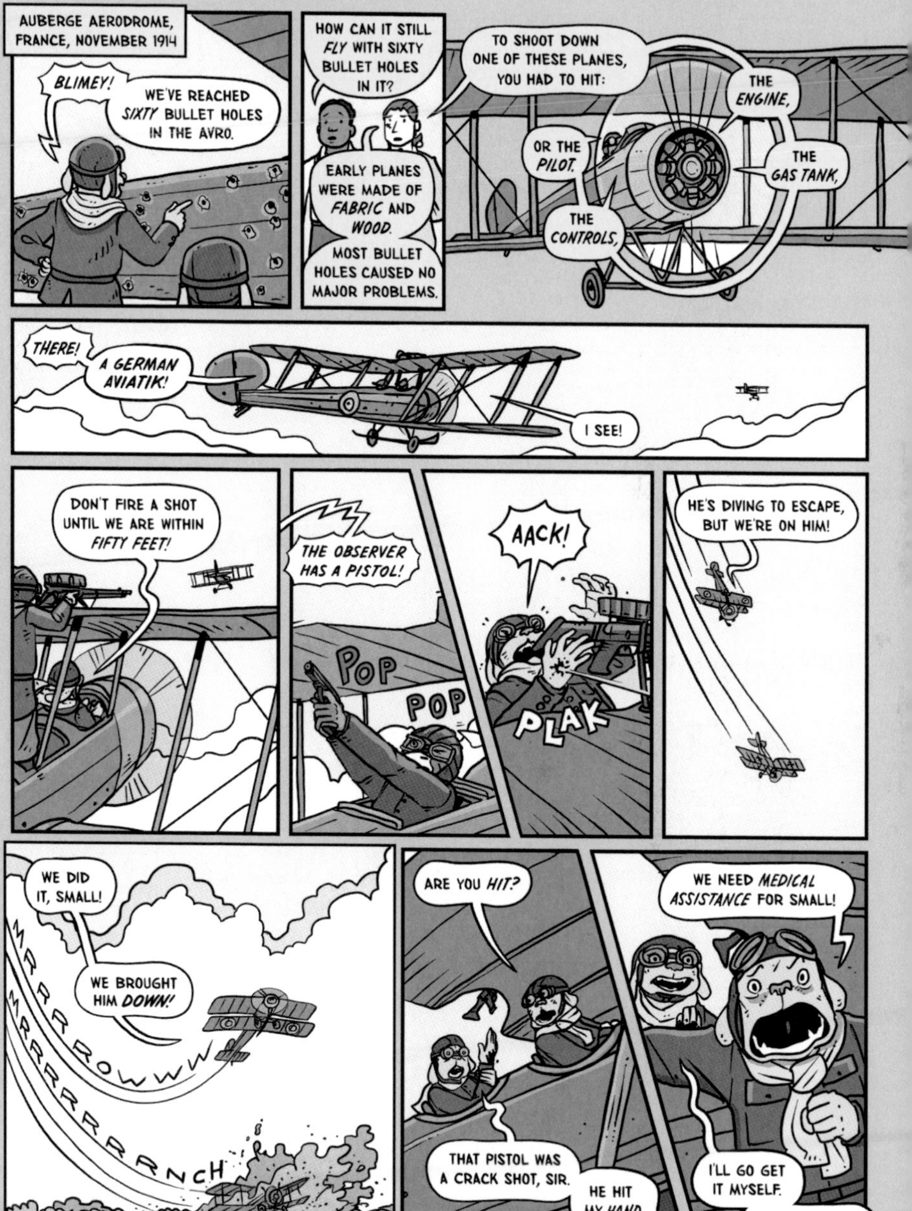
AUBERGE AERODROME, FRANCE, NOVEMBER 1914
BLIMEY!
WE'VE REACHED *SIXTY* BULLET HOLES IN THE AVRO.
HOW CAN IT STILL *FLY* WITH SIXTY BULLET HOLES IN IT?
EARLY PLANES WERE MADE OF *FABRIC* AND *WOOD*.
MOST BULLET HOLES CAUSED NO MAJOR PROBLEMS.
TO SHOOT DOWN ONE OF THESE PLANES, YOU HAD TO HIT:
THE *ENGINE*,
THE *GAS TANK*,
THE *CONTROLS*,
OR THE *PILOT*.
THERE!
A GERMAN AVIATIK!
I SEE!
DON'T FIRE A SHOT UNTIL WE ARE WITHIN *FIFTY FEET*!
THE OBSERVER HAS A PISTOL!
POP
POP
AACK!
PLAK
HE'S DIVING TO ESCAPE, BUT WE'RE ON HIM!
WE DID IT, SMALL!
WE BROUGHT HIM *DOWN*!
MRRRROWWW
MRRRRRRRRRRNCH
ARE YOU *HIT*?
THAT PISTOL WAS A CRACK SHOT, SIR.
HE HIT MY *HAND*.
WE NEED *MEDICAL ASSISTANCE* FOR SMALL!
I'LL GO GET IT MYSELF.
YOU GO CAPTURE THAT *AVIATIK*!

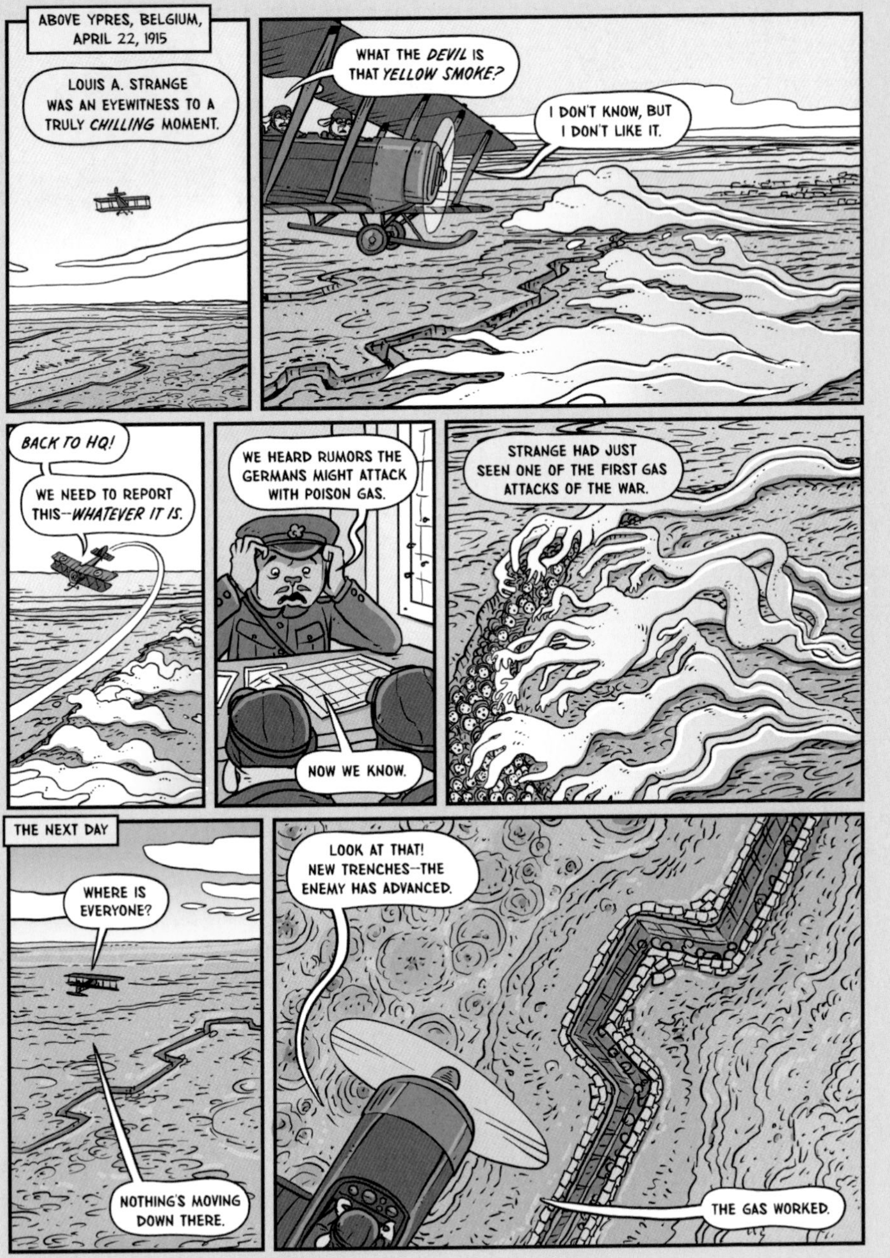
ABOVE YPRES, BELGIUM, APRIL 22, 1915
LOUIS A. STRANGE WAS AN EYEWITNESS TO A TRULY *CHILLING* MOMENT.
WHAT THE *DEVIL* IS THAT *YELLOW SMOKE?*
I DON'T KNOW, BUT I DON'T LIKE IT.
BACK TO HQ!
WE NEED TO REPORT THIS--*WHATEVER IT IS.*
WE HEARD RUMORS THE GERMANS MIGHT ATTACK WITH POISON GAS.
NOW WE KNOW.
STRANGE HAD JUST SEEN ONE OF THE FIRST GAS ATTACKS OF THE WAR.
THE NEXT DAY
WHERE IS EVERYONE?
NOTHING'S MOVING DOWN THERE.
LOOK AT THAT! NEW TRENCHES--THE ENEMY HAS ADVANCED.
THE GAS WORKED.

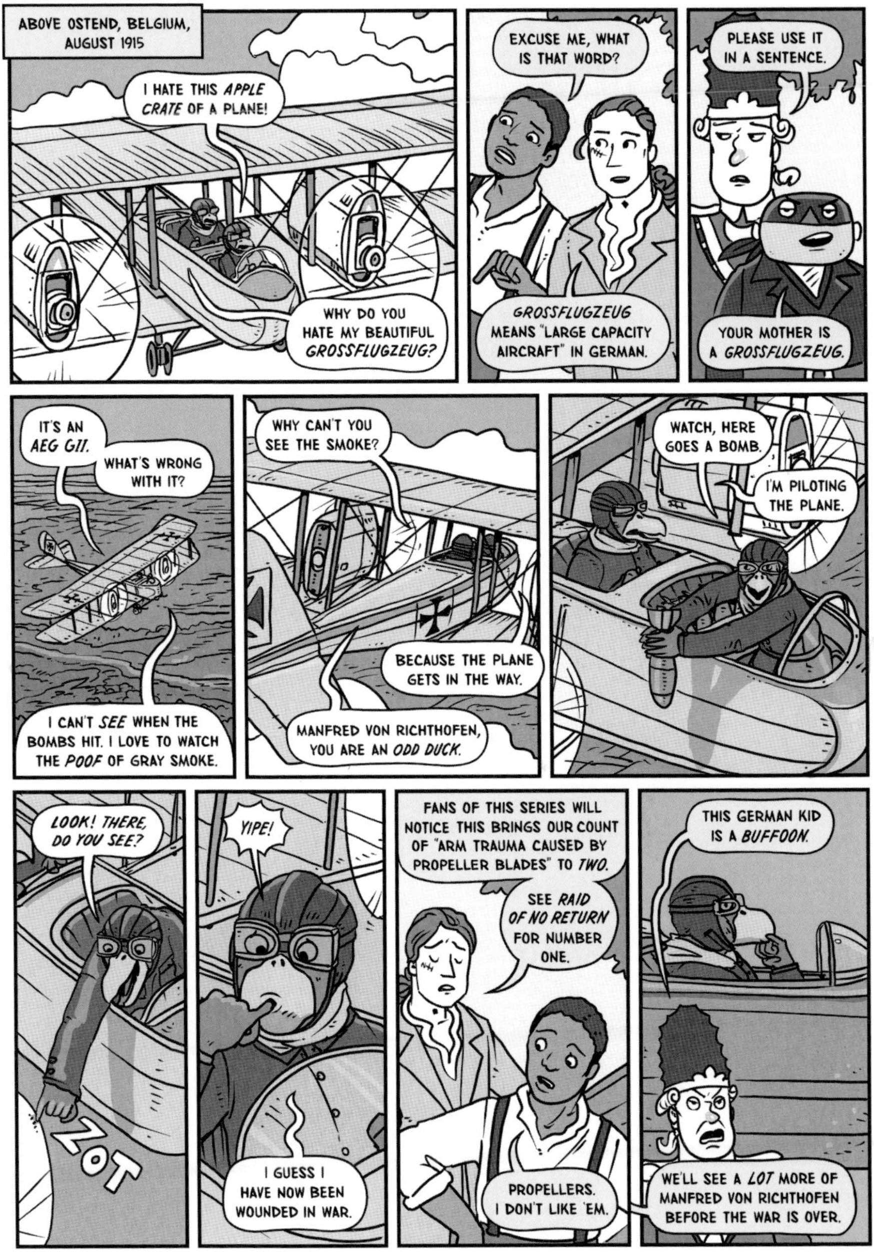
ABOVE OSTEND, BELGIUM, AUGUST 1915
I HATE THIS *APPLE CRATE* OF A PLANE!
WHY DO YOU HATE MY BEAUTIFUL *GROSSFLUGZEUG?*
EXCUSE ME, WHAT IS THAT WORD?
GROSSFLUGZEUG MEANS "LARGE CAPACITY AIRCRAFT" IN GERMAN.
PLEASE USE IT IN A SENTENCE.
YOUR MOTHER IS A *GROSSFLUGZEUG.*
IT'S AN *AEG GII.*
WHAT'S WRONG WITH IT?
I CAN'T *SEE* WHEN THE BOMBS HIT. I LOVE TO WATCH THE *POOF* OF GRAY SMOKE.
WHY CAN'T YOU SEE THE SMOKE?
BECAUSE THE PLANE GETS IN THE WAY.
MANFRED VON RICHTHOFEN, YOU ARE AN *ODD DUCK.*
WATCH, HERE GOES A BOMB.
I'M PILOTING THE PLANE.
LOOK! THERE, DO YOU SEE?
ZOT
YIPE!
I GUESS I HAVE NOW BEEN WOUNDED IN WAR.
FANS OF THIS SERIES WILL NOTICE THIS BRINGS OUR COUNT OF "ARM TRAUMA CAUSED BY PROPELLER BLADES" TO *TWO.*
SEE *RAID OF NO RETURN* FOR NUMBER ONE.
PROPELLERS. I DON'T LIKE 'EM.
THIS GERMAN KID IS A *BUFFOON.*
WE'LL SEE A *LOT* MORE OF MANFRED VON RICHTHOFEN BEFORE THE WAR IS OVER.

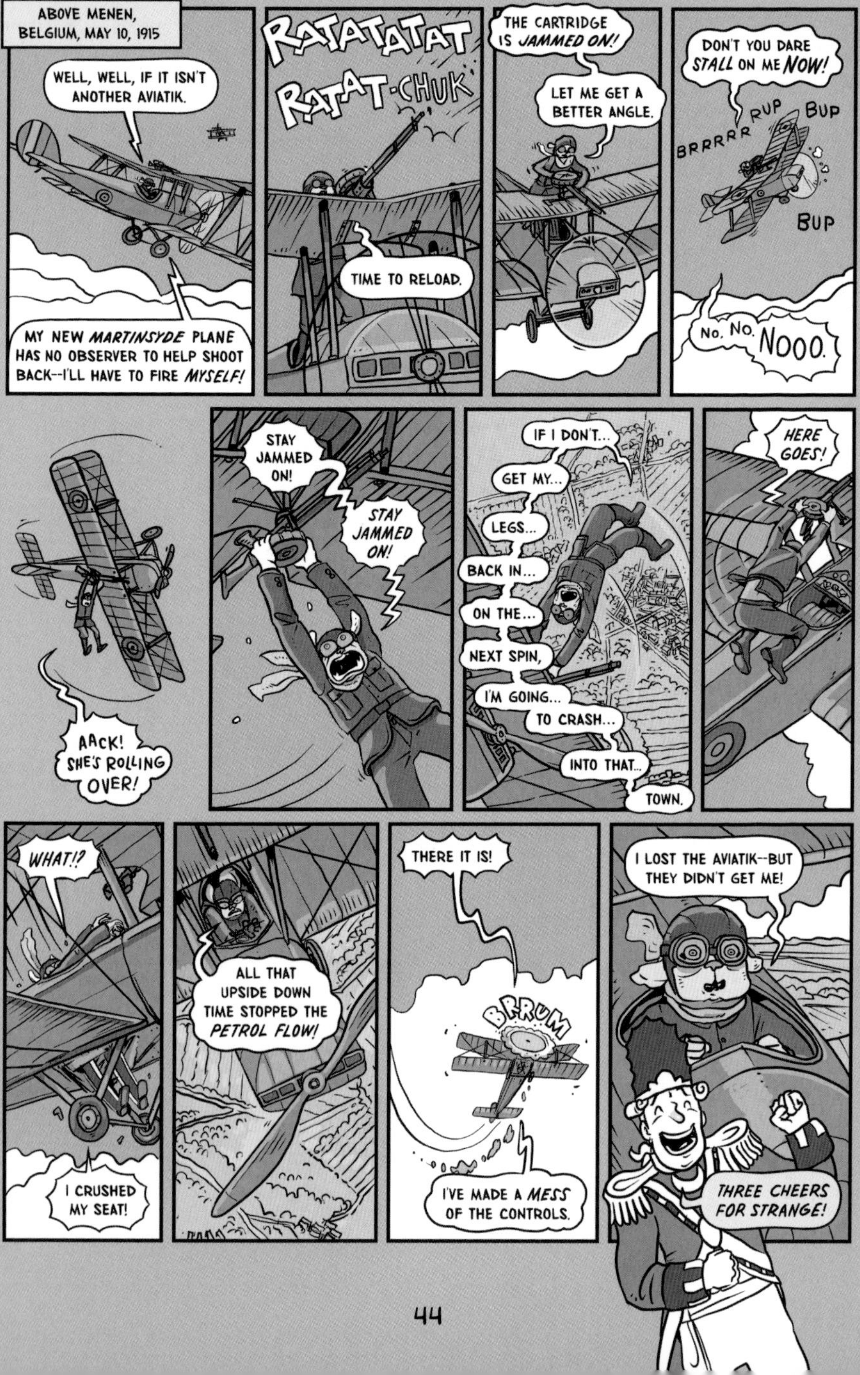
ABOVE MENEN, BELGIUM, MAY 10, 1915
WELL, WELL, IF IT ISN'T ANOTHER AVIATIK.
MY NEW MARTINSYDE PLANE HAS NO OBSERVER TO HELP SHOOT BACK--I'LL HAVE TO FIRE MYSELF!
RATATATAT
RATAT-CHUK
TIME TO RELOAD.
THE CARTRIDGE IS JAMMED ON!
LET ME GET A BETTER ANGLE.
DON'T YOU DARE STALL ON ME NOW!
BRRRRR RUP
BUP
BUP
No. No. NOOO.
AACK! SHE'S ROLLING OVER!
STAY JAMMED ON!
STAY JAMMED ON!
IF I DON'T...
GET MY...
LEGS...
BACK IN...
ON THE...
NEXT SPIN,
I'M GOING...
TO CRASH...
INTO THAT...
TOWN.
HERE GOES!
WHAT!?
I CRUSHED MY SEAT!
ALL THAT UPSIDE DOWN TIME STOPPED THE PETROL FLOW!
THERE IT IS!
BRRUM
I'VE MADE A MESS OF THE CONTROLS.
I LOST THE AVIATIK--BUT THEY DIDN'T GET ME!
THREE CHEERS FOR STRANGE!

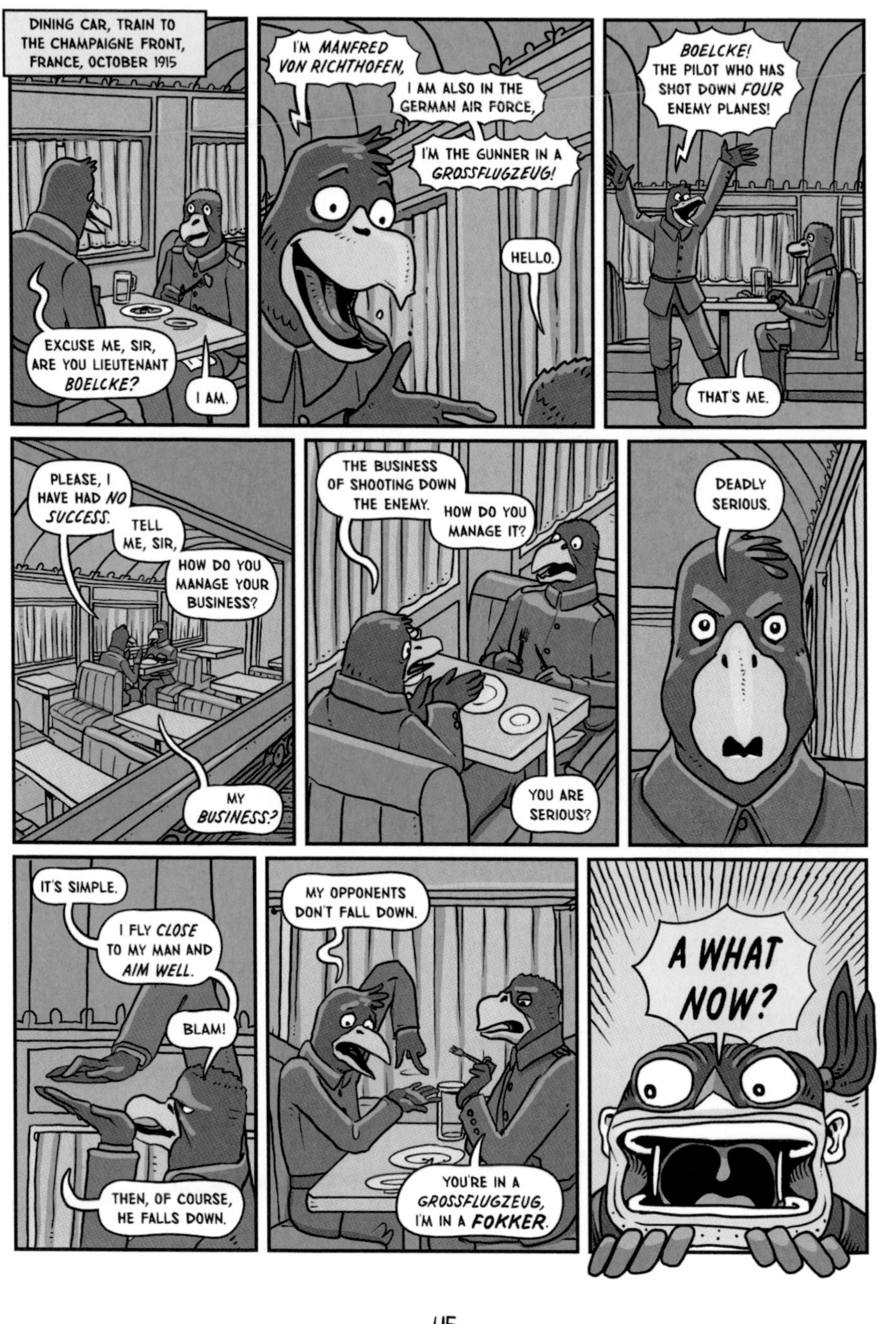
DINING CAR, TRAIN TO THE CHAMPAIGNE FRONT, FRANCE, OCTOBER 1915
EXCUSE ME, SIR, ARE YOU LIEUTENANT *BOELCKE?*
I AM.
I'M *MANFRED VON RICHTHOFEN,*
I AM ALSO IN THE GERMAN AIR FORCE,
I'M THE GUNNER IN A *GROSSFLUGZEUG!*
HELLO.
BOELCKE! THE PILOT WHO HAS SHOT DOWN *FOUR* ENEMY PLANES!
THAT'S ME.
PLEASE, I HAVE HAD *NO SUCCESS.*
TELL ME, SIR,
HOW DO YOU MANAGE YOUR BUSINESS?
MY *BUSINESS?*
THE BUSINESS OF SHOOTING DOWN THE ENEMY.
HOW DO YOU MANAGE IT?
YOU ARE SERIOUS?
DEADLY SERIOUS.
IT'S SIMPLE.
I FLY *CLOSE* TO MY MAN AND *AIM WELL.*
BLAM!
THEN, OF COURSE, HE FALLS DOWN.
MY OPPONENTS DON'T FALL DOWN.
YOU'RE IN A *GROSSFLUGZEUG,* I'M IN A ***FOKKER.***
A WHAT NOW?

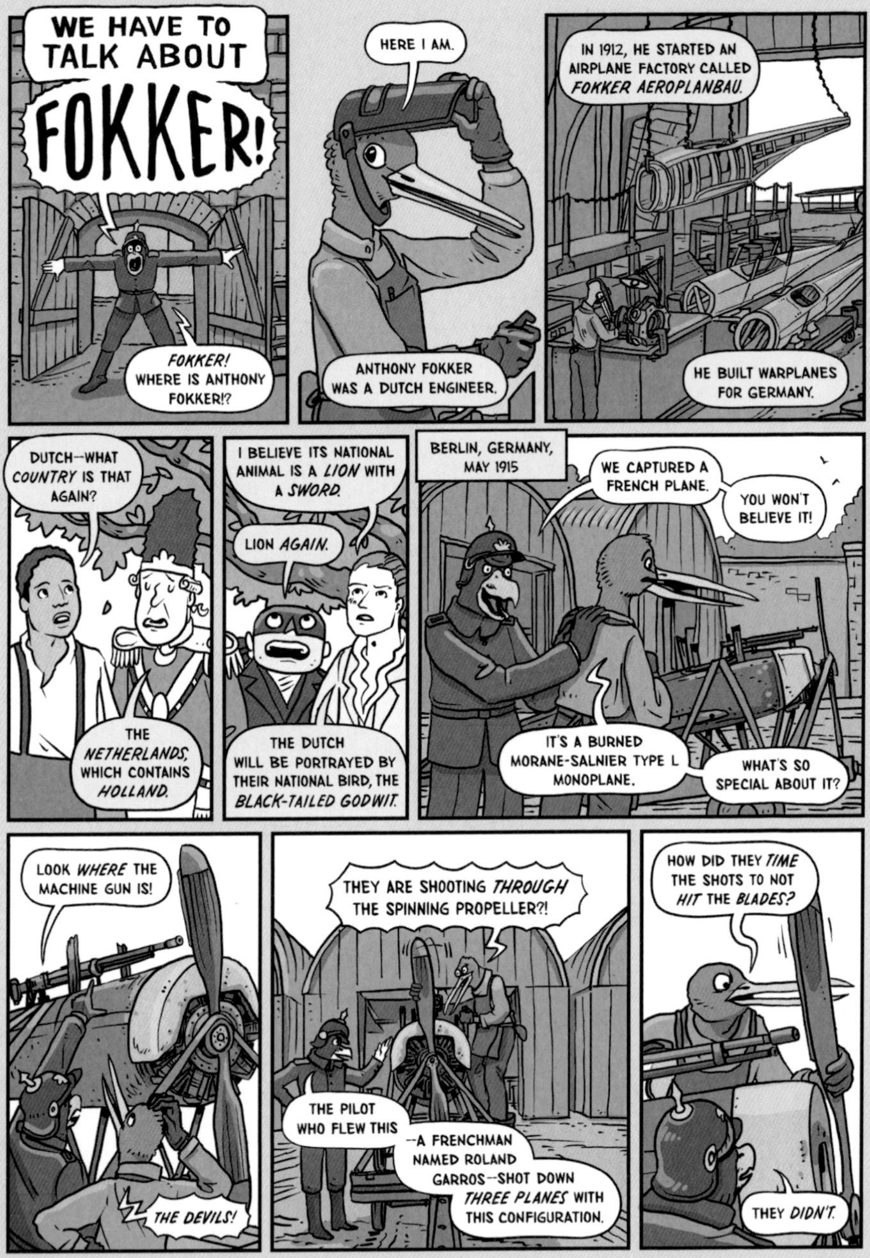
WE HAVE TO TALK ABOUT
FOKKER!
FOKKER! WHERE IS ANTHONY FOKKER!?
HERE I AM.
ANTHONY FOKKER WAS A DUTCH ENGINEER.
IN 1912, HE STARTED AN AIRPLANE FACTORY CALLED FOKKER AEROPLANBAU.
HE BUILT WARPLANES FOR GERMANY.
DUTCH--WHAT COUNTRY IS THAT AGAIN?
THE NETHERLANDS, WHICH CONTAINS HOLLAND.
I BELIEVE ITS NATIONAL ANIMAL IS A LION WITH A SWORD.
LION AGAIN.
THE DUTCH WILL BE PORTRAYED BY THEIR NATIONAL BIRD, THE BLACK-TAILED GODWIT.
BERLIN, GERMANY, MAY 1915
WE CAPTURED A FRENCH PLANE.
YOU WON'T BELIEVE IT!
IT'S A BURNED MORANE-SALNIER TYPE L MONOPLANE.
WHAT'S SO SPECIAL ABOUT IT?
LOOK WHERE THE MACHINE GUN IS!
THE DEVILS!
THEY ARE SHOOTING THROUGH THE SPINNING PROPELLER?!
THE PILOT WHO FLEW THIS
--A FRENCHMAN NAMED ROLAND GARROS--SHOT DOWN THREE PLANES WITH THIS CONFIGURATION.
HOW DID THEY TIME THE SHOTS TO NOT HIT THE BLADES?
THEY DIDN'T.

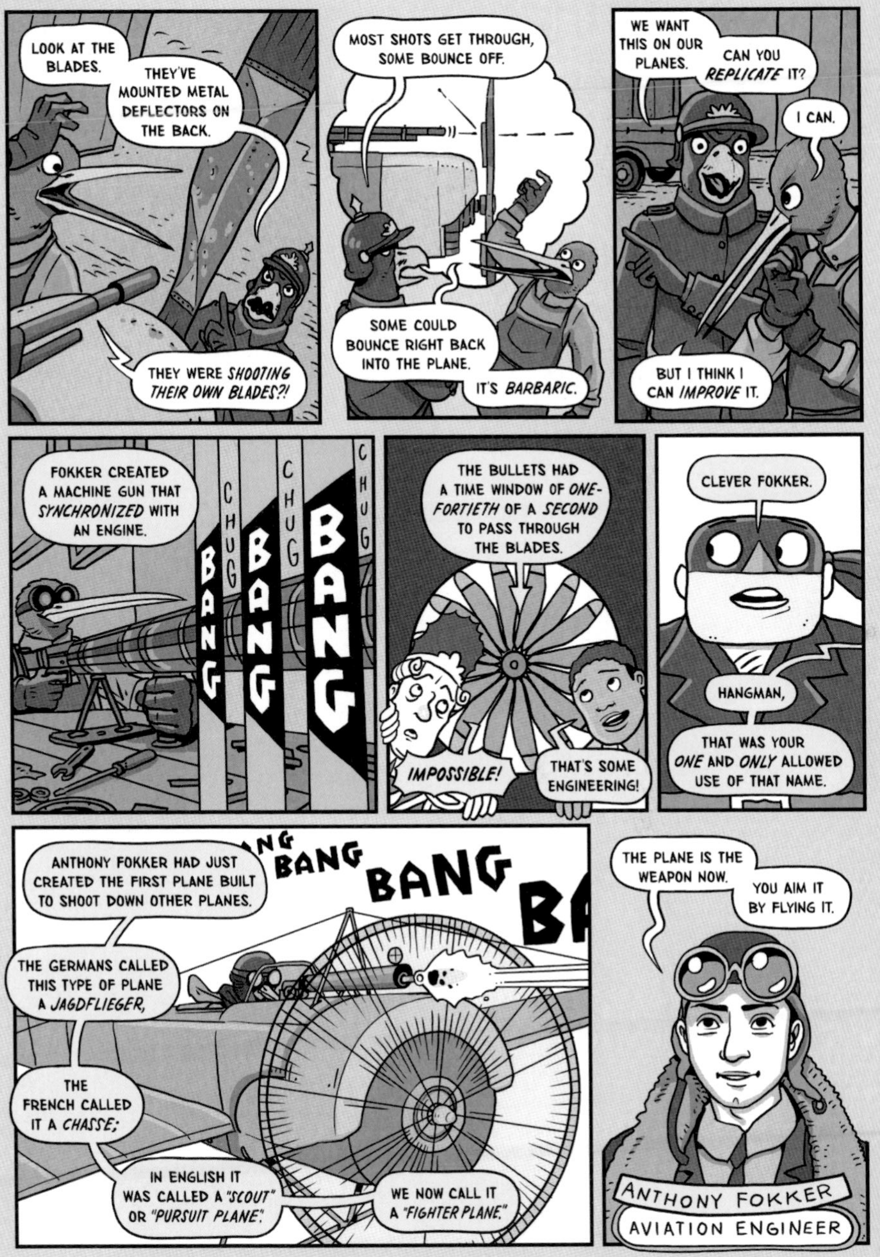
LOOK AT THE BLADES.
THEY'VE MOUNTED METAL DEFLECTORS ON THE BACK.
THEY WERE *SHOOTING THEIR OWN BLADES?!*
MOST SHOTS GET THROUGH, SOME BOUNCE OFF.
SOME COULD BOUNCE RIGHT BACK INTO THE PLANE.
IT'S *BARBARIC.*
WE WANT THIS ON OUR PLANES.
CAN YOU *REPLICATE* IT?
I CAN.
BUT I THINK I CAN *IMPROVE* IT.
FOKKER CREATED A MACHINE GUN THAT *SYNCHRONIZED* WITH AN ENGINE.
CHUG
BANG
CHUG
BANG
CHUG
BANG
THE BULLETS HAD A TIME WINDOW OF *ONE-FORTIETH* OF A *SECOND* TO PASS THROUGH THE BLADES.
IMPOSSIBLE!
THAT'S SOME ENGINEERING!
CLEVER FOKKER.
HANGMAN,
THAT WAS YOUR *ONE* AND *ONLY* ALLOWED USE OF THAT NAME.
ANTHONY FOKKER HAD JUST CREATED THE FIRST PLANE BUILT TO SHOOT DOWN OTHER PLANES.
BANG
BANG
BANG
THE GERMANS CALLED THIS TYPE OF PLANE A *JAGDFLIEGER,*
THE FRENCH CALLED IT A *CHASSE;*
IN ENGLISH IT WAS CALLED A *"SCOUT"* OR *"PURSUIT PLANE".*
WE NOW CALL IT A *"FIGHTER PLANE."*
THE PLANE IS THE WEAPON NOW.
YOU AIM IT BY FLYING IT.
ANTHONY FOKKER
AVIATION ENGINEER

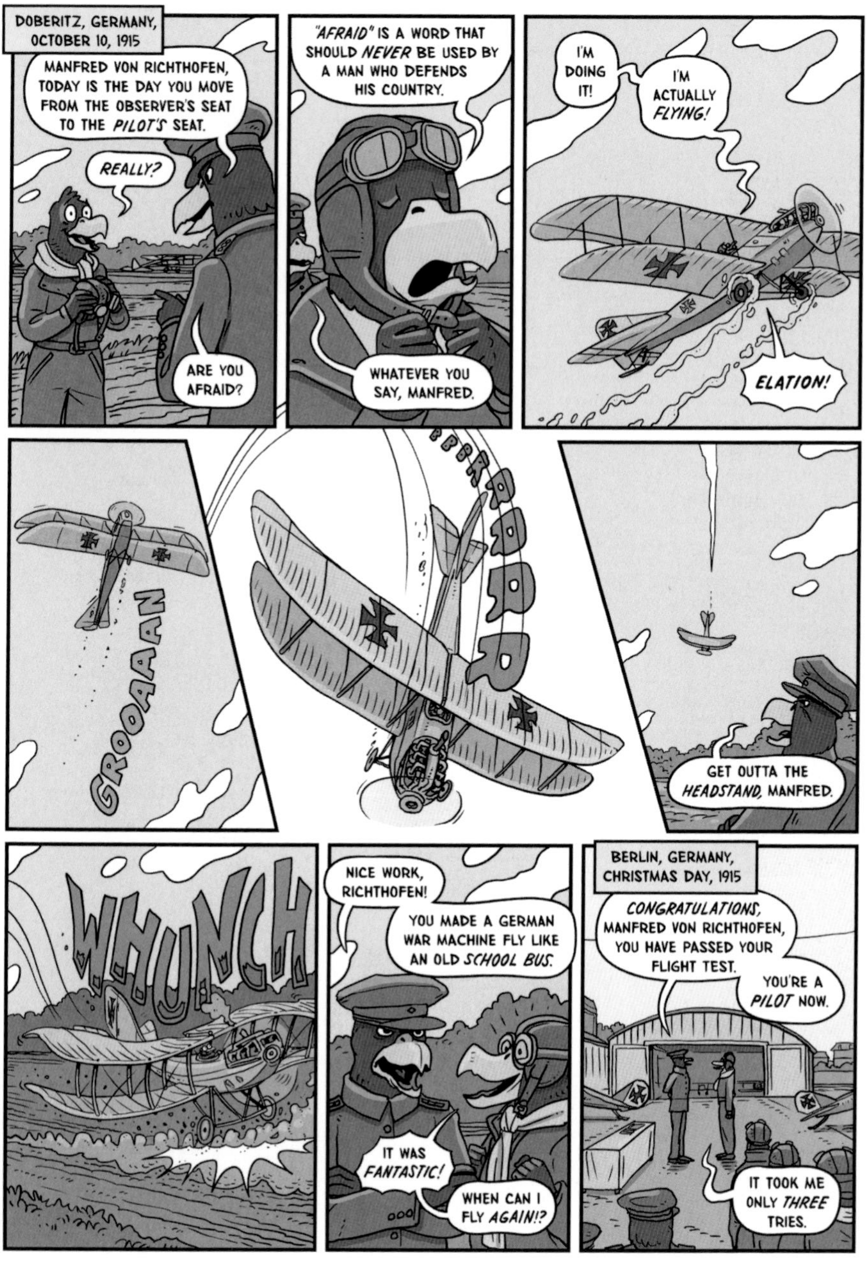
DOBERITZ, GERMANY, OCTOBER 10, 1915
MANFRED VON RICHTHOFEN, TODAY IS THE DAY YOU MOVE FROM THE OBSERVER'S SEAT TO THE PILOT'S SEAT.
REALLY?
ARE YOU AFRAID?
"AFRAID" IS A WORD THAT SHOULD NEVER BE USED BY A MAN WHO DEFENDS HIS COUNTRY.
WHATEVER YOU SAY, MANFRED.
I'M DOING IT!
I'M ACTUALLY FLYING!
ELATION!
GROOAAAN
RRRRRRRRR
GET OUTTA THE HEADSTAND, MANFRED.
WHUNCH
NICE WORK, RICHTHOFEN!
YOU MADE A GERMAN WAR MACHINE FLY LIKE AN OLD SCHOOL BUS.
IT WAS FANTASTIC!
WHEN CAN I FLY AGAIN!?
BERLIN, GERMANY, CHRISTMAS DAY, 1915
CONGRATULATIONS, MANFRED VON RICHTHOFEN, YOU HAVE PASSED YOUR FLIGHT TEST.
YOU'RE A PILOT NOW.
IT TOOK ME ONLY THREE TRIES.

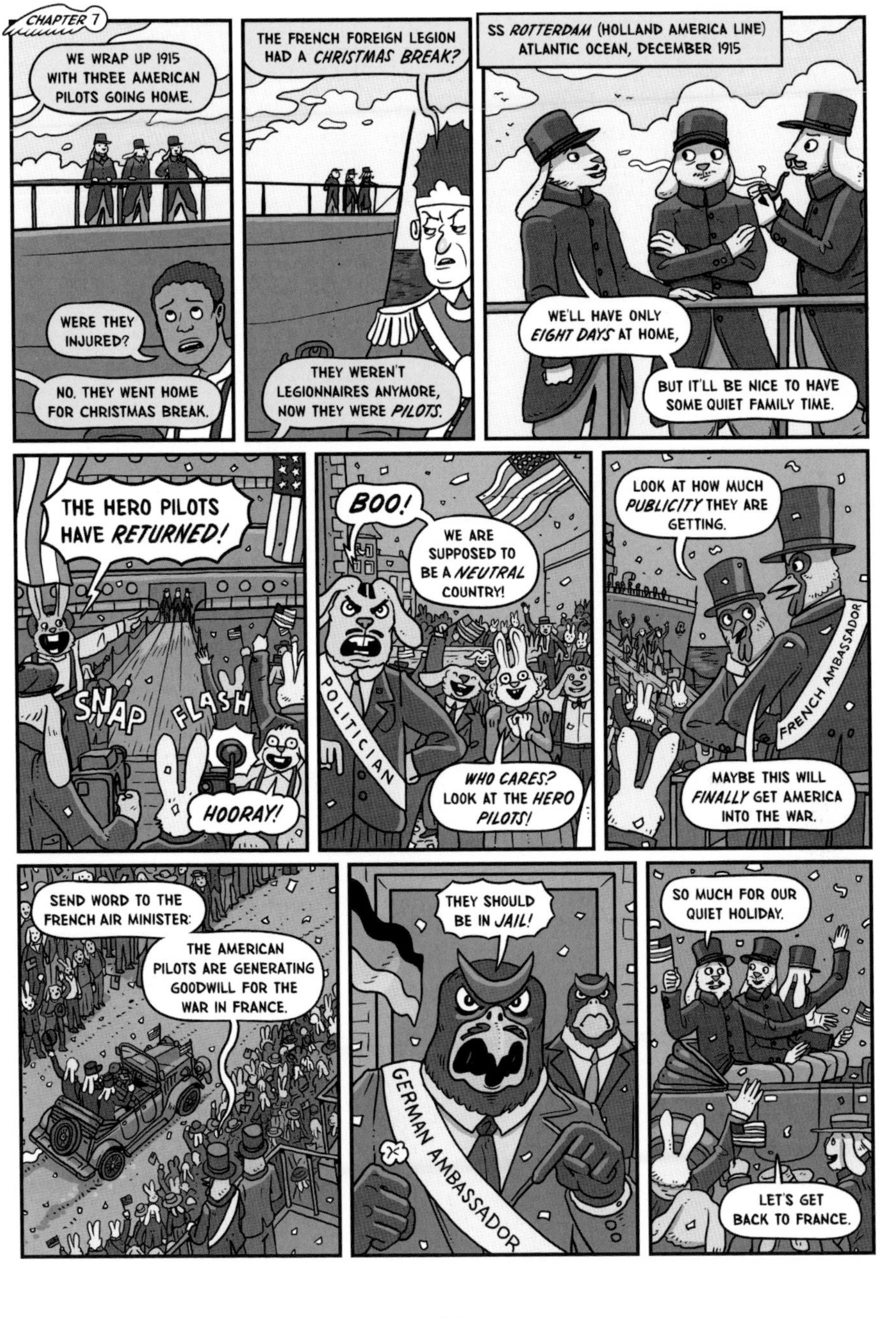
CHAPTER 7
WE WRAP UP 1915 WITH THREE AMERICAN PILOTS GOING HOME.
WERE THEY INJURED?
NO. THEY WENT HOME FOR CHRISTMAS BREAK.
THE FRENCH FOREIGN LEGION HAD A *CHRISTMAS BREAK?*
THEY WEREN'T LEGIONNAIRES ANYMORE, NOW THEY WERE *PILOTS.*
SS *ROTTERDAM* (HOLLAND AMERICA LINE) ATLANTIC OCEAN, DECEMBER 1915
WE'LL HAVE ONLY *EIGHT DAYS* AT HOME,
BUT IT'LL BE NICE TO HAVE SOME QUIET FAMILY TIME.
THE HERO PILOTS HAVE *RETURNED!*
SNAP
FLASH
HOORAY!
BOO!
WE ARE SUPPOSED TO BE A *NEUTRAL* COUNTRY!
POLITICIAN
WHO CARES? LOOK AT THE *HERO PILOTS!*
LOOK AT HOW MUCH *PUBLICITY* THEY ARE GETTING.
FRENCH AMBASSADOR
MAYBE THIS WILL *FINALLY* GET AMERICA INTO THE WAR.
SEND WORD TO THE FRENCH AIR MINISTER:
THE AMERICAN PILOTS ARE GENERATING GOODWILL FOR THE WAR IN FRANCE.
THEY SHOULD BE IN *JAIL!*
GERMAN AMBASSADOR
SO MUCH FOR OUR QUIET HOLIDAY.
LET'S GET BACK TO FRANCE.

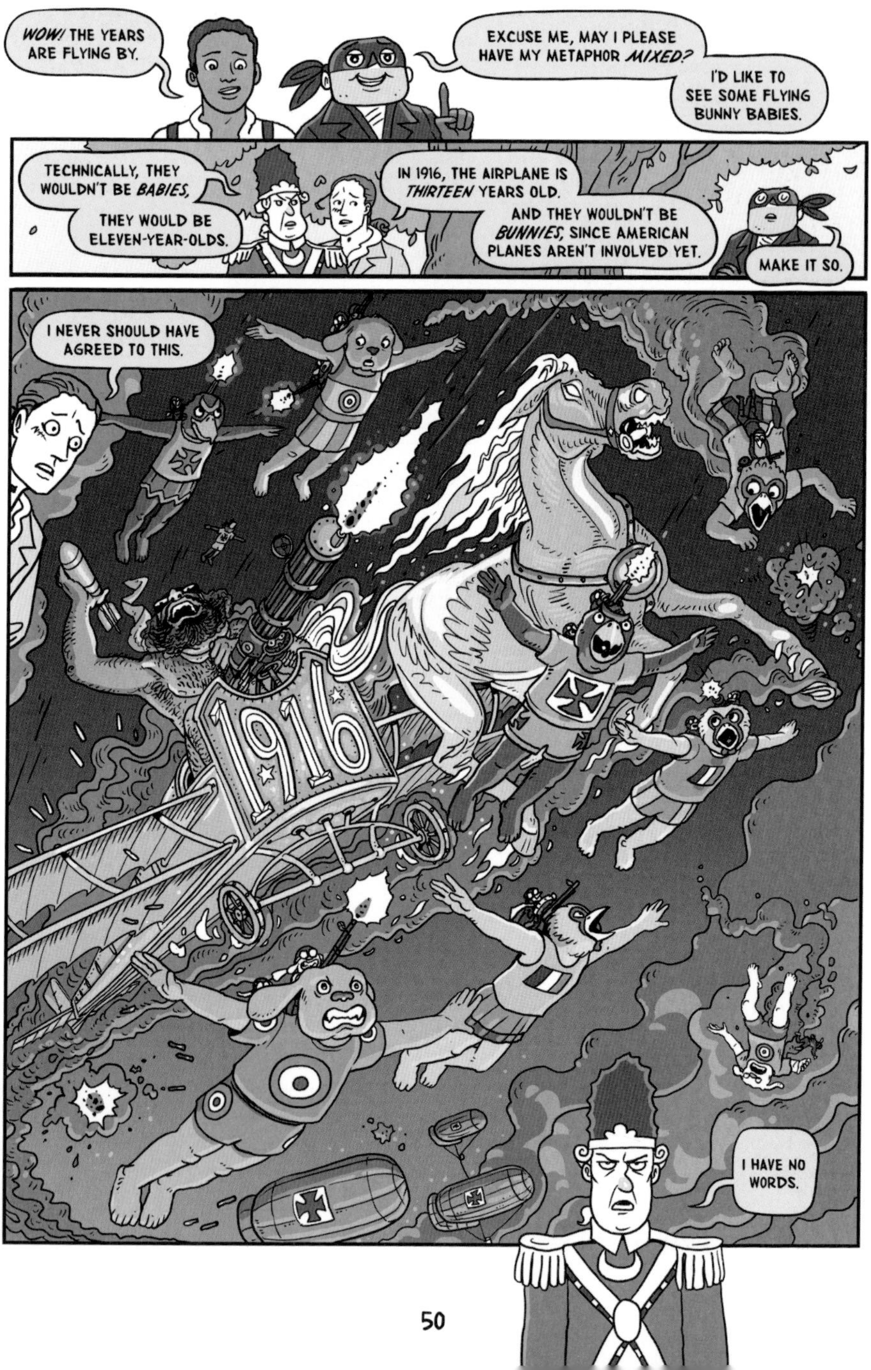
WOW! THE YEARS ARE FLYING BY.
EXCUSE ME, MAY I PLEASE HAVE MY METAPHOR MIXED?
I'D LIKE TO SEE SOME FLYING BUNNY BABIES.
TECHNICALLY, THEY WOULDN'T BE BABIES,
THEY WOULD BE ELEVEN-YEAR-OLDS.
IN 1916, THE AIRPLANE IS THIRTEEN YEARS OLD.
AND THEY WOULDN'T BE BUNNIES, SINCE AMERICAN PLANES AREN'T INVOLVED YET.
MAKE IT SO.
I NEVER SHOULD HAVE AGREED TO THIS.
1916
I HAVE NO WORDS.

IN JANUARY OF 1916, GERMANY'S TOP PILOTS, *OSWALD BOELCKE* AND *MAX IMMELMANN*,

WERE AWARDED THE *POUR LE MÉRITE*—

KNOWN AS THE *BLUE MAX.*

HEY, THAT'S MANFRED'S BUDDY!

GERMAN PAPERS MADE THESE MEN INTO STARS.

THEIR VICTORIES AND KILL COUNTS BECAME A SOURCE OF NATIONAL PRIDE.

Pour le Mé. rite

PARIS, FRANCE, JANUARY 1916

FRANCE DECIDED TO INVEST IN PILOT PUBLICITY TOO.

GEORGES GUYNEMER SCORES FOURTH VICTORY! IN HIS SINGLE SEAT NIEUPORT PLANE THE BRAVE ARISTOCRAT BROUGHT DOWN AN AVIAT...

FRENCH PILOTS BECAME FAMOUS.

IT WAS EVEN DECIDED THAT HAVING AN AMERICAN SQUADRON WOULD BE *GOOD PUBLICITY.*

YOUR REQUEST FOR AN ESCADRILLE MADE ENTIRELY OF AMERICAN PILOTS IS *GRANTED.*

EXCELLENT!

YOU MUST BE ABLE TO PASS FRENCH FLIGHT TRAINING AND FOLLOW FRENCH MILITARY REGULATIONS.

YES, SIR.

AND THOUGH THE PILOTS WILL BE AMERICAN, THE *OFFICERS* WILL BE *FRENCH.*

YOU WILL BE ESCADRILLE N 124.

"N" FOR *NIEUPORT* PLANES, SIR?

YES, AS YOU KNOW, EACH ESCADRILLE NAME HAS THE INITIAL OF THE PLANES IT USES.

YOU WILL FLY NIEUPORTS.

VER-SUR-LAUNETTE

ÉVE

LE PLESSIS-BELLEVILLE

LAGNY-LE-SEC

SAINT-PATHUS OISE

GATHER ALL THE AMERICAN PILOTS TO THE TOWN OF LE PLESSIS-BELLEVILLE UNTIL WE FIND AN AERODROME FOR YOU.

51

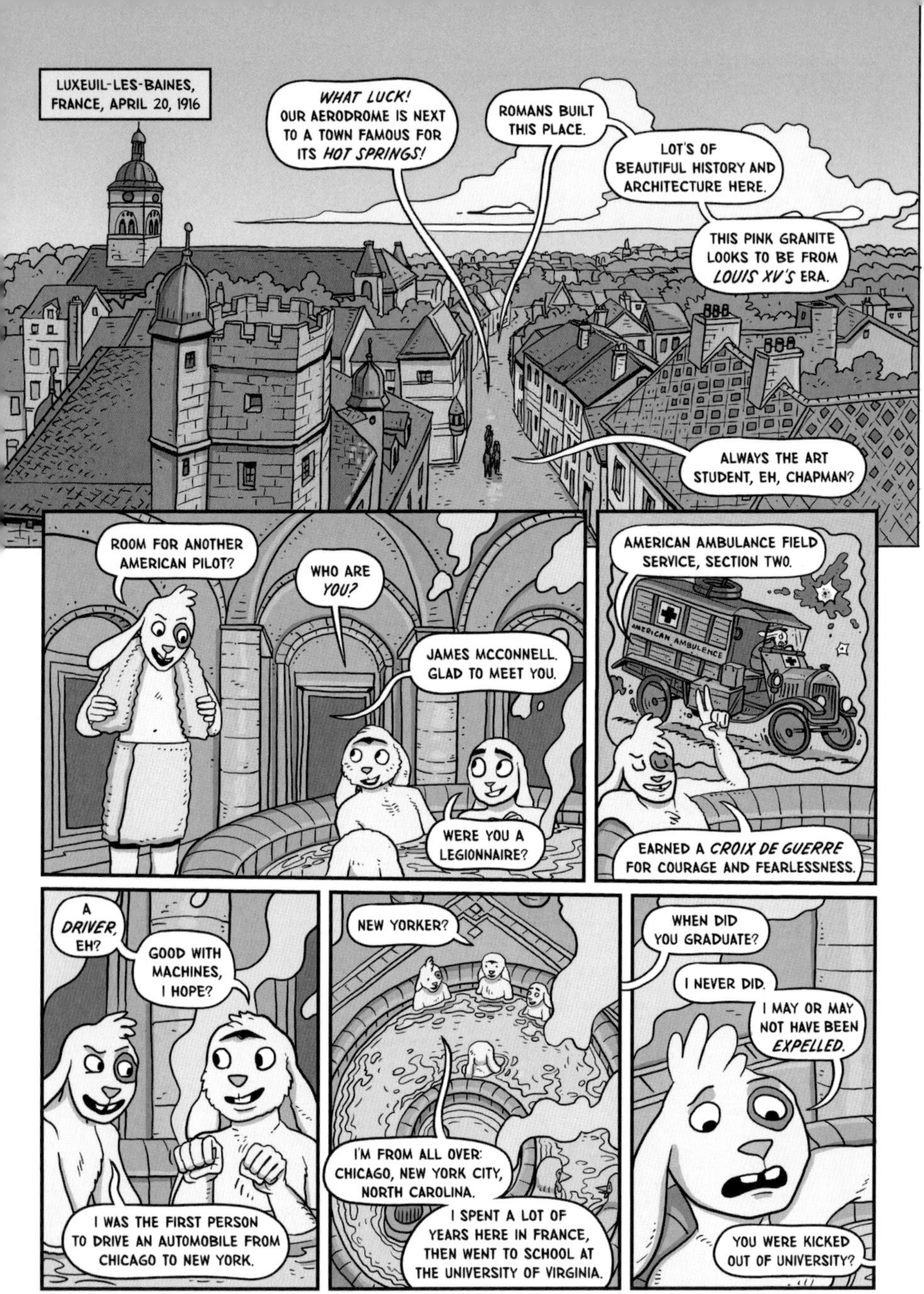
LUXEUIL-LES-BAINES, FRANCE, APRIL 20, 1916
WHAT LUCK! OUR AERODROME IS NEXT TO A TOWN FAMOUS FOR ITS HOT SPRINGS!
ROMANS BUILT THIS PLACE.
LOT'S OF BEAUTIFUL HISTORY AND ARCHITECTURE HERE.
THIS PINK GRANITE LOOKS TO BE FROM LOUIS XV'S ERA.
ALWAYS THE ART STUDENT, EH, CHAPMAN?
ROOM FOR ANOTHER AMERICAN PILOT?
WHO ARE YOU?
JAMES MCCONNELL. GLAD TO MEET YOU.
WERE YOU A LEGIONNAIRE?
AMERICAN AMBULANCE FIELD SERVICE, SECTION TWO.
AMERICAN AMBULENCE
EARNED A CROIX DE GUERRE FOR COURAGE AND FEARLESSNESS.
A DRIVER, EH?
GOOD WITH MACHINES, I HOPE?
I WAS THE FIRST PERSON TO DRIVE AN AUTOMOBILE FROM CHICAGO TO NEW YORK.
NEW YORKER?
I'M FROM ALL OVER: CHICAGO, NEW YORK CITY, NORTH CAROLINA.
I SPENT A LOT OF YEARS HERE IN FRANCE, THEN WENT TO SCHOOL AT THE UNIVERSITY OF VIRGINIA.
WHEN DID YOU GRADUATE?
I NEVER DID.
I MAY OR MAY NOT HAVE BEEN EXPELLED.
YOU WERE KICKED OUT OF UNIVERSITY?

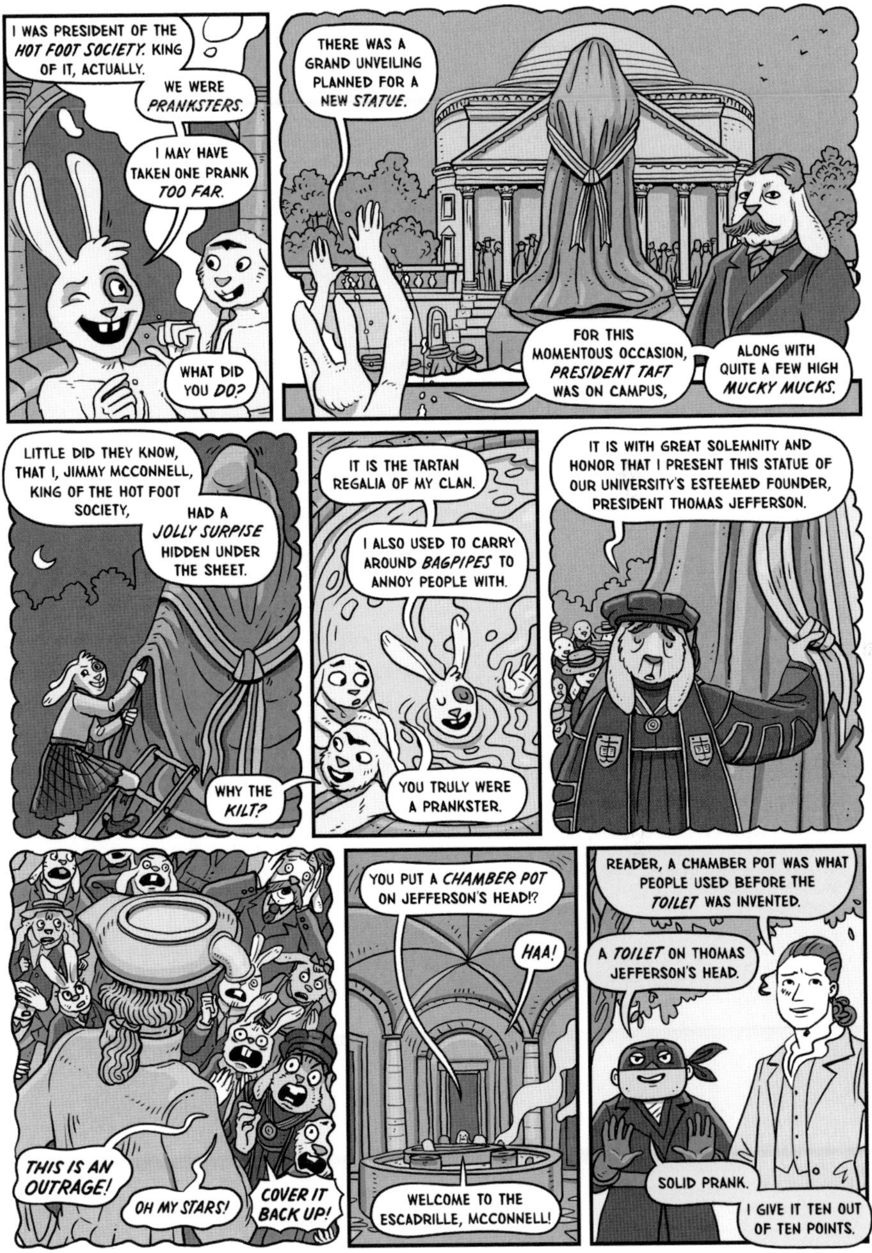
I WAS PRESIDENT OF THE HOT FOOT SOCIETY. KING OF IT, ACTUALLY.
WE WERE PRANKSTERS.
I MAY HAVE TAKEN ONE PRANK TOO FAR.
WHAT DID YOU DO?
THERE WAS A GRAND UNVEILING PLANNED FOR A NEW STATUE.
FOR THIS MOMENTOUS OCCASION, PRESIDENT TAFT WAS ON CAMPUS,
ALONG WITH QUITE A FEW HIGH MUCKY MUCKS.
LITTLE DID THEY KNOW, THAT I, JIMMY MCCONNELL, KING OF THE HOT FOOT SOCIETY,
HAD A JOLLY SURPISE HIDDEN UNDER THE SHEET.
WHY THE KILT?
IT IS THE TARTAN REGALIA OF MY CLAN.
I ALSO USED TO CARRY AROUND BAGPIPES TO ANNOY PEOPLE WITH.
YOU TRULY WERE A PRANKSTER.
IT IS WITH GREAT SOLEMNITY AND HONOR THAT I PRESENT THIS STATUE OF OUR UNIVERSITY'S ESTEEMED FOUNDER, PRESIDENT THOMAS JEFFERSON.
THIS IS AN OUTRAGE!
OH MY STARS!
COVER IT BACK UP!
YOU PUT A CHAMBER POT ON JEFFERSON'S HEAD!?
HAA!
WELCOME TO THE ESCADRILLE, MCCONNELL!
READER, A CHAMBER POT WAS WHAT PEOPLE USED BEFORE THE TOILET WAS INVENTED.
A TOILET ON THOMAS JEFFERSON'S HEAD.
SOLID PRANK.
I GIVE IT TEN OUT OF TEN POINTS.

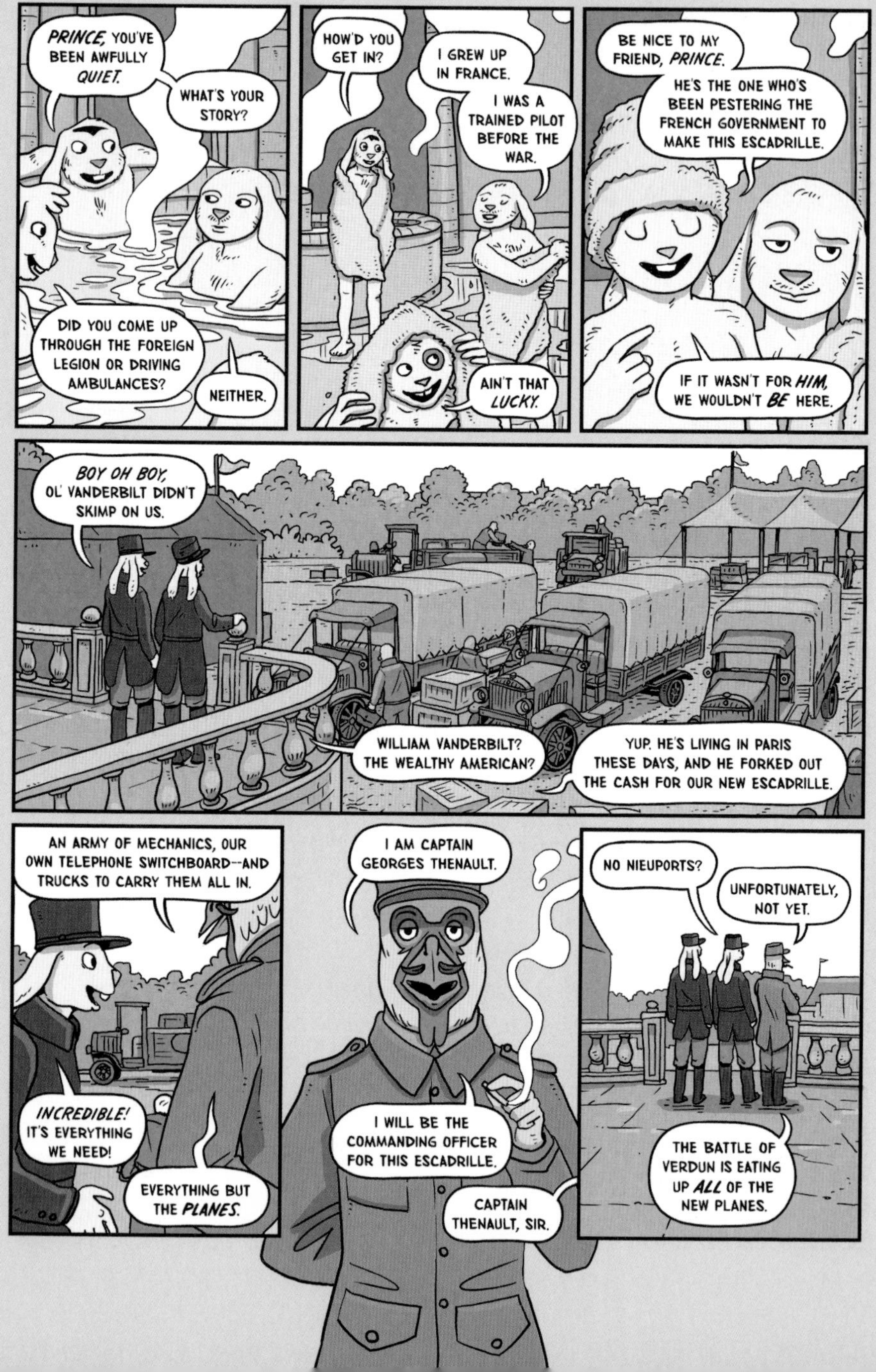
PRINCE, YOU'VE BEEN AWFULLY QUIET.
WHAT'S YOUR STORY?
DID YOU COME UP THROUGH THE FOREIGN LEGION OR DRIVING AMBULANCES?
NEITHER.
HOW'D YOU GET IN?
I GREW UP IN FRANCE.
I WAS A TRAINED PILOT BEFORE THE WAR.
AIN'T THAT LUCKY.
BE NICE TO MY FRIEND, PRINCE.
HE'S THE ONE WHO'S BEEN PESTERING THE FRENCH GOVERNMENT TO MAKE THIS ESCADRILLE.
IF IT WASN'T FOR HIM, WE WOULDN'T BE HERE.
BOY OH BOY, OL' VANDERBILT DIDN'T SKIMP ON US.
WILLIAM VANDERBILT? THE WEALTHY AMERICAN?
YUP. HE'S LIVING IN PARIS THESE DAYS, AND HE FORKED OUT THE CASH FOR OUR NEW ESCADRILLE.
AN ARMY OF MECHANICS, OUR OWN TELEPHONE SWITCHBOARD--AND TRUCKS TO CARRY THEM ALL IN.
INCREDIBLE! IT'S EVERYTHING WE NEED!
EVERYTHING BUT THE PLANES.
I AM CAPTAIN GEORGES THENAULT.
I WILL BE THE COMMANDING OFFICER FOR THIS ESCADRILLE.
CAPTAIN THENAULT, SIR.
NO NIEUPORTS?
UNFORTUNATELY, NOT YET.
THE BATTLE OF VERDUN IS EATING UP ALL OF THE NEW PLANES.

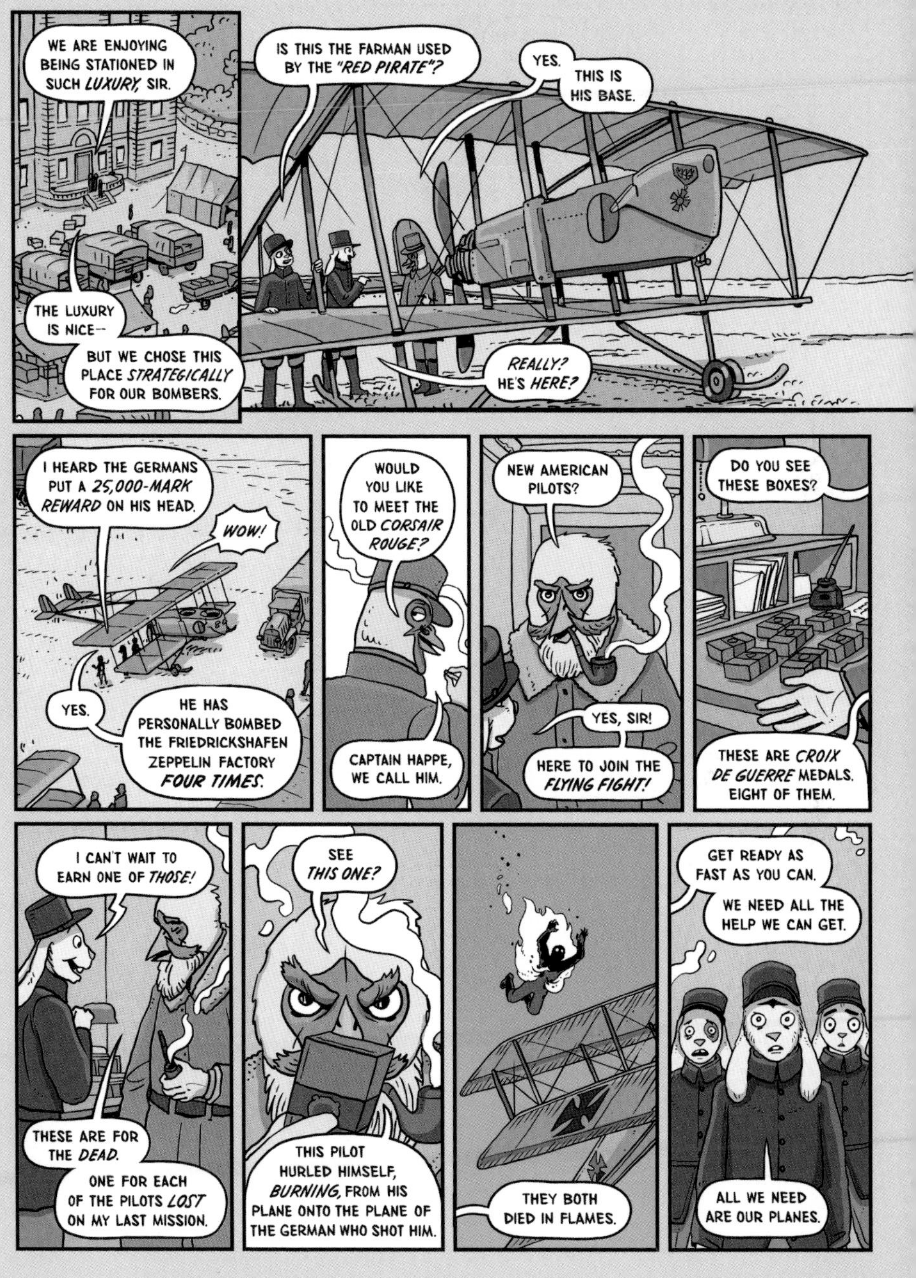

WE ARE ENJOYING BEING STATIONED IN SUCH LUXURY, SIR.
THE LUXURY IS NICE--
BUT WE CHOSE THIS PLACE STRATEGICALLY FOR OUR BOMBERS.
IS THIS THE FARMAN USED BY THE "RED PIRATE"?
YES.
THIS IS HIS BASE.
REALLY? HE'S HERE?
I HEARD THE GERMANS PUT A 25,000-MARK REWARD ON HIS HEAD.
WOW!
YES.
HE HAS PERSONALLY BOMBED THE FRIEDRICKSHAFEN ZEPPELIN FACTORY FOUR TIMES.
WOULD YOU LIKE TO MEET THE OLD CORSAIR ROUGE?
CAPTAIN HAPPE, WE CALL HIM.
NEW AMERICAN PILOTS?
YES, SIR!
HERE TO JOIN THE FLYING FIGHT!
DO YOU SEE THESE BOXES?
THESE ARE CROIX DE GUERRE MEDALS. EIGHT OF THEM.
I CAN'T WAIT TO EARN ONE OF THOSE!
THESE ARE FOR THE DEAD.
ONE FOR EACH OF THE PILOTS LOST ON MY LAST MISSION.
SEE THIS ONE?
THIS PILOT HURLED HIMSELF, BURNING, FROM HIS PLANE ONTO THE PLANE OF THE GERMAN WHO SHOT HIM.
THEY BOTH DIED IN FLAMES.
GET READY AS FAST AS YOU CAN.
WE NEED ALL THE HELP WE CAN GET.
ALL WE NEED ARE OUR PLANES.

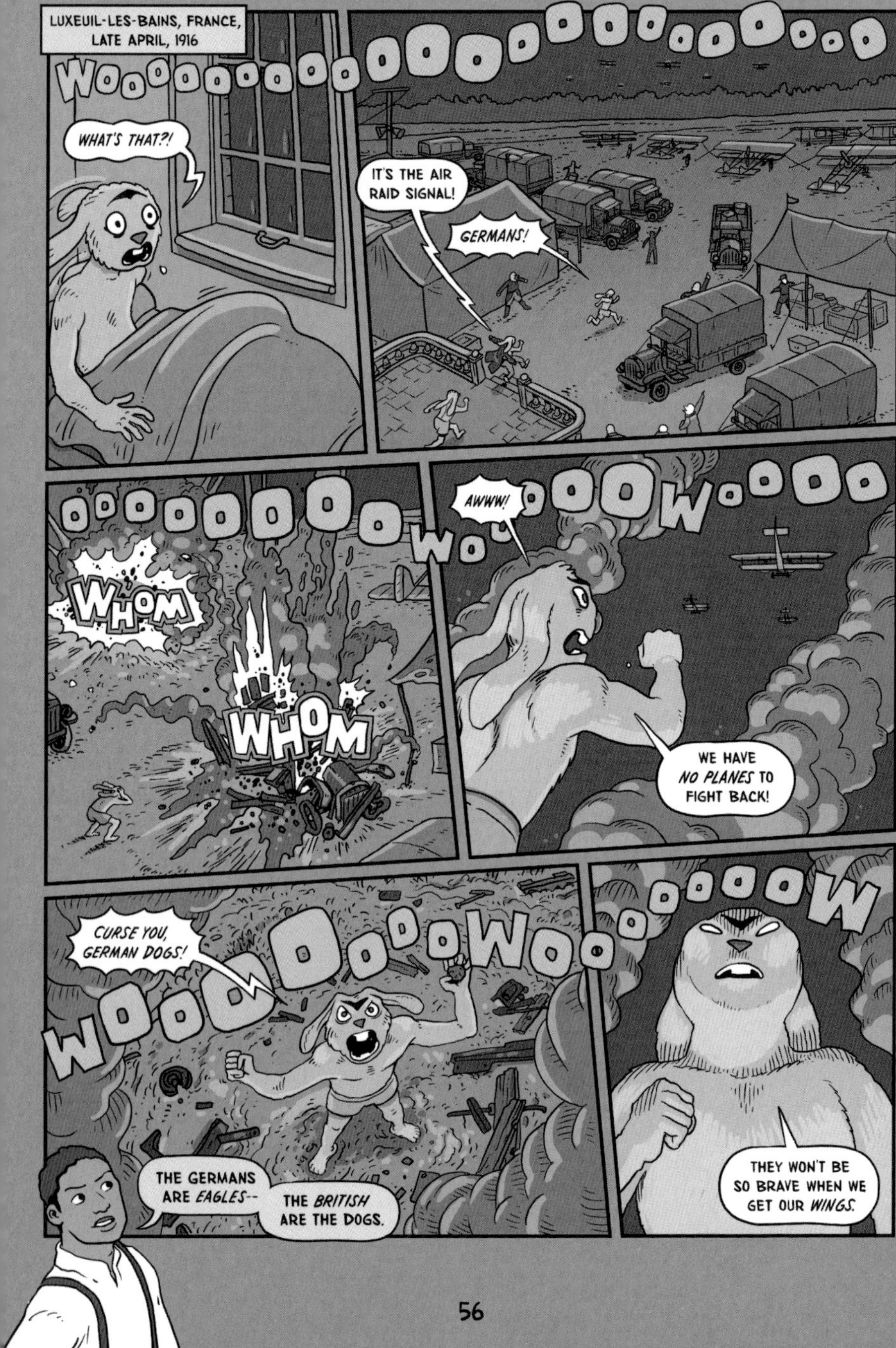
LUXEUIL-LES-BAINS, FRANCE, LATE APRIL, 1916
WOOOOOOOOOOOOOOOOOOOOOOOOOO
WHAT'S THAT?!
IT'S THE AIR RAID SIGNAL!
GERMANS!
OOOOOOOOOOOOOWOO
WHOM
WHOM
AWWW!
OOOOW OOOO
WE HAVE *NO PLANES* TO FIGHT BACK!
CURSE YOU, GERMAN DOGS!
WOOOOOOOOWOOOOOOOOOOW
THE GERMANS ARE *EAGLES*--
THE *BRITISH* ARE THE DOGS.
THEY WON'T BE SO BRAVE WHEN WE GET OUR *WINGS*.

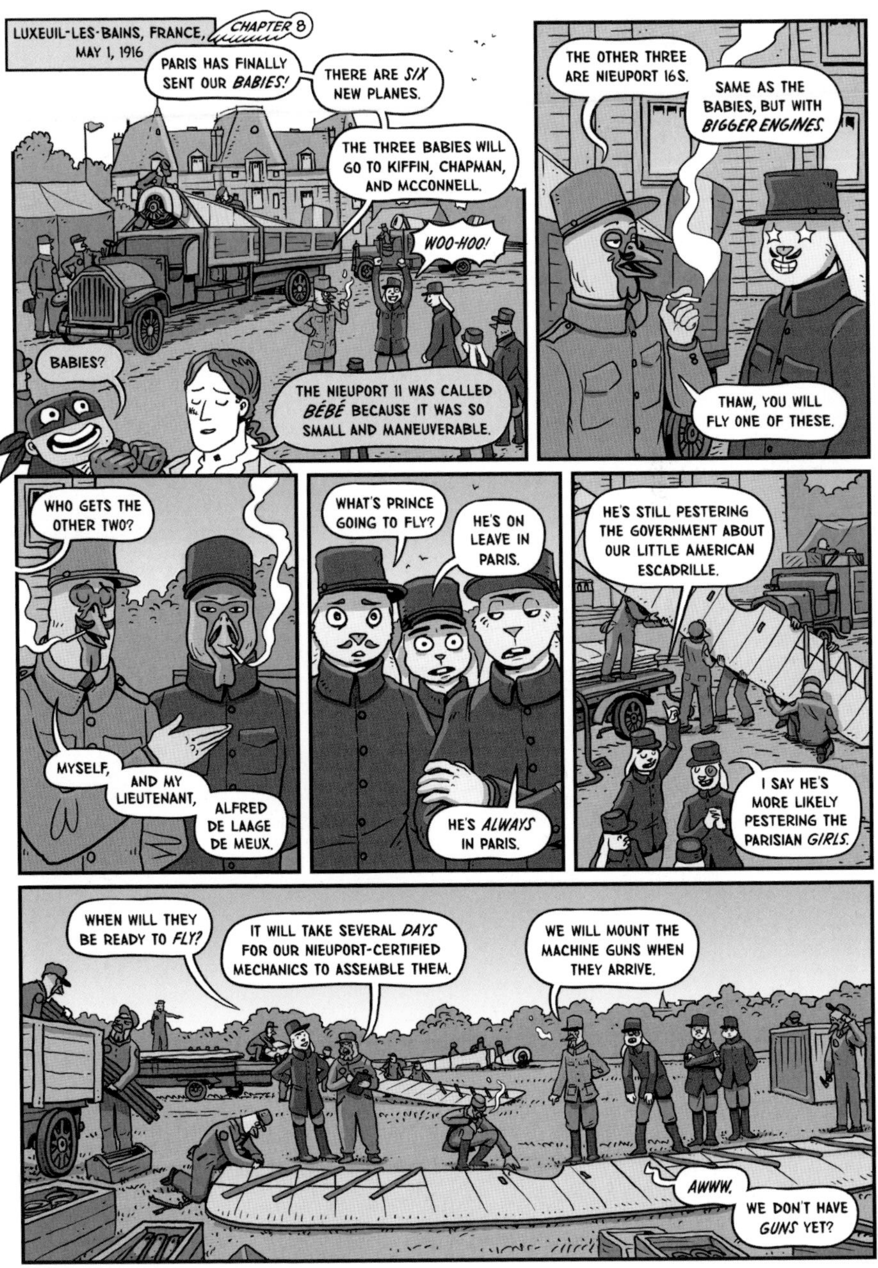

CHAPTER 8
LUXEUIL-LES-BAINS, FRANCE, MAY 1, 1916
PARIS HAS FINALLY SENT OUR BABIES!
THERE ARE SIX NEW PLANES.
THE THREE BABIES WILL GO TO KIFFIN, CHAPMAN, AND MCCONNELL.
WOO-HOO!
BABIES?
THE NIEUPORT 11 WAS CALLED BÉBÉ BECAUSE IT WAS SO SMALL AND MANEUVERABLE.
THE OTHER THREE ARE NIEUPORT 16S.
SAME AS THE BABIES, BUT WITH BIGGER ENGINES.
THAW, YOU WILL FLY ONE OF THESE.
WHO GETS THE OTHER TWO?
MYSELF,
AND MY LIEUTENANT,
ALFRED DE LAAGE DE MEUX.
WHAT'S PRINCE GOING TO FLY?
HE'S ON LEAVE IN PARIS.
HE'S ALWAYS IN PARIS.
HE'S STILL PESTERING THE GOVERNMENT ABOUT OUR LITTLE AMERICAN ESCADRILLE.
I SAY HE'S MORE LIKELY PESTERING THE PARISIAN GIRLS.
WHEN WILL THEY BE READY TO FLY?
IT WILL TAKE SEVERAL DAYS FOR OUR NIEUPORT-CERTIFIED MECHANICS TO ASSEMBLE THEM.
WE WILL MOUNT THE MACHINE GUNS WHEN THEY ARRIVE.
AWWW.
WE DON'T HAVE GUNS YET?

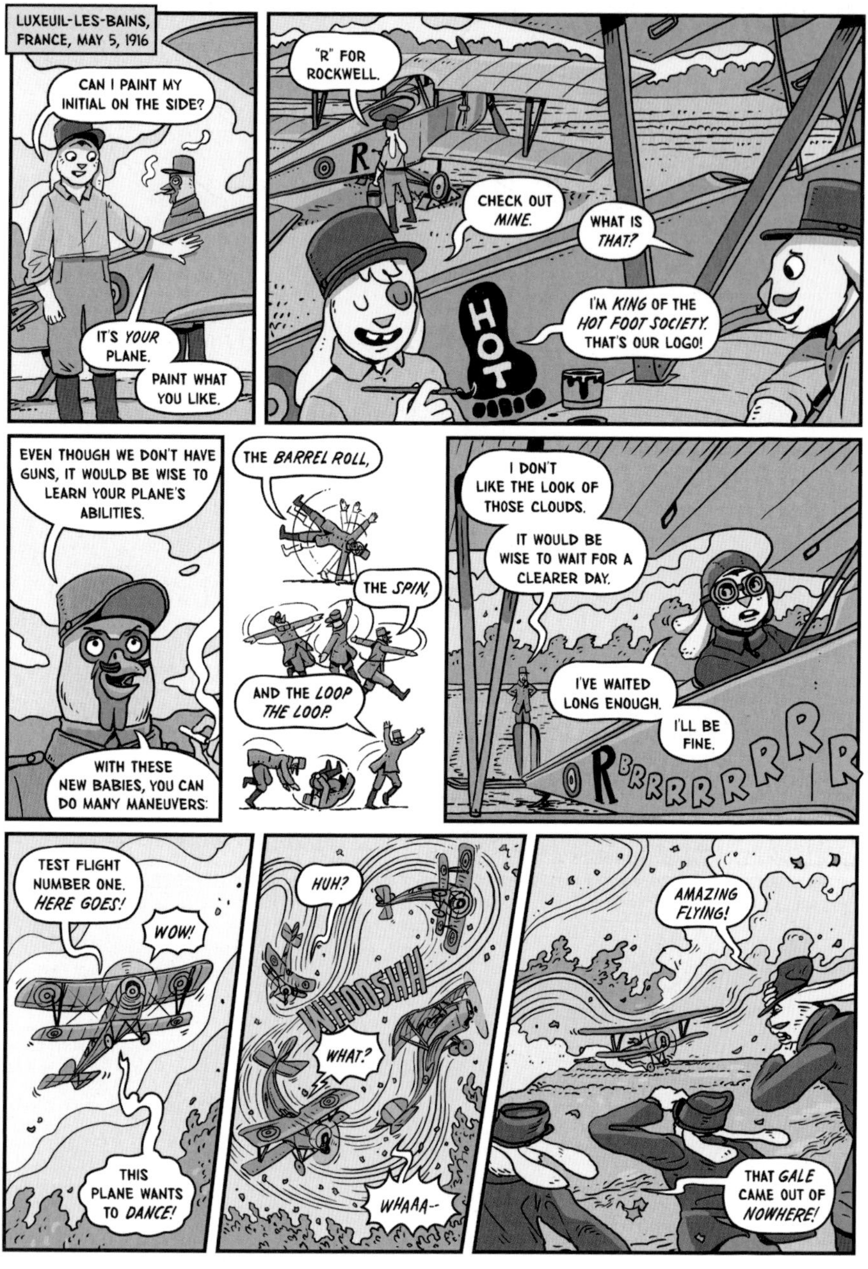
LUXEUIL-LES-BAINS, FRANCE, MAY 5, 1916
CAN I PAINT MY INITIAL ON THE SIDE?
IT'S *YOUR* PLANE.
PAINT WHAT YOU LIKE.
"R" FOR ROCKWELL.
CHECK OUT *MINE*.
WHAT IS *THAT?*
HOT
I'M *KING* OF THE *HOT FOOT SOCIETY*. THAT'S OUR LOGO!
EVEN THOUGH WE DON'T HAVE GUNS, IT WOULD BE WISE TO LEARN YOUR PLANE'S ABILITIES.
WITH THESE NEW BABIES, YOU CAN DO MANY MANEUVERS:
THE *BARREL ROLL*,
THE *SPIN*,
AND THE *LOOP THE LOOP*.
I DON'T LIKE THE LOOK OF THOSE CLOUDS.
IT WOULD BE WISE TO WAIT FOR A CLEARER DAY.
I'VE WAITED LONG ENOUGH.
I'LL BE FINE.
RBRRRRRRRRR
TEST FLIGHT NUMBER ONE. *HERE GOES!*
WOW!
THIS PLANE WANTS TO *DANCE!*
HUH?
WHOOSHH
WHAT?
WHAAA--
AMAZING FLYING!
THAT *GALE* CAME OUT OF *NOWHERE!*

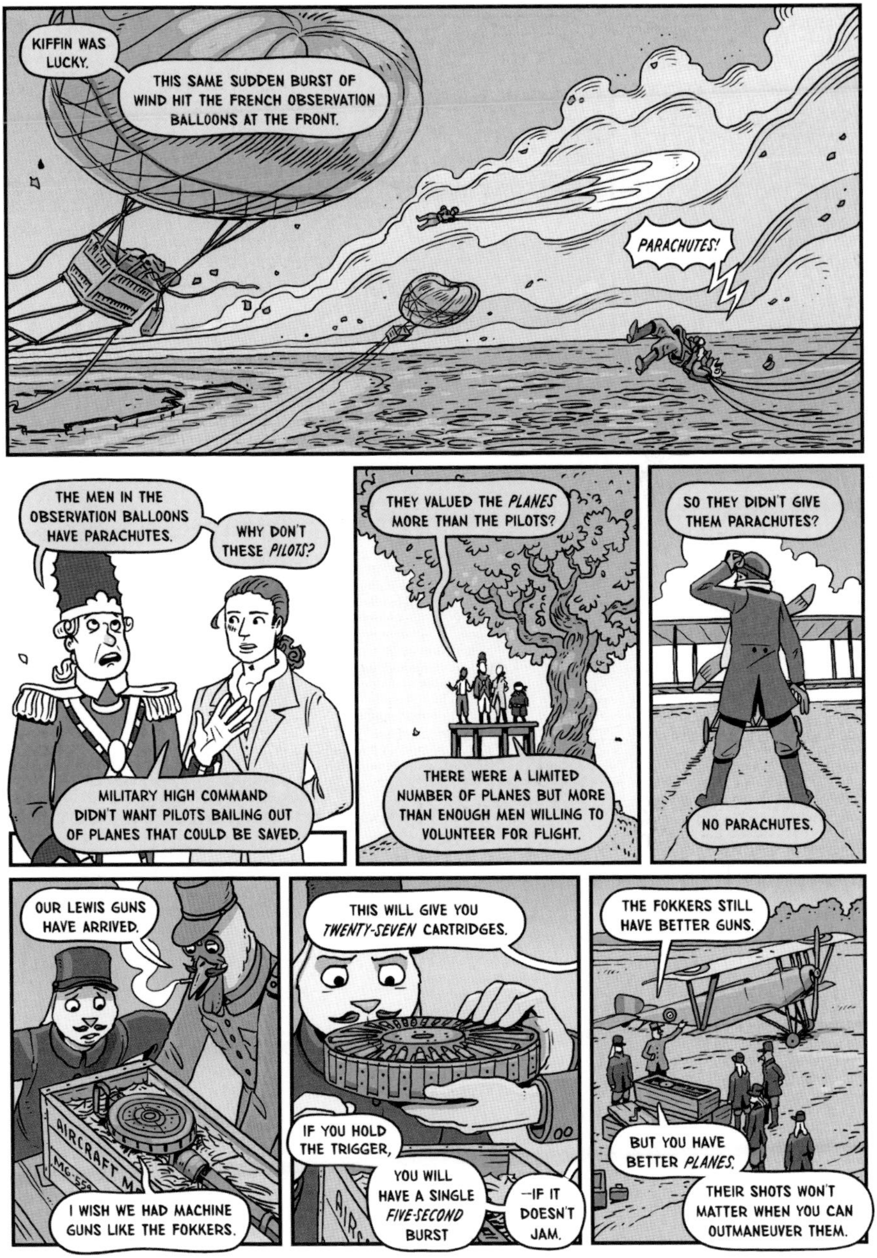
KIFFIN WAS LUCKY.
THIS SAME SUDDEN BURST OF WIND HIT THE FRENCH OBSERVATION BALLOONS AT THE FRONT.
PARACHUTES!
THE MEN IN THE OBSERVATION BALLOONS HAVE PARACHUTES.
WHY DON'T THESE *PILOTS*?
MILITARY HIGH COMMAND DIDN'T WANT PILOTS BAILING OUT OF PLANES THAT COULD BE SAVED.
THEY VALUED THE *PLANES* MORE THAN THE PILOTS?
THERE WERE A LIMITED NUMBER OF PLANES BUT MORE THAN ENOUGH MEN WILLING TO VOLUNTEER FOR FLIGHT.
SO THEY DIDN'T GIVE THEM PARACHUTES?
NO PARACHUTES.
OUR LEWIS GUNS HAVE ARRIVED.
AIRCRAFT M
MG-559
I WISH WE HAD MACHINE GUNS LIKE THE FOKKERS.
THIS WILL GIVE YOU *TWENTY-SEVEN* CARTRIDGES.
IF YOU HOLD THE TRIGGER,
YOU WILL HAVE A SINGLE *FIVE-SECOND* BURST
--IF IT DOESN'T JAM.
THE FOKKERS STILL HAVE BETTER GUNS.
BUT YOU HAVE BETTER *PLANES*.
THEIR SHOTS WON'T MATTER WHEN YOU CAN OUTMANEUVER THEM.

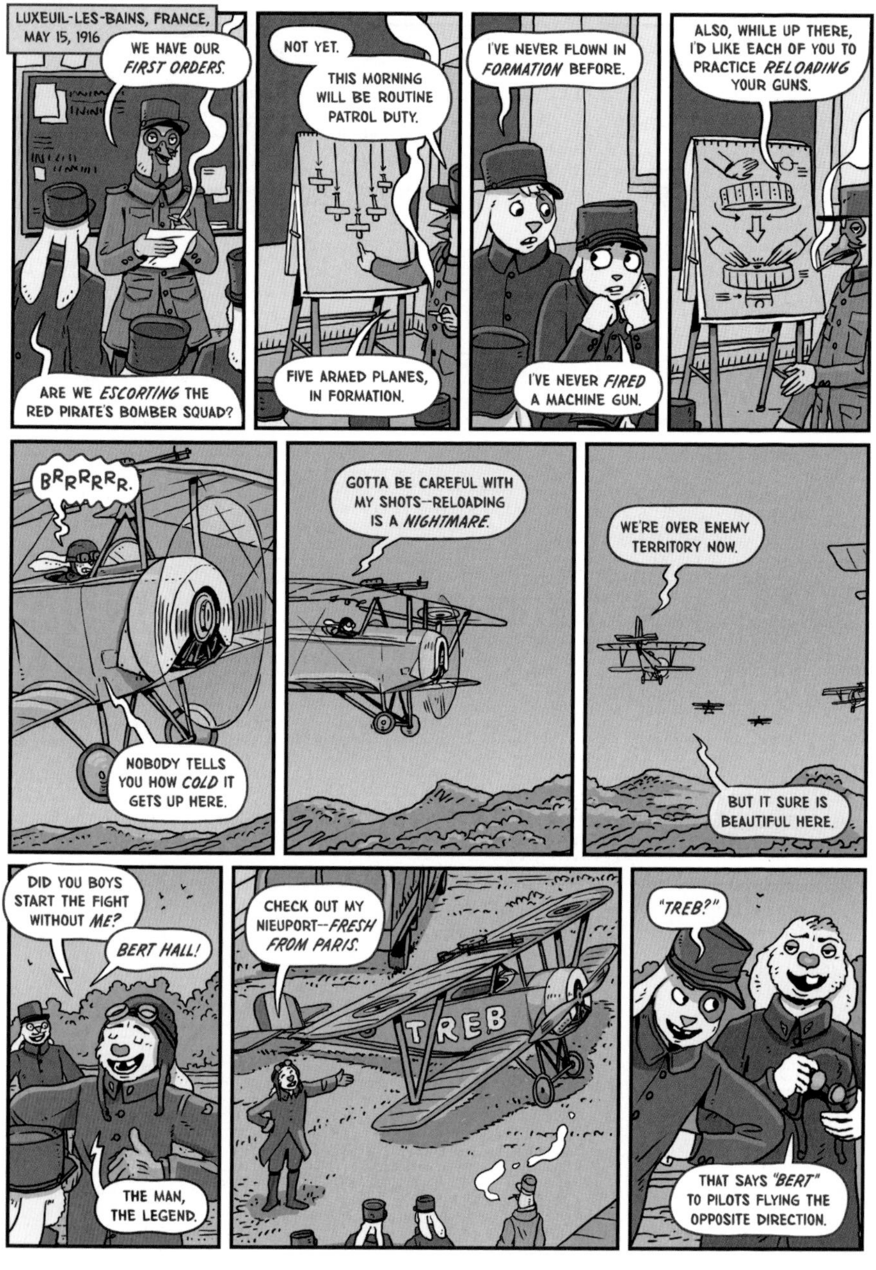

LUXEUIL-LES-BAINS, FRANCE, MAY 15, 1916
WE HAVE OUR *FIRST ORDERS.*
ARE WE *ESCORTING* THE RED PIRATE'S BOMBER SQUAD?
NOT YET.
THIS MORNING WILL BE ROUTINE PATROL DUTY.
FIVE ARMED PLANES, IN FORMATION.
I'VE NEVER FLOWN IN *FORMATION* BEFORE.
I'VE NEVER *FIRED* A MACHINE GUN.
ALSO, WHILE UP THERE, I'D LIKE EACH OF YOU TO PRACTICE *RELOADING* YOUR GUNS.
BRRRRRR.
NOBODY TELLS YOU HOW *COLD* IT GETS UP HERE.
GOTTA BE CAREFUL WITH MY SHOTS--RELOADING IS A *NIGHTMARE.*
WE'RE OVER ENEMY TERRITORY NOW.
BUT IT SURE IS BEAUTIFUL HERE.
DID YOU BOYS START THE FIGHT WITHOUT *ME?*
BERT HALL!
THE MAN, THE LEGEND.
CHECK OUT MY NIEUPORT--*FRESH FROM PARIS.*
TREB
"TREB?"
THAT SAYS *"BERT"* TO PILOTS FLYING THE OPPOSITE DIRECTION.

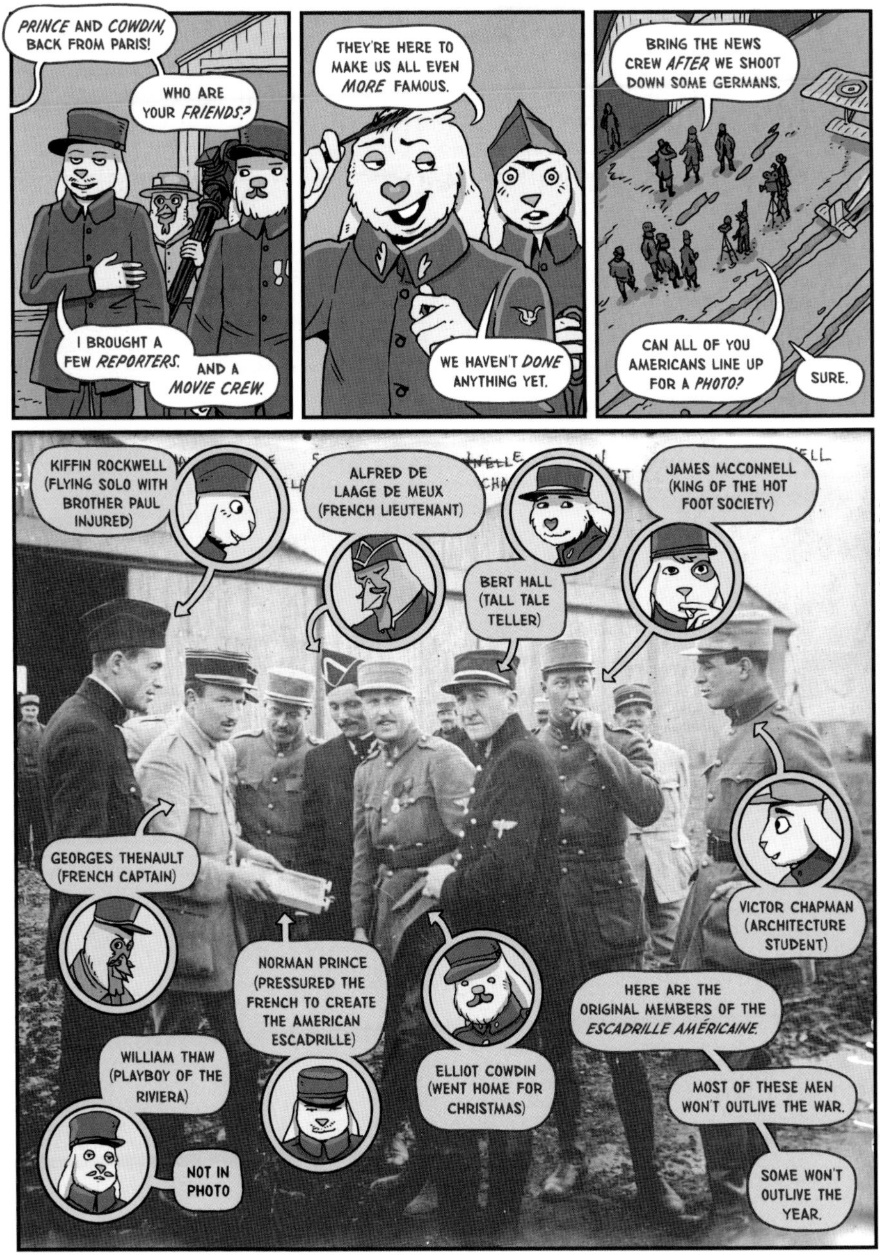

PRINCE AND COWDIN, BACK FROM PARIS!
WHO ARE YOUR FRIENDS?
I BROUGHT A FEW REPORTERS.
AND A MOVIE CREW.
THEY'RE HERE TO MAKE US ALL EVEN MORE FAMOUS.
WE HAVEN'T DONE ANYTHING YET.
BRING THE NEWS CREW AFTER WE SHOOT DOWN SOME GERMANS.
CAN ALL OF YOU AMERICANS LINE UP FOR A PHOTO?
SURE.
KIFFIN ROCKWELL (FLYING SOLO WITH BROTHER PAUL INJURED)
ALFRED DE LAAGE DE MEUX (FRENCH LIEUTENANT)
BERT HALL (TALL TALE TELLER)
JAMES MCCONNELL (KING OF THE HOT FOOT SOCIETY)
GEORGES THENAULT (FRENCH CAPTAIN)
NORMAN PRINCE (PRESSURED THE FRENCH TO CREATE THE AMERICAN ESCADRILLE)
ELLIOT COWDIN (WENT HOME FOR CHRISTMAS)
VICTOR CHAPMAN (ARCHITECTURE STUDENT)
WILLIAM THAW (PLAYBOY OF THE RIVIERA)
NOT IN PHOTO
HERE ARE THE ORIGINAL MEMBERS OF THE ESCADRILLE AMÉRICAINE.
MOST OF THESE MEN WON'T OUTLIVE THE WAR.
SOME WON'T OUTLIVE THE YEAR.

BAIN NEWS SERVICE PHOTOGRAPH COLLECTION, LIBRARY OF CONGRESS PRINTS AND PHOTOGRAPHS DIVISION WASHINGTON, D.C.

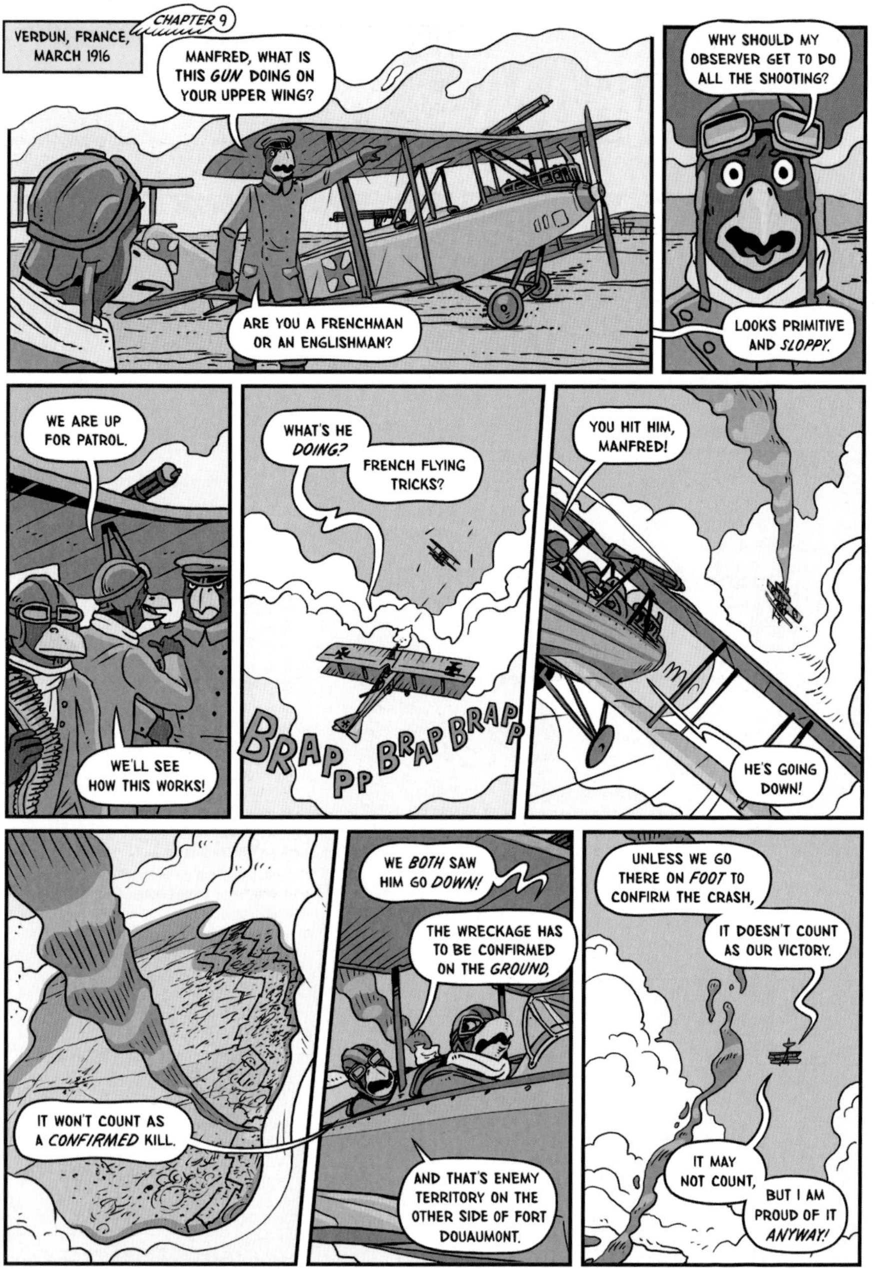
CHAPTER 9
VERDUN, FRANCE, MARCH 1916
MANFRED, WHAT IS THIS GUN DOING ON YOUR UPPER WING?
ARE YOU A FRENCHMAN OR AN ENGLISHMAN?
WHY SHOULD MY OBSERVER GET TO DO ALL THE SHOOTING?
LOOKS PRIMITIVE AND SLOPPY.
WE ARE UP FOR PATROL.
WE'LL SEE HOW THIS WORKS!
WHAT'S HE DOING?
FRENCH FLYING TRICKS?
BRAPPP BRAP BRAPP
YOU HIT HIM, MANFRED!
HE'S GOING DOWN!
IT WON'T COUNT AS A CONFIRMED KILL.
WE BOTH SAW HIM GO DOWN!
THE WRECKAGE HAS TO BE CONFIRMED ON THE GROUND,
AND THAT'S ENEMY TERRITORY ON THE OTHER SIDE OF FORT DOUAUMONT.
UNLESS WE GO THERE ON FOOT TO CONFIRM THE CRASH,
IT DOESN'T COUNT AS OUR VICTORY.
IT MAY NOT COUNT,
BUT I AM PROUD OF IT ANYWAY!

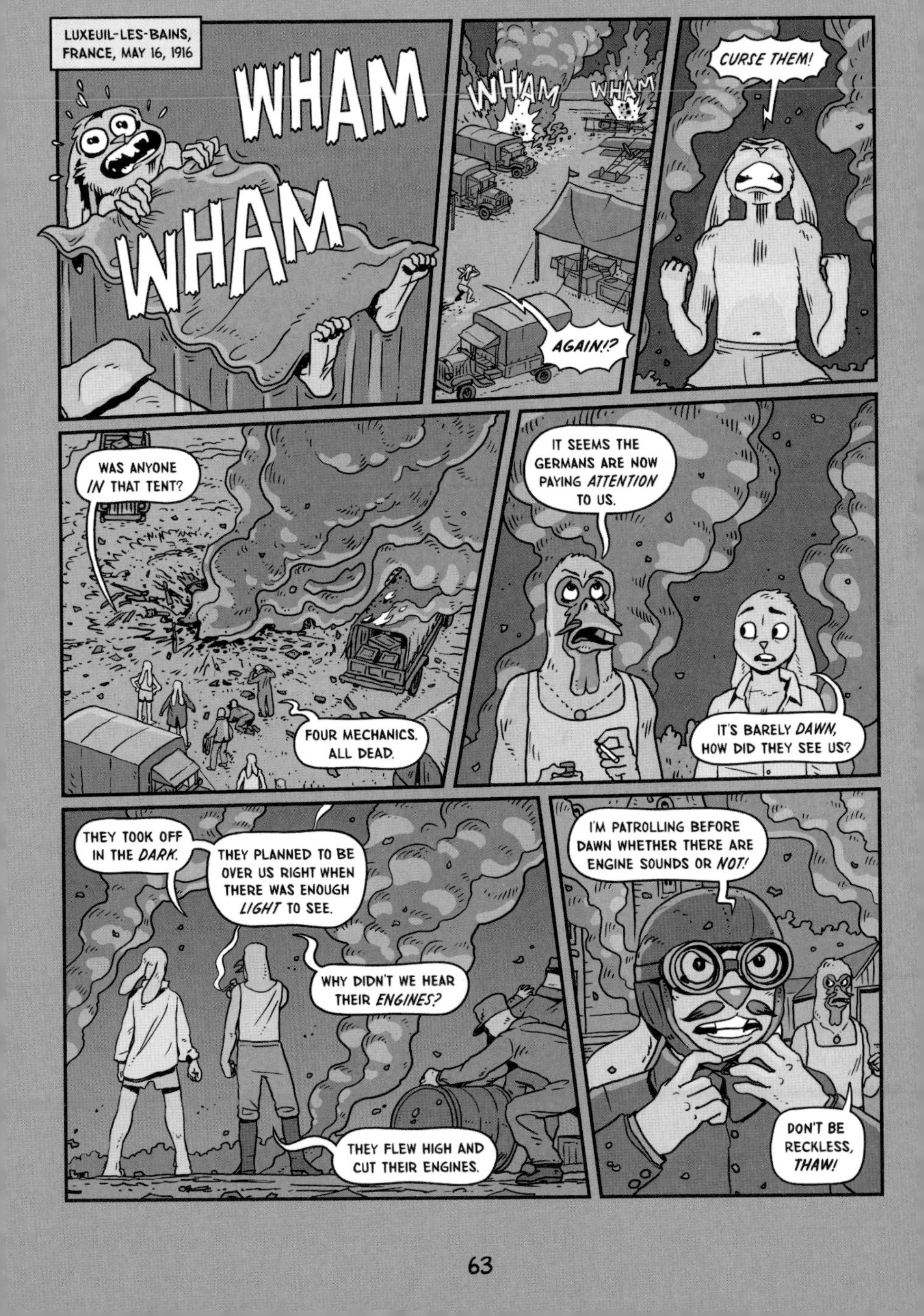
LUXEUIL-LES-BAINS, FRANCE, MAY 16, 1916
WHAM
WHAM
WHAM
WHAM
AGAIN!?
CURSE THEM!
WAS ANYONE *IN* THAT TENT?
FOUR MECHANICS. ALL DEAD.
IT SEEMS THE GERMANS ARE NOW PAYING *ATTENTION* TO US.
IT'S BARELY *DAWN*, HOW DID THEY SEE US?
THEY TOOK OFF IN THE *DARK*.
THEY PLANNED TO BE OVER US RIGHT WHEN THERE WAS ENOUGH *LIGHT* TO SEE.
WHY DIDN'T WE HEAR THEIR *ENGINES?*
THEY FLEW HIGH AND CUT THEIR ENGINES.
I'M PATROLLING BEFORE DAWN WHETHER THERE ARE ENGINE SOUNDS OR *NOT!*
DON'T BE RECKLESS, *THAW!*

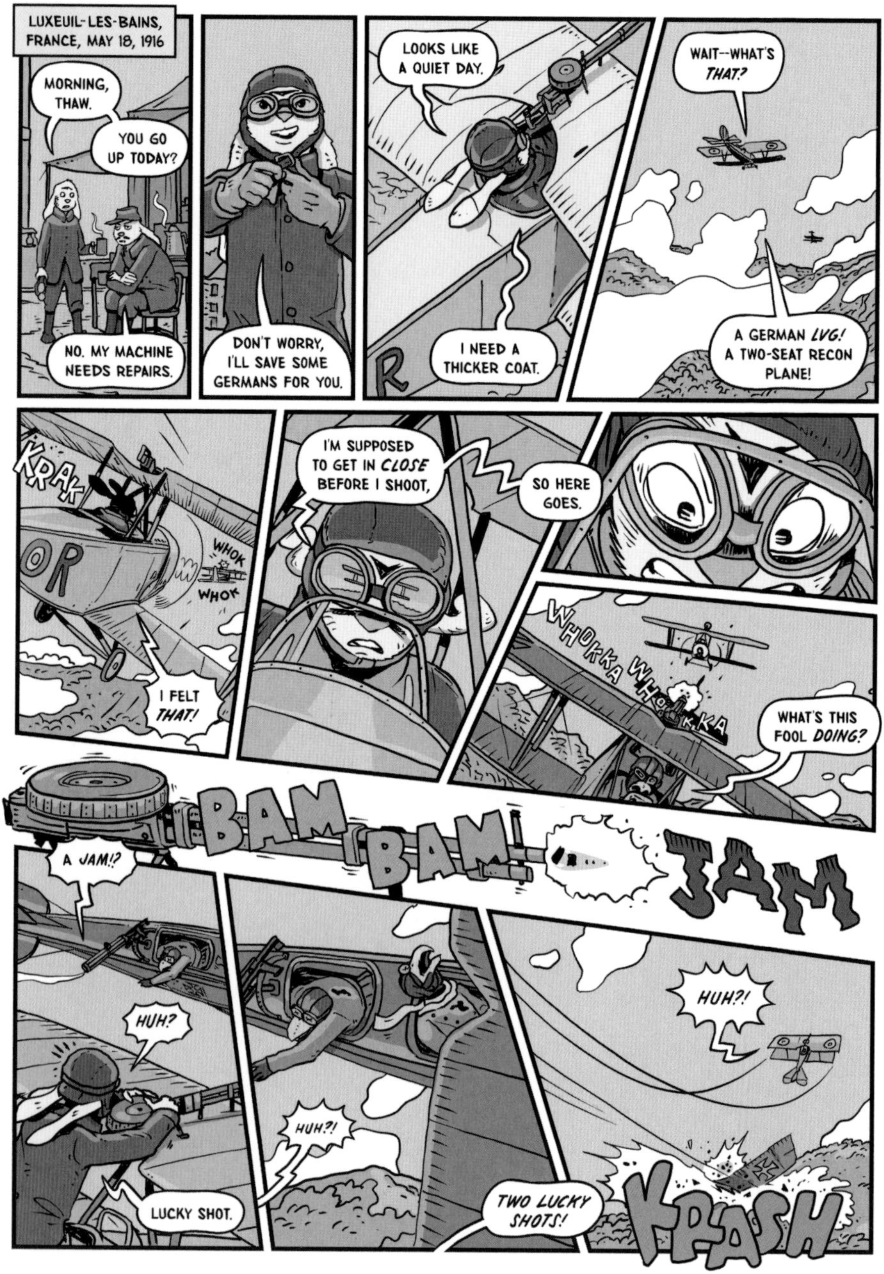

LUXEUIL-LES-BAINS, FRANCE, MAY 18, 1916
MORNING, THAW.
YOU GO UP TODAY?
NO. MY MACHINE NEEDS REPAIRS.
DON'T WORRY, I'LL SAVE SOME GERMANS FOR YOU.
LOOKS LIKE A QUIET DAY.
I NEED A THICKER COAT.
WAIT--WHAT'S *THAT?*
A GERMAN *LVG!* A TWO-SEAT RECON PLANE!
KRAK
WHOK
WHOK
I FELT *THAT!*
I'M SUPPOSED TO GET IN *CLOSE* BEFORE I SHOOT,
SO HERE GOES.
WHOKKA WHOKKA
WHAT'S THIS FOOL *DOING?*
BAM BAM
JAM
A JAM!?
HUH?
HUH?!
LUCKY SHOT.
TWO LUCKY SHOTS!
HUH?!
KRASH

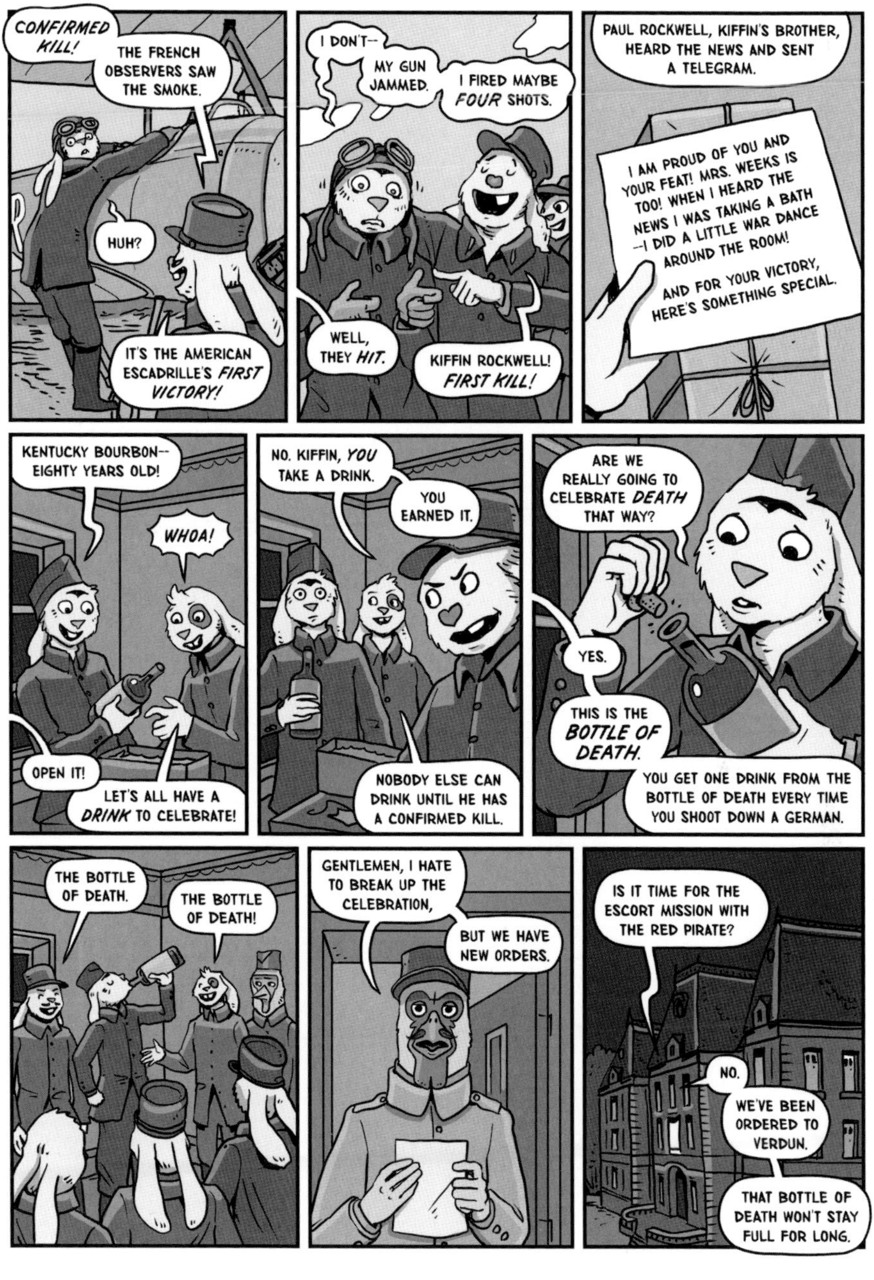
CONFIRMED KILL!
THE FRENCH OBSERVERS SAW THE SMOKE.
HUH?
IT'S THE AMERICAN ESCADRILLE'S FIRST VICTORY!
I DON'T--
MY GUN JAMMED.
I FIRED MAYBE FOUR SHOTS.
WELL, THEY HIT.
KIFFIN ROCKWELL! FIRST KILL!
PAUL ROCKWELL, KIFFIN'S BROTHER, HEARD THE NEWS AND SENT A TELEGRAM.
I AM PROUD OF YOU AND YOUR FEAT! MRS. WEEKS IS TOO! WHEN I HEARD THE NEWS I WAS TAKING A BATH --I DID A LITTLE WAR DANCE AROUND THE ROOM!
AND FOR YOUR VICTORY, HERE'S SOMETHING SPECIAL.
KENTUCKY BOURBON-- EIGHTY YEARS OLD!
WHOA!
OPEN IT!
LET'S ALL HAVE A DRINK TO CELEBRATE!
NO. KIFFIN, YOU TAKE A DRINK.
YOU EARNED IT.
NOBODY ELSE CAN DRINK UNTIL HE HAS A CONFIRMED KILL.
ARE WE REALLY GOING TO CELEBRATE DEATH THAT WAY?
YES.
THIS IS THE BOTTLE OF DEATH.
YOU GET ONE DRINK FROM THE BOTTLE OF DEATH EVERY TIME YOU SHOOT DOWN A GERMAN.
THE BOTTLE OF DEATH.
THE BOTTLE OF DEATH!
GENTLEMEN, I HATE TO BREAK UP THE CELEBRATION,
BUT WE HAVE NEW ORDERS.
IS IT TIME FOR THE ESCORT MISSION WITH THE RED PIRATE?
NO.
WE'VE BEEN ORDERED TO VERDUN.
THAT BOTTLE OF DEATH WON'T STAY FULL FOR LONG.

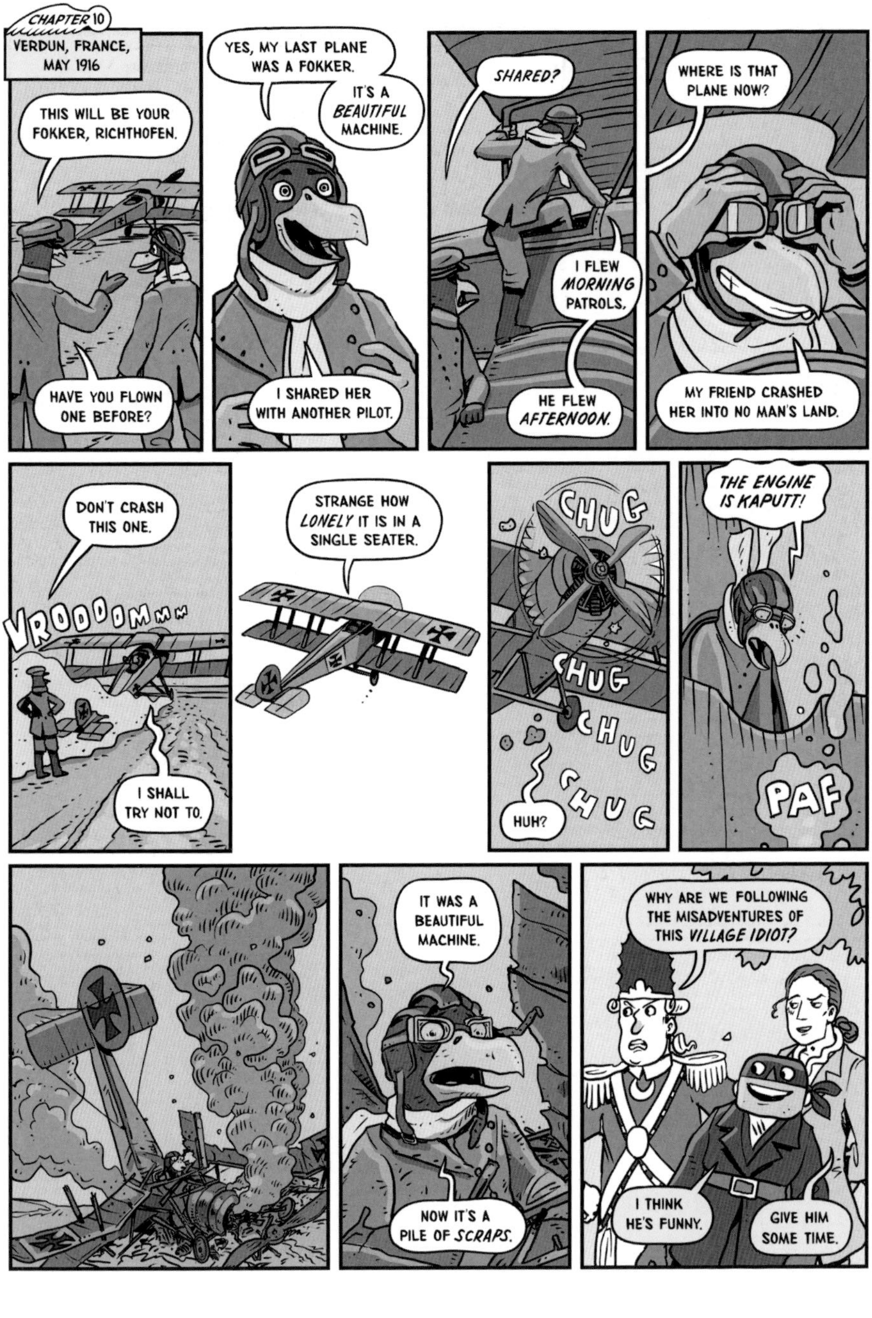
CHAPTER 10
VERDUN, FRANCE, MAY 1916
THIS WILL BE YOUR FOKKER, RICHTHOFEN.
HAVE YOU FLOWN ONE BEFORE?
YES, MY LAST PLANE WAS A FOKKER.
IT'S A *BEAUTIFUL* MACHINE.
I SHARED HER WITH ANOTHER PILOT.
SHARED?
I FLEW *MORNING* PATROLS.
HE FLEW *AFTERNOON.*
WHERE IS THAT PLANE NOW?
MY FRIEND CRASHED HER INTO NO MAN'S LAND.
DON'T CRASH THIS ONE.
VROOOOMMM
I SHALL TRY NOT TO.
STRANGE HOW *LONELY* IT IS IN A SINGLE SEATER.
CHUG
CHUG
CHUG
CHUG
HUH?
THE ENGINE IS KAPUTT!
PAF
IT WAS A BEAUTIFUL MACHINE.
NOW IT'S A PILE OF *SCRAPS.*
WHY ARE WE FOLLOWING THE MISADVENTURES OF THIS *VILLAGE IDIOT?*
I THINK HE'S FUNNY.
GIVE HIM SOME TIME.

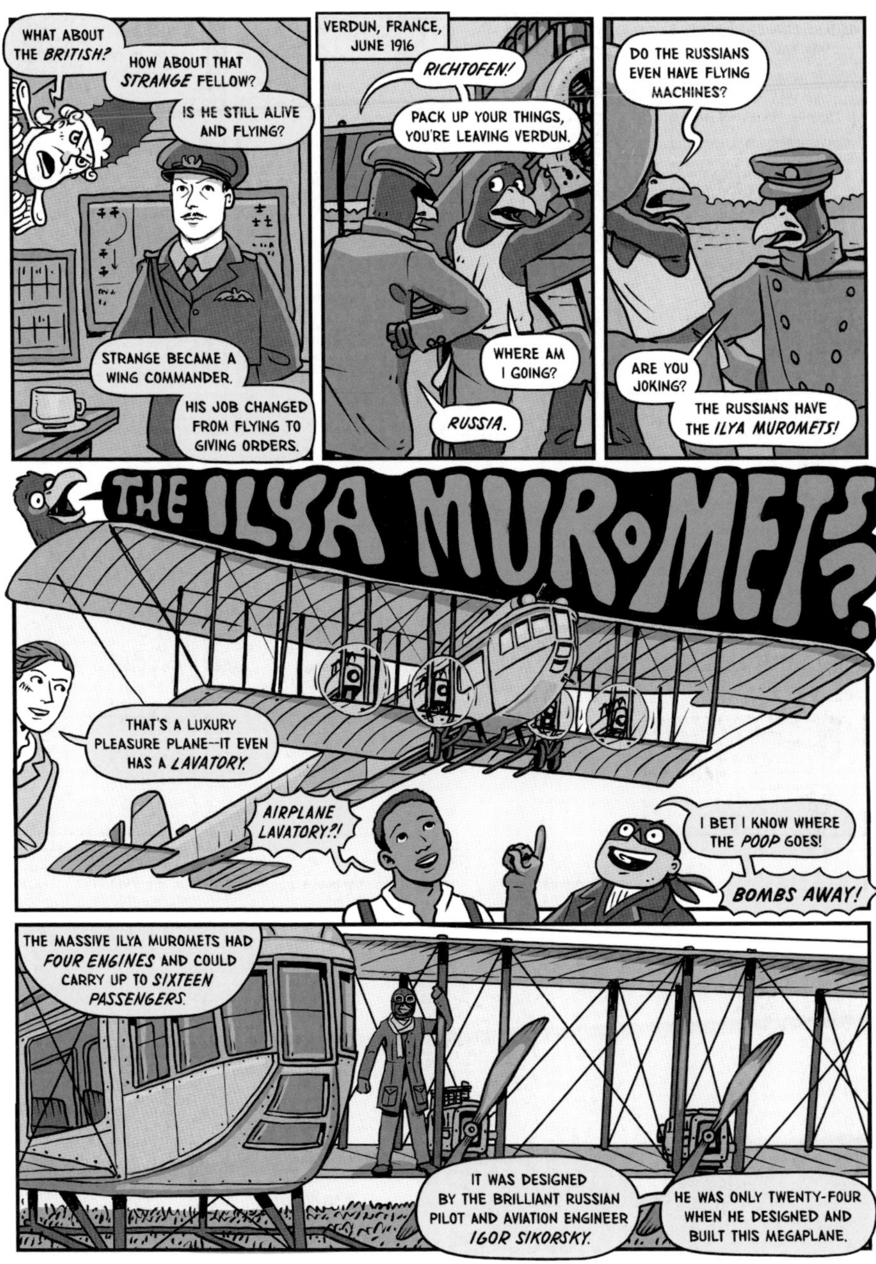
WHAT ABOUT THE *BRITISH?*
HOW ABOUT THAT *STRANGE* FELLOW?
IS HE STILL ALIVE AND FLYING?
STRANGE BECAME A WING COMMANDER.
HIS JOB CHANGED FROM FLYING TO GIVING ORDERS.
VERDUN, FRANCE, JUNE 1916
RICHTOFEN!
PACK UP YOUR THINGS, YOU'RE LEAVING VERDUN.
WHERE AM I GOING?
RUSSIA.
DO THE RUSSIANS EVEN HAVE FLYING MACHINES?
ARE YOU JOKING?
THE RUSSIANS HAVE THE *ILYA MUROMETS!*
THE ILYA MUROMETS?
THAT'S A LUXURY PLEASURE PLANE--IT EVEN HAS A *LAVATORY.*
AIRPLANE LAVATORY?!
I BET I KNOW WHERE THE *POOP* GOES!
BOMBS AWAY!
THE MASSIVE ILYA MUROMETS HAD *FOUR ENGINES* AND COULD CARRY UP TO *SIXTEEN PASSENGERS.*
IT WAS DESIGNED BY THE BRILLIANT RUSSIAN PILOT AND AVIATION ENGINEER *IGOR SIKORSKY.*
HE WAS ONLY TWENTY-FOUR WHEN HE DESIGNED AND BUILT THIS MEGAPLANE.

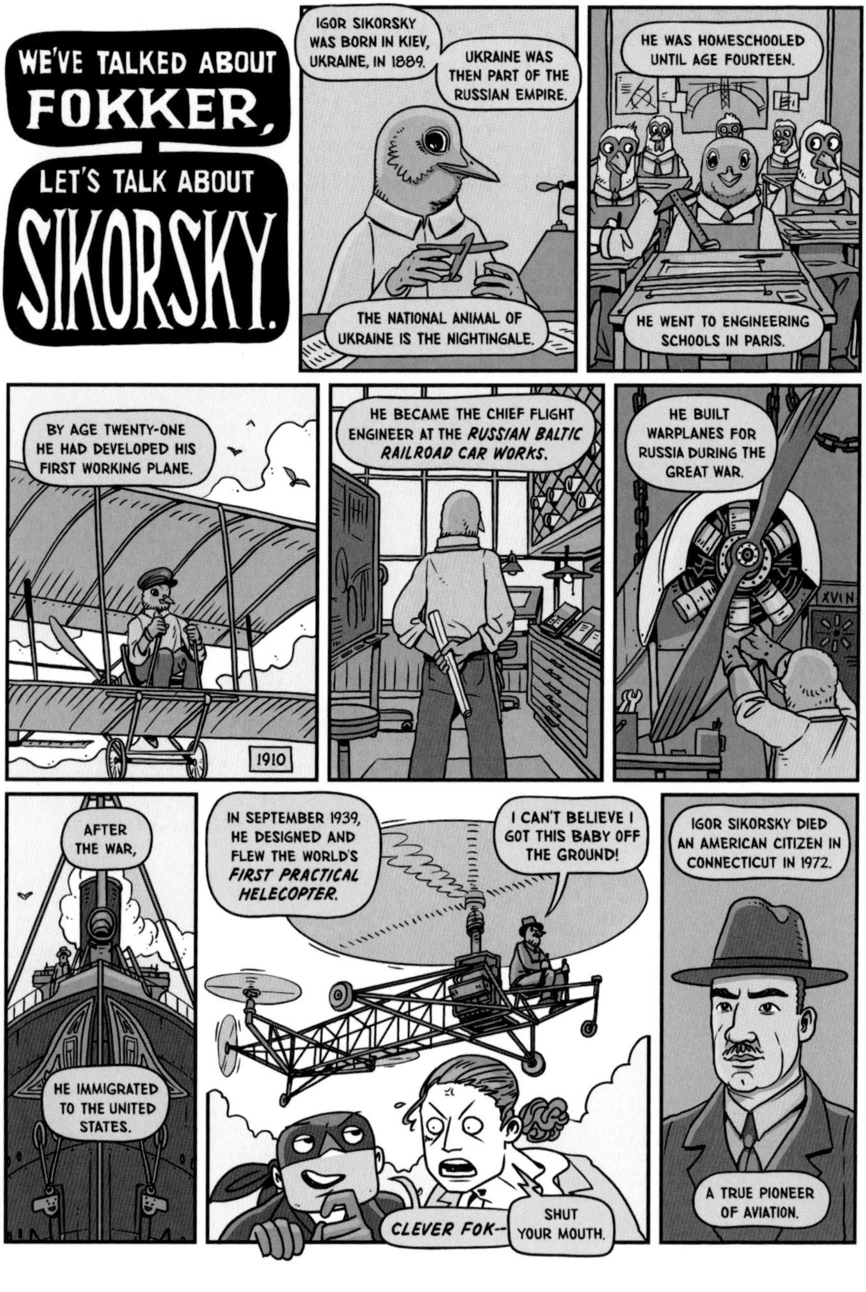
WE'VE TALKED ABOUT
FOKKER,
LET'S TALK ABOUT
SIKORSKY.
IGOR SIKORSKY WAS BORN IN KIEV, UKRAINE, IN 1889.
UKRAINE WAS THEN PART OF THE RUSSIAN EMPIRE.
THE NATIONAL ANIMAL OF UKRAINE IS THE NIGHTINGALE.
HE WAS HOMESCHOOLED UNTIL AGE FOURTEEN.
HE WENT TO ENGINEERING SCHOOLS IN PARIS.
BY AGE TWENTY-ONE HE HAD DEVELOPED HIS FIRST WORKING PLANE.
1910
HE BECAME THE CHIEF FLIGHT ENGINEER AT THE *RUSSIAN BALTIC RAILROAD CAR WORKS*.
HE BUILT WARPLANES FOR RUSSIA DURING THE GREAT WAR.
XVIN
AFTER THE WAR,
HE IMMIGRATED TO THE UNITED STATES.
IN SEPTEMBER 1939, HE DESIGNED AND FLEW THE WORLD'S *FIRST PRACTICAL HELECOPTER*.
I CAN'T BELIEVE I GOT THIS BABY OFF THE GROUND!
CLEVER FOK--
SHUT YOUR MOUTH.
IGOR SIKORSKY DIED AN AMERICAN CITIZEN IN CONNECTICUT IN 1972.
A TRUE PIONEER OF AVIATION.

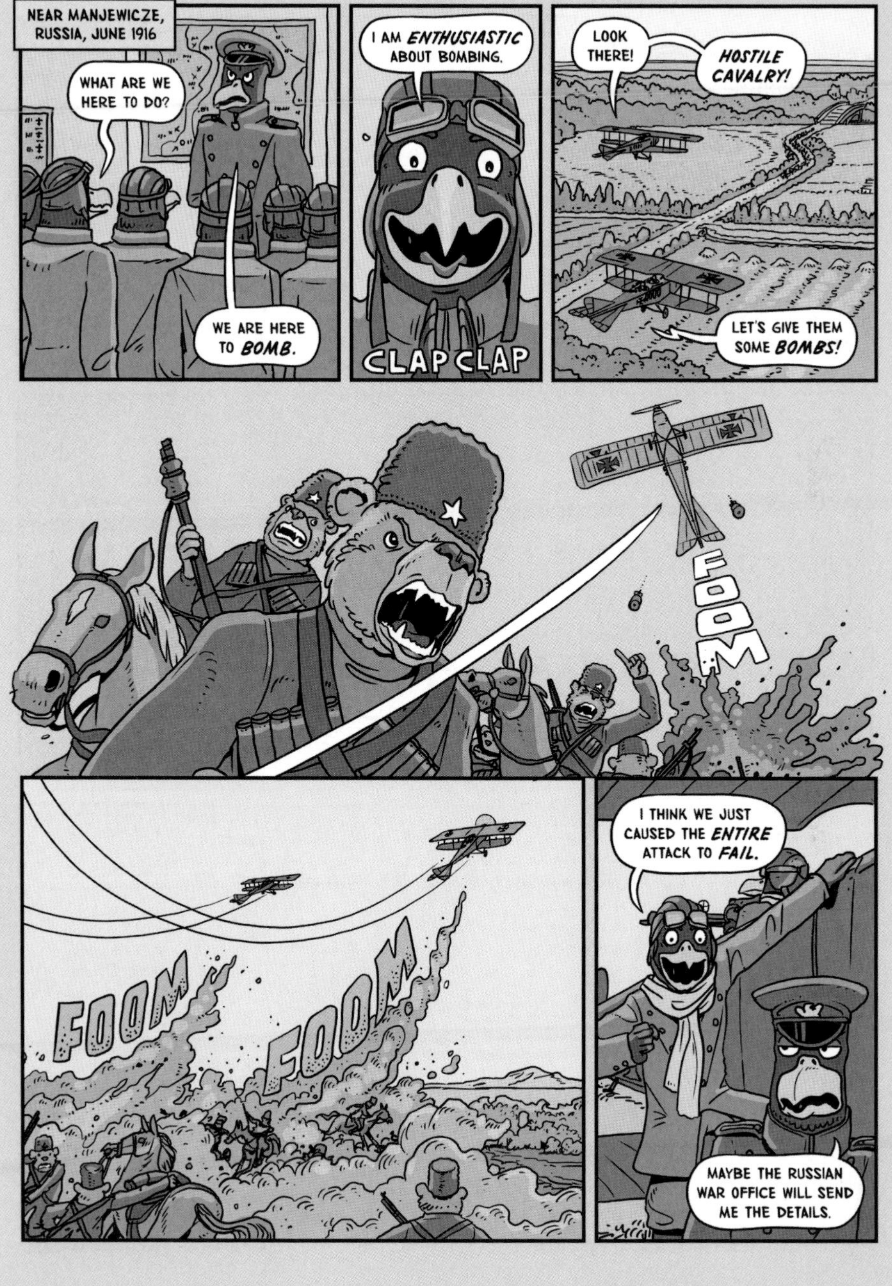
NEAR MANJEWICZE, RUSSIA, JUNE 1916
WHAT ARE WE HERE TO DO?
WE ARE HERE TO *BOMB.*
I AM *ENTHUSIASTIC* ABOUT BOMBING.
CLAP CLAP
LOOK THERE!
HOSTILE CAVALRY!
LET'S GIVE THEM SOME *BOMBS!*
FOOM
FOOM
FOOM
I THINK WE JUST CAUSED THE *ENTIRE* ATTACK TO *FAIL.*
MAYBE THE RUSSIAN WAR OFFICE WILL SEND ME THE DETAILS.

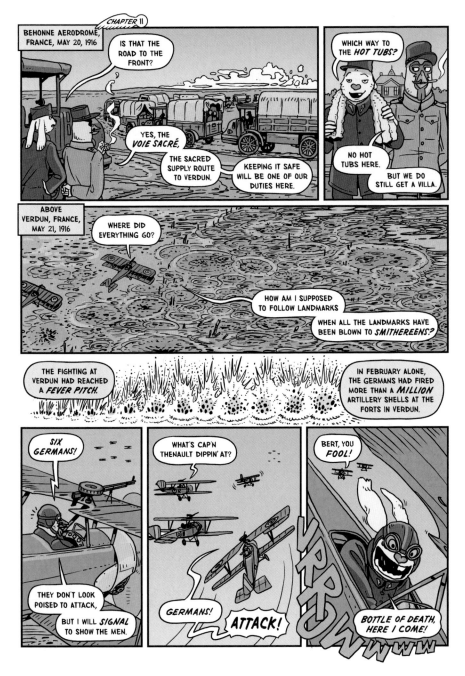

CHAPTER 11

BEHONNE AERODROME, FRANCE, MAY 20, 1916

IS THAT THE ROAD TO THE FRONT?

YES, THE *VOIE SACRÉ*,

THE SACRED SUPPLY ROUTE TO VERDUN.

KEEPING IT SAFE WILL BE ONE OF OUR DUTIES HERE.

WHICH WAY TO THE *HOT TUBS*?

NO HOT TUBS HERE.

BUT WE DO STILL GET A VILLA.

ABOVE VERDUN, FRANCE, MAY 21, 1916

WHERE DID EVERYTHING GO?

HOW AM I SUPPOSED TO FOLLOW LANDMARKS

WHEN ALL THE LANDMARKS HAVE BEEN BLOWN TO *SMITHEREENS?*

THE FIGHTING AT VERDUN HAD REACHED A *FEVER PITCH*.

IN FEBRUARY ALONE, THE GERMANS HAD FIRED MORE THAN A *MILLION* ARTILLERY SHELLS AT THE FORTS IN VERDUN.

SIX GERMANS!

THEY DON'T LOOK POISED TO ATTACK,

BUT I WILL *SIGNAL* TO SHOW THE MEN.

WHAT'S CAP'N THENAULT DIPPIN' AT?

GERMANS!

ATTACK!

BERT, YOU *FOOL!*

VRRRMMM

BOTTLE OF DEATH, HERE I COME!

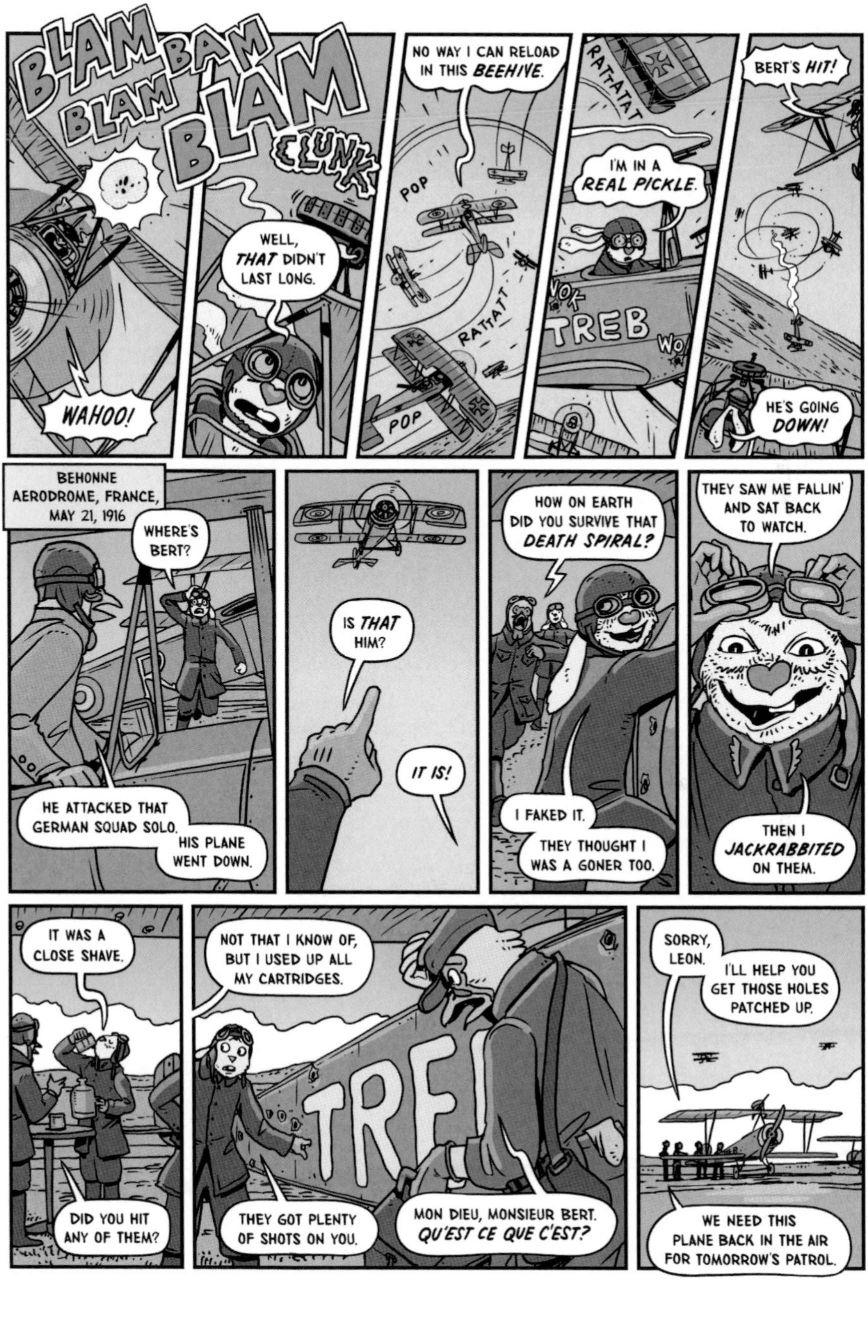
BLAM BAM BLAM BLAM BLAM
WAHOO!
CLUNK
WELL, THAT DIDN'T LAST LONG.
NO WAY I CAN RELOAD IN THIS BEEHIVE.
POP
RATTATT
POP
RATTATAT
I'M IN A REAL PICKLE.
TREB
BERT'S HIT!
HE'S GOING DOWN!
BEHONNE AERODROME, FRANCE, MAY 21, 1916
WHERE'S BERT?
HE ATTACKED THAT GERMAN SQUAD SOLO.
HIS PLANE WENT DOWN.
IS THAT HIM?
IT IS!
HOW ON EARTH DID YOU SURVIVE THAT DEATH SPIRAL?
I FAKED IT.
THEY THOUGHT I WAS A GONER TOO.
THEY SAW ME FALLIN' AND SAT BACK TO WATCH.
THEN I JACKRABBITED ON THEM.
IT WAS A CLOSE SHAVE.
DID YOU HIT ANY OF THEM?
NOT THAT I KNOW OF, BUT I USED UP ALL MY CARTRIDGES.
THEY GOT PLENTY OF SHOTS ON YOU.
MON DIEU, MONSIEUR BERT. QU'EST CE QUE C'EST?
SORRY, LEON.
I'LL HELP YOU GET THOSE HOLES PATCHED UP.
WE NEED THIS PLANE BACK IN THE AIR FOR TOMORROW'S PATROL.

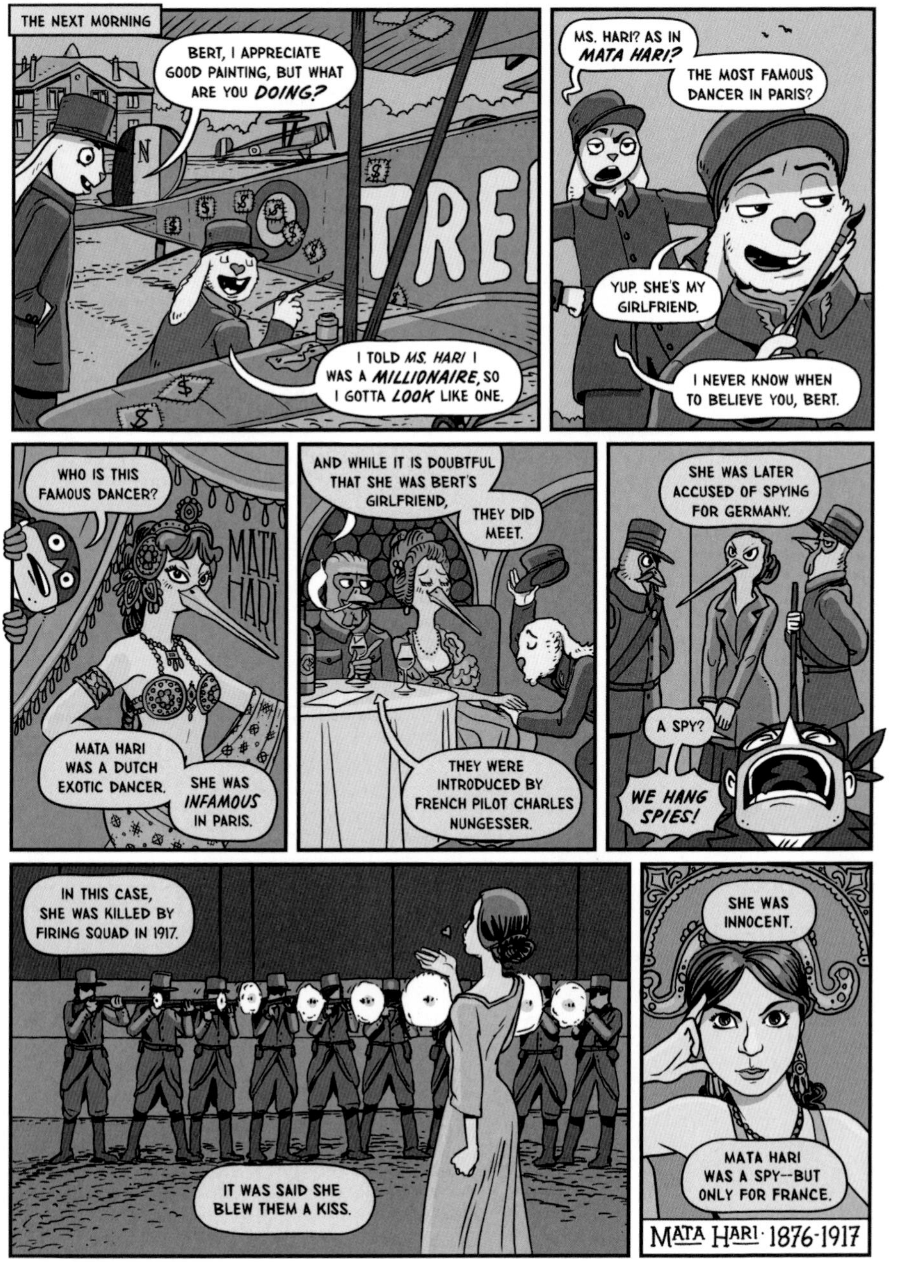
THE NEXT MORNING
BERT, I APPRECIATE GOOD PAINTING, BUT WHAT ARE YOU DOING?
I TOLD MS. HARI I WAS A MILLIONAIRE, SO I GOTTA LOOK LIKE ONE.
MS. HARI? AS IN MATA HARI?
THE MOST FAMOUS DANCER IN PARIS?
YUP. SHE'S MY GIRLFRIEND.
I NEVER KNOW WHEN TO BELIEVE YOU, BERT.
WHO IS THIS FAMOUS DANCER?
MATA HARI
MATA HARI WAS A DUTCH EXOTIC DANCER.
SHE WAS INFAMOUS IN PARIS.
AND WHILE IT IS DOUBTFUL THAT SHE WAS BERT'S GIRLFRIEND,
THEY DID MEET.
THEY WERE INTRODUCED BY FRENCH PILOT CHARLES NUNGESSER.
SHE WAS LATER ACCUSED OF SPYING FOR GERMANY.
A SPY?
WE HANG SPIES!
IN THIS CASE, SHE WAS KILLED BY FIRING SQUAD IN 1917.
IT WAS SAID SHE BLEW THEM A KISS.
SHE WAS INNOCENT.
MATA HARI WAS A SPY--BUT ONLY FOR FRANCE.
MATA HARI · 1876-1917

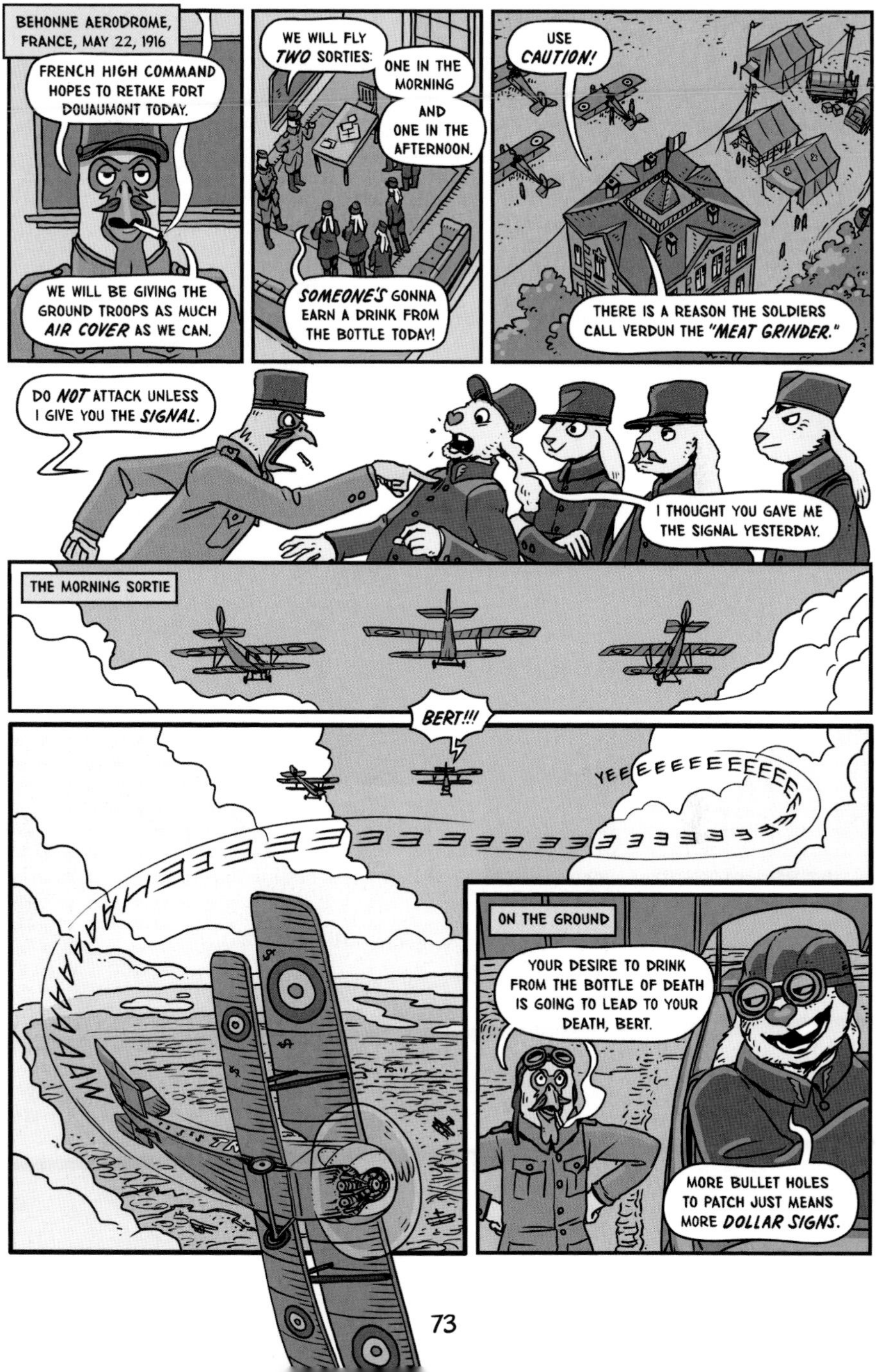
BEHONNE AERODROME, FRANCE, MAY 22, 1916
FRENCH HIGH COMMAND HOPES TO RETAKE FORT DOUAUMONT TODAY.
WE WILL BE GIVING THE GROUND TROOPS AS MUCH AIR COVER AS WE CAN.
WE WILL FLY TWO SORTIES:
ONE IN THE MORNING
AND ONE IN THE AFTERNOON.
SOMEONE'S GONNA EARN A DRINK FROM THE BOTTLE TODAY!
USE CAUTION!
THERE IS A REASON THE SOLDIERS CALL VERDUN THE "MEAT GRINDER."
DO NOT ATTACK UNLESS I GIVE YOU THE SIGNAL.
I THOUGHT YOU GAVE ME THE SIGNAL YESTERDAY.
THE MORNING SORTIE
BERT!!!
YEEEEEEEEEEEEEEEEEEEEEEEEEEEEEEEEEEHAAAAAAAAW
ON THE GROUND
YOUR DESIRE TO DRINK FROM THE BOTTLE OF DEATH IS GOING TO LEAD TO YOUR DEATH, BERT.
MORE BULLET HOLES TO PATCH JUST MEANS MORE DOLLAR SIGNS.

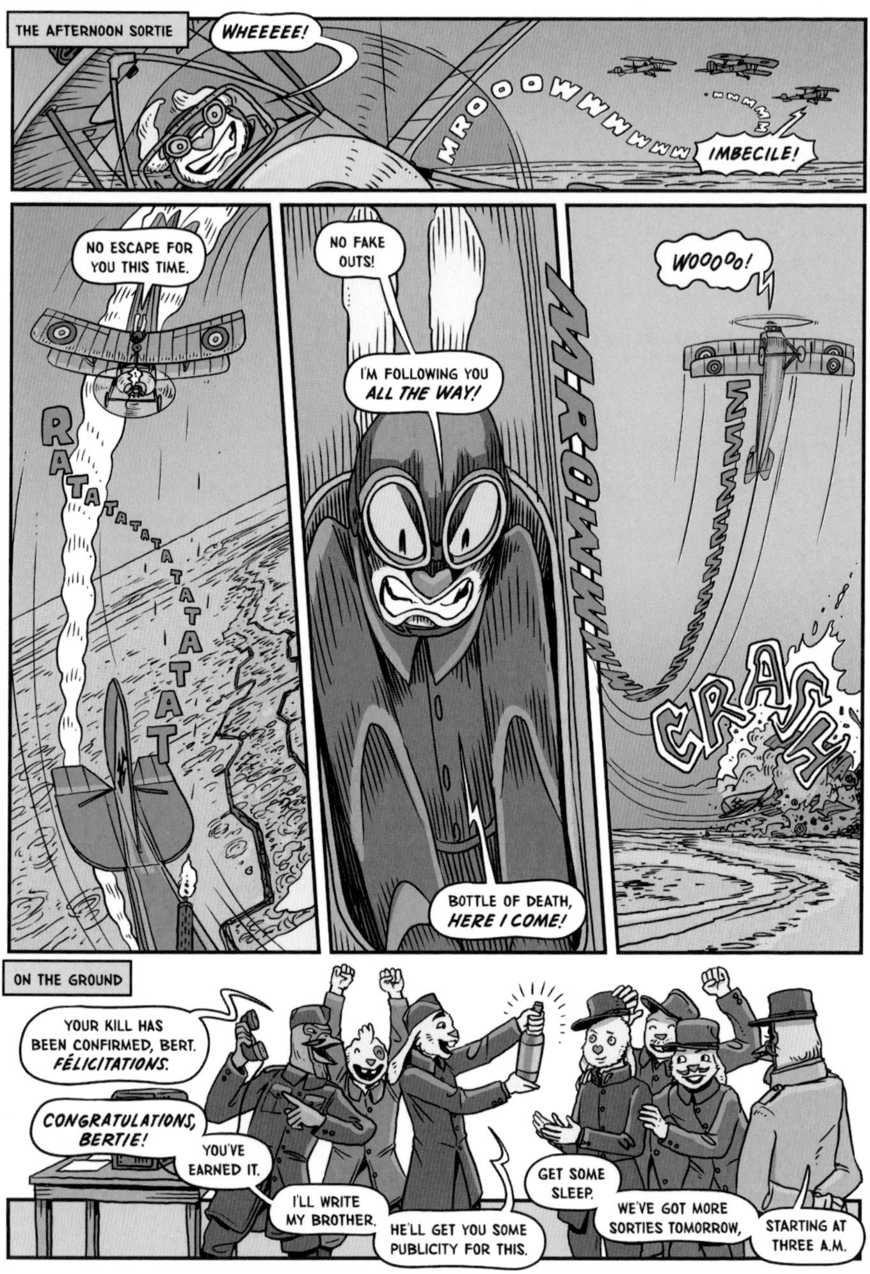
THE AFTERNOON SORTIE
WHEEEEE!
MROOOOWMMMMMMMMMMM...
IMBECILE!
NO ESCAPE FOR YOU THIS TIME.
RATATATATATATATATAT
NO FAKE OUTS!
I'M FOLLOWING YOU ALL THE WAY!
BOTTLE OF DEATH, HERE I COME!
WOOOoo!
CRASH
ON THE GROUND
YOUR KILL HAS BEEN CONFIRMED, BERT. FÉLICITATIONS.
CONGRATULATIONS, BERTIE!
YOU'VE EARNED IT.
I'LL WRITE MY BROTHER.
HE'LL GET YOU SOME PUBLICITY FOR THIS.
GET SOME SLEEP.
WE'VE GOT MORE SORTIES TOMORROW,
STARTING AT THREE A.M.

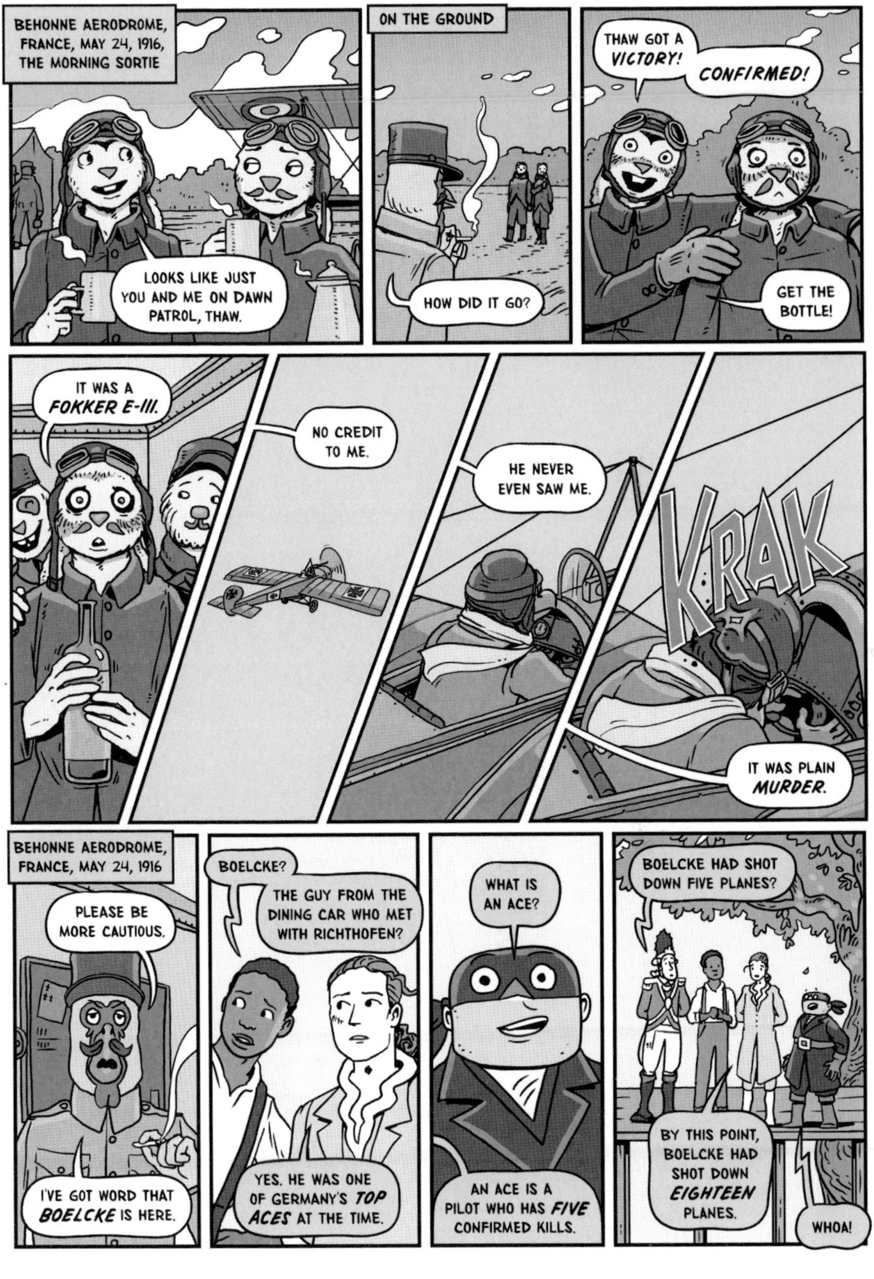
BEHONNE AERODROME, FRANCE, MAY 24, 1916, THE MORNING SORTIE
LOOKS LIKE JUST YOU AND ME ON DAWN PATROL, THAW.
ON THE GROUND
HOW DID IT GO?
THAW GOT A VICTORY!
CONFIRMED!
GET THE BOTTLE!
IT WAS A FOKKER E-III.
NO CREDIT TO ME.
HE NEVER EVEN SAW ME.
KRAK
IT WAS PLAIN MURDER.
BEHONNE AERODROME, FRANCE, MAY 24, 1916
PLEASE BE MORE CAUTIOUS.
I'VE GOT WORD THAT BOELCKE IS HERE.
BOELCKE?
THE GUY FROM THE DINING CAR WHO MET WITH RICHTHOFEN?
YES. HE WAS ONE OF GERMANY'S TOP ACES AT THE TIME.
WHAT IS AN ACE?
AN ACE IS A PILOT WHO HAS FIVE CONFIRMED KILLS.
BOELCKE HAD SHOT DOWN FIVE PLANES?
BY THIS POINT, BOELCKE HAD SHOT DOWN EIGHTEEN PLANES.
WHOA!

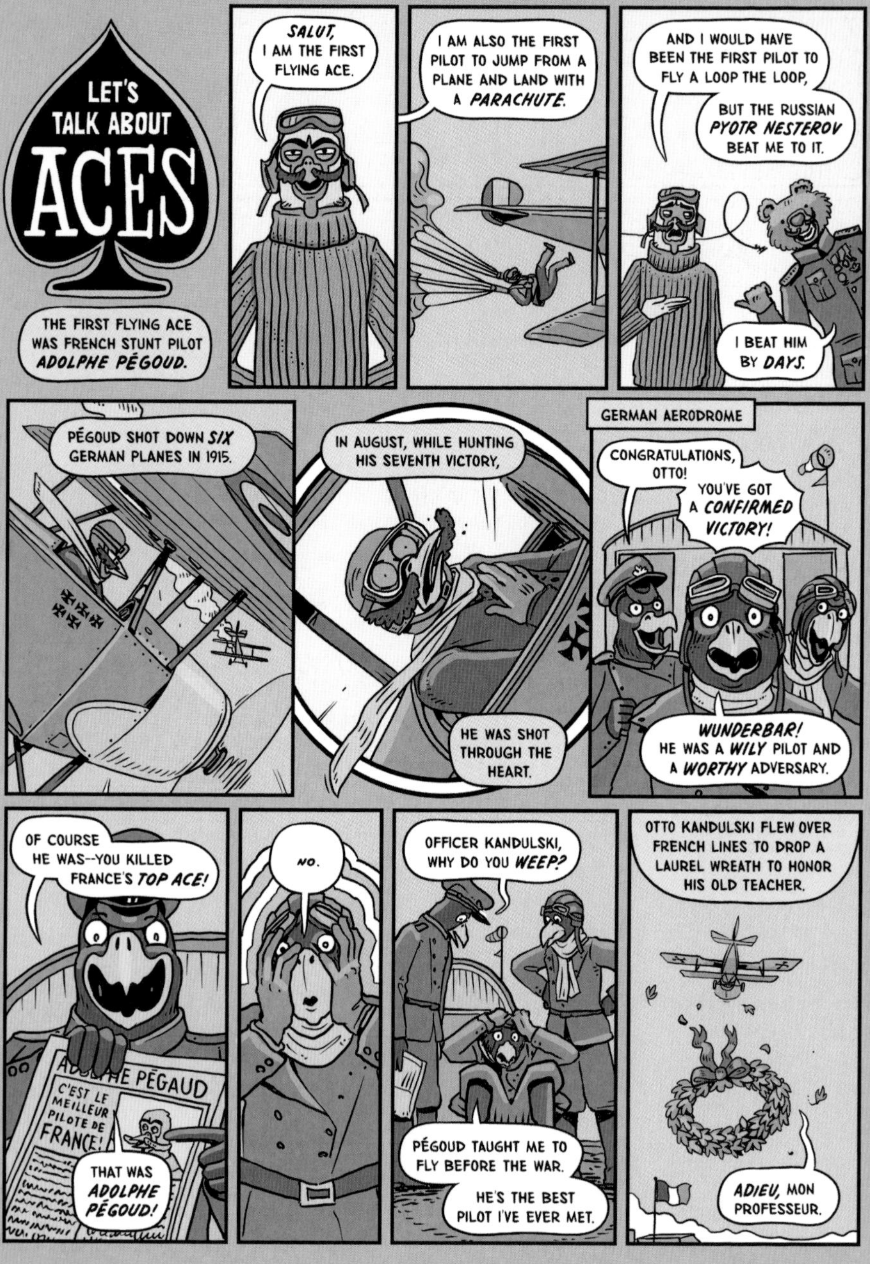
LET'S TALK ABOUT ACES
THE FIRST FLYING ACE WAS FRENCH STUNT PILOT ADOLPHE PÉGOUD.
SALUT, I AM THE FIRST FLYING ACE.
I AM ALSO THE FIRST PILOT TO JUMP FROM A PLANE AND LAND WITH A PARACHUTE.
AND I WOULD HAVE BEEN THE FIRST PILOT TO FLY A LOOP THE LOOP,
BUT THE RUSSIAN PYOTR NESTEROV BEAT ME TO IT.
I BEAT HIM BY DAYS.
PÉGOUD SHOT DOWN SIX GERMAN PLANES IN 1915.
IN AUGUST, WHILE HUNTING HIS SEVENTH VICTORY,
HE WAS SHOT THROUGH THE HEART.
GERMAN AERODROME
CONGRATULATIONS, OTTO!
YOU'VE GOT A CONFIRMED VICTORY!
WUNDERBAR! HE WAS A WILY PILOT AND A WORTHY ADVERSARY.
OF COURSE HE WAS--YOU KILLED FRANCE'S TOP ACE!
ADOLPHE PÉGAUD
C'EST LE MEILLEUR PILOTE DE FRANCE!
THAT WAS ADOLPHE PÉGOUD!
NO.
OFFICER KANDULSKI, WHY DO YOU WEEP?
PÉGOUD TAUGHT ME TO FLY BEFORE THE WAR.
HE'S THE BEST PILOT I'VE EVER MET.
OTTO KANDULSKI FLEW OVER FRENCH LINES TO DROP A LAUREL WREATH TO HONOR HIS OLD TEACHER.
ADIEU, MON PROFESSEUR.

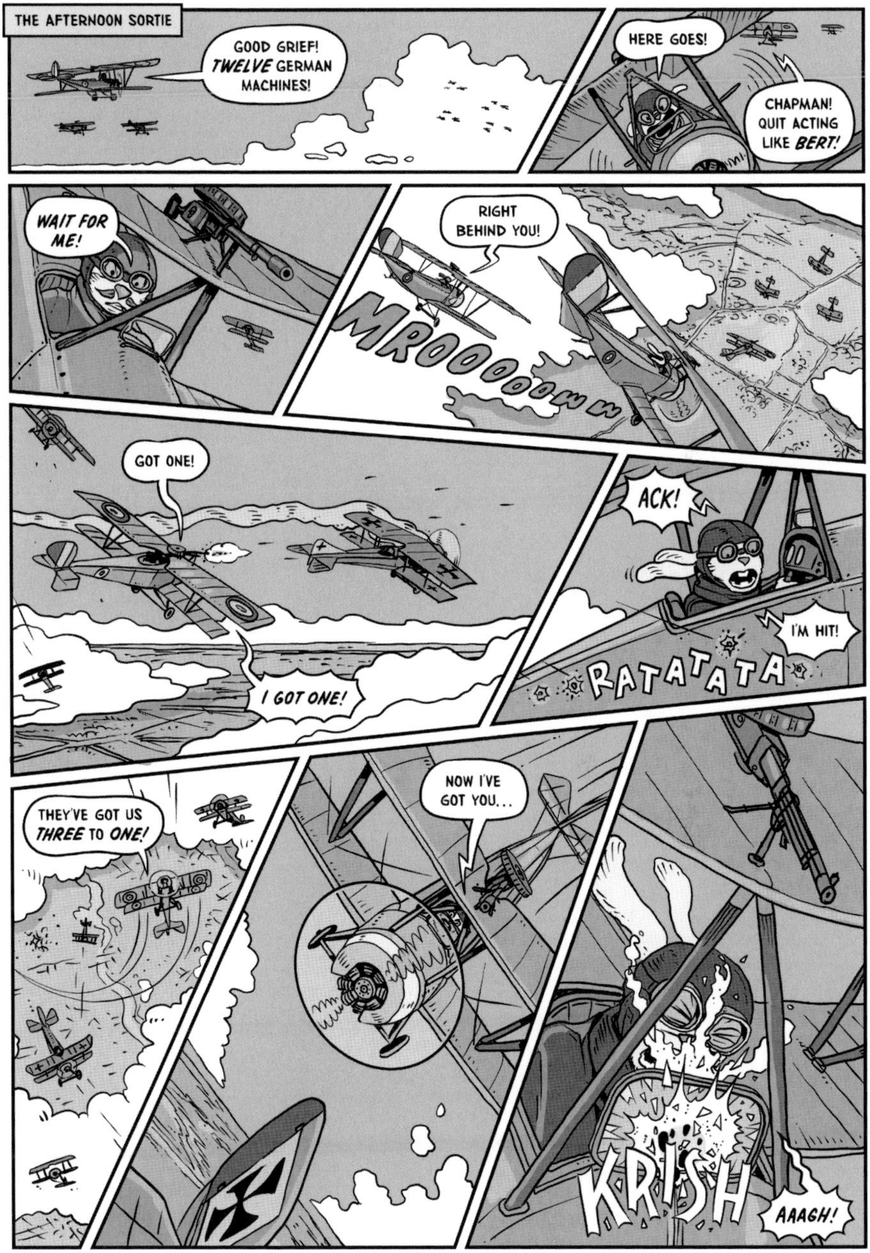
THE AFTERNOON SORTIE
GOOD GRIEF! TWELVE GERMAN MACHINES!
HERE GOES!
CHAPMAN! QUIT ACTING LIKE BERT!
WAIT FOR ME!
RIGHT BEHIND YOU!
MROOOOoooWW
GOT ONE!
I GOT ONE!
ACK!
I'M HIT!
RATATATA
THEY'VE GOT US THREE TO ONE!
NOW I'VE GOT YOU...
KRISH
AAAGH!

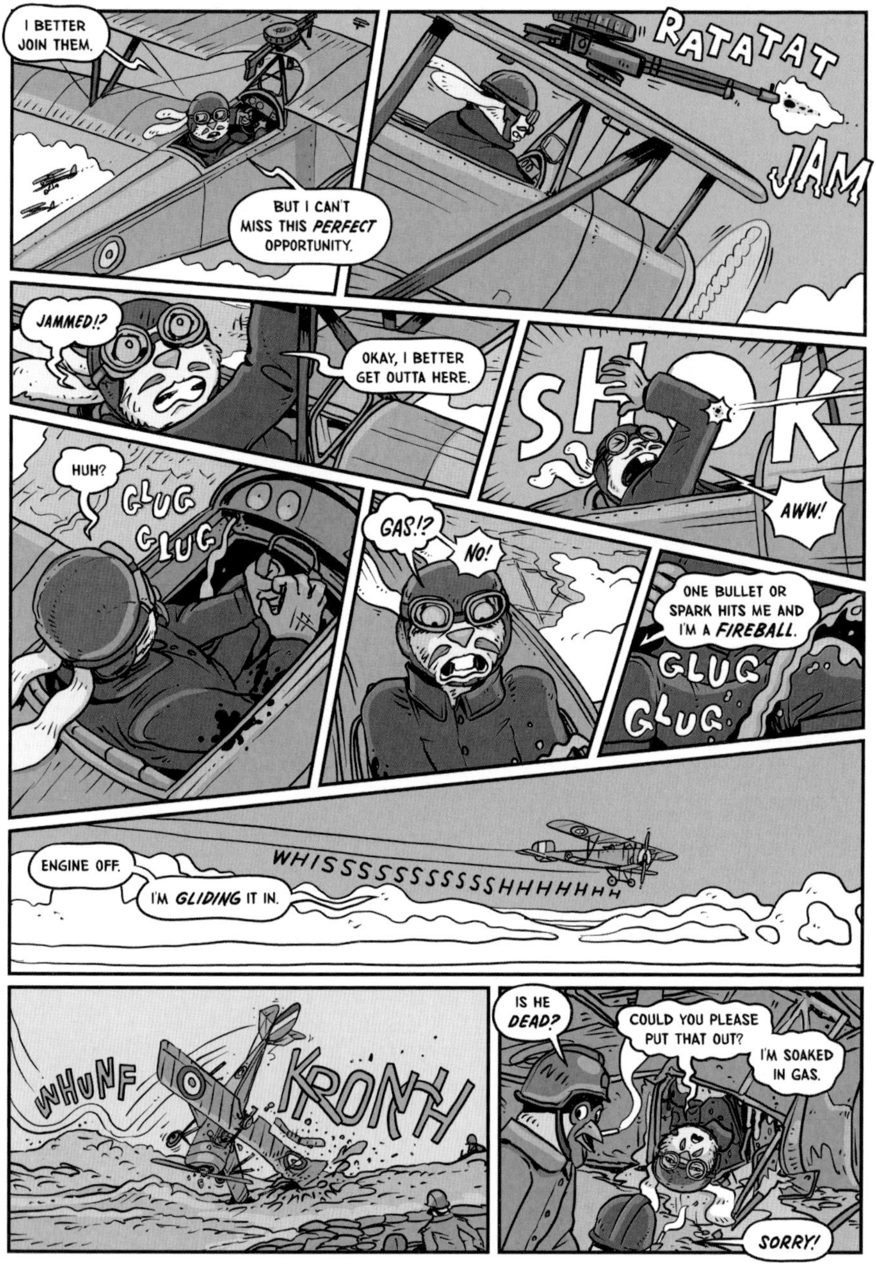
I BETTER JOIN THEM.
BUT I CAN'T MISS THIS *PERFECT* OPPORTUNITY.
RATATAT
JAM
JAMMED!?
OKAY, I BETTER GET OUTTA HERE.
SHOK
AWW!
HUH?
GLUG GLUG
GAS!?
NO!
ONE BULLET OR SPARK HITS ME AND I'M A *FIREBALL*.
GLUG GLUG
ENGINE OFF.
I'M *GLIDING* IT IN.
WHISSSSSSSSSSSSHHHHHHH
WHUNF
KRONCH
IS HE *DEAD?*
COULD YOU PLEASE PUT THAT OUT?
I'M SOAKED IN GAS.
SORRY!

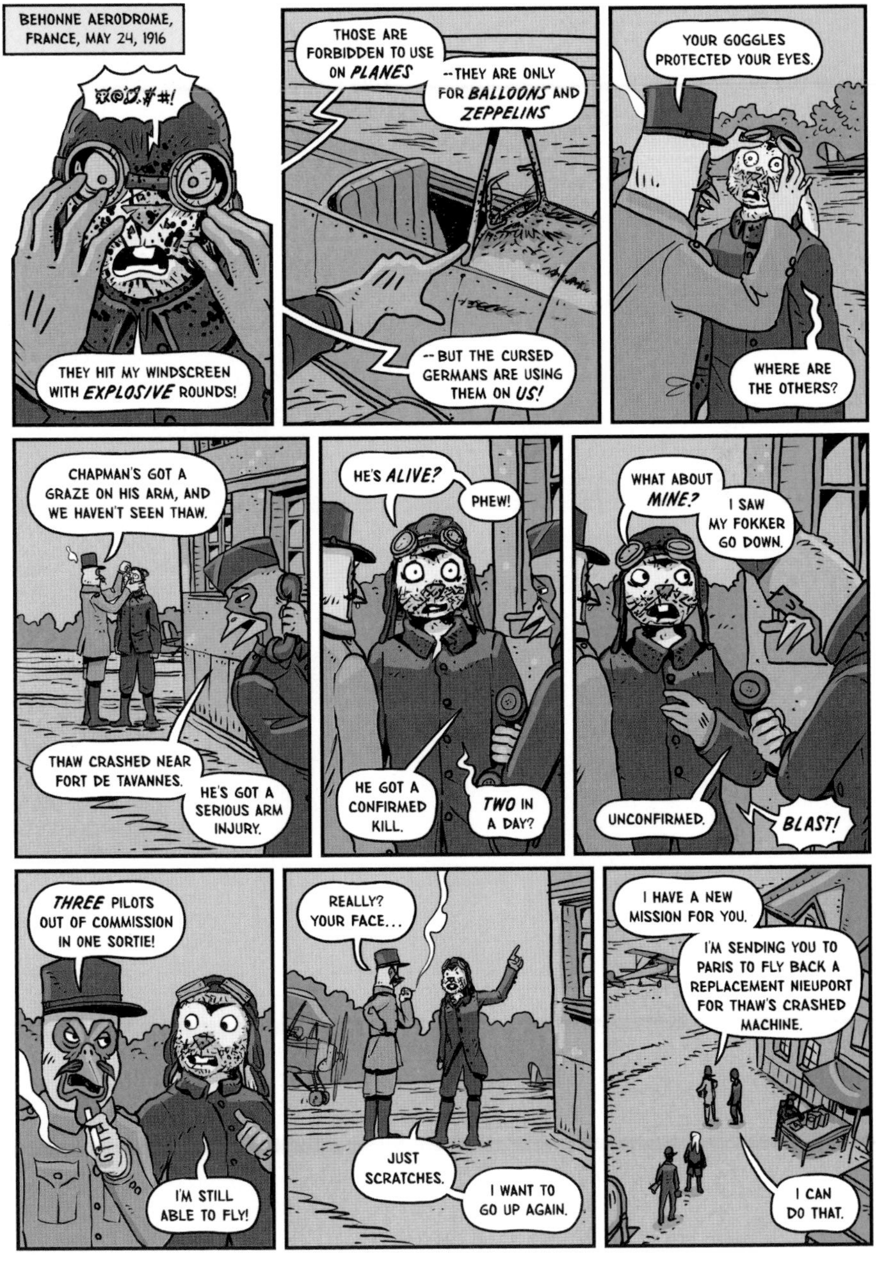
BEHONNE AERODROME, FRANCE, MAY 24, 1916
THEY HIT MY WINDSCREEN WITH EXPLOSIVE ROUNDS!
THOSE ARE FORBIDDEN TO USE ON PLANES
--THEY ARE ONLY FOR BALLOONS AND ZEPPELINS
--BUT THE CURSED GERMANS ARE USING THEM ON US!
YOUR GOGGLES PROTECTED YOUR EYES.
WHERE ARE THE OTHERS?
CHAPMAN'S GOT A GRAZE ON HIS ARM, AND WE HAVEN'T SEEN THAW.
THAW CRASHED NEAR FORT DE TAVANNES.
HE'S GOT A SERIOUS ARM INJURY.
HE'S ALIVE?
PHEW!
HE GOT A CONFIRMED KILL.
TWO IN A DAY?
WHAT ABOUT MINE?
I SAW MY FOKKER GO DOWN.
UNCONFIRMED.
BLAST!
THREE PILOTS OUT OF COMMISSION IN ONE SORTIE!
I'M STILL ABLE TO FLY!
REALLY? YOUR FACE...
JUST SCRATCHES.
I WANT TO GO UP AGAIN.
I HAVE A NEW MISSION FOR YOU.
I'M SENDING YOU TO PARIS TO FLY BACK A REPLACEMENT NIEUPORT FOR THAW'S CRASHED MACHINE.
I CAN DO THAT.

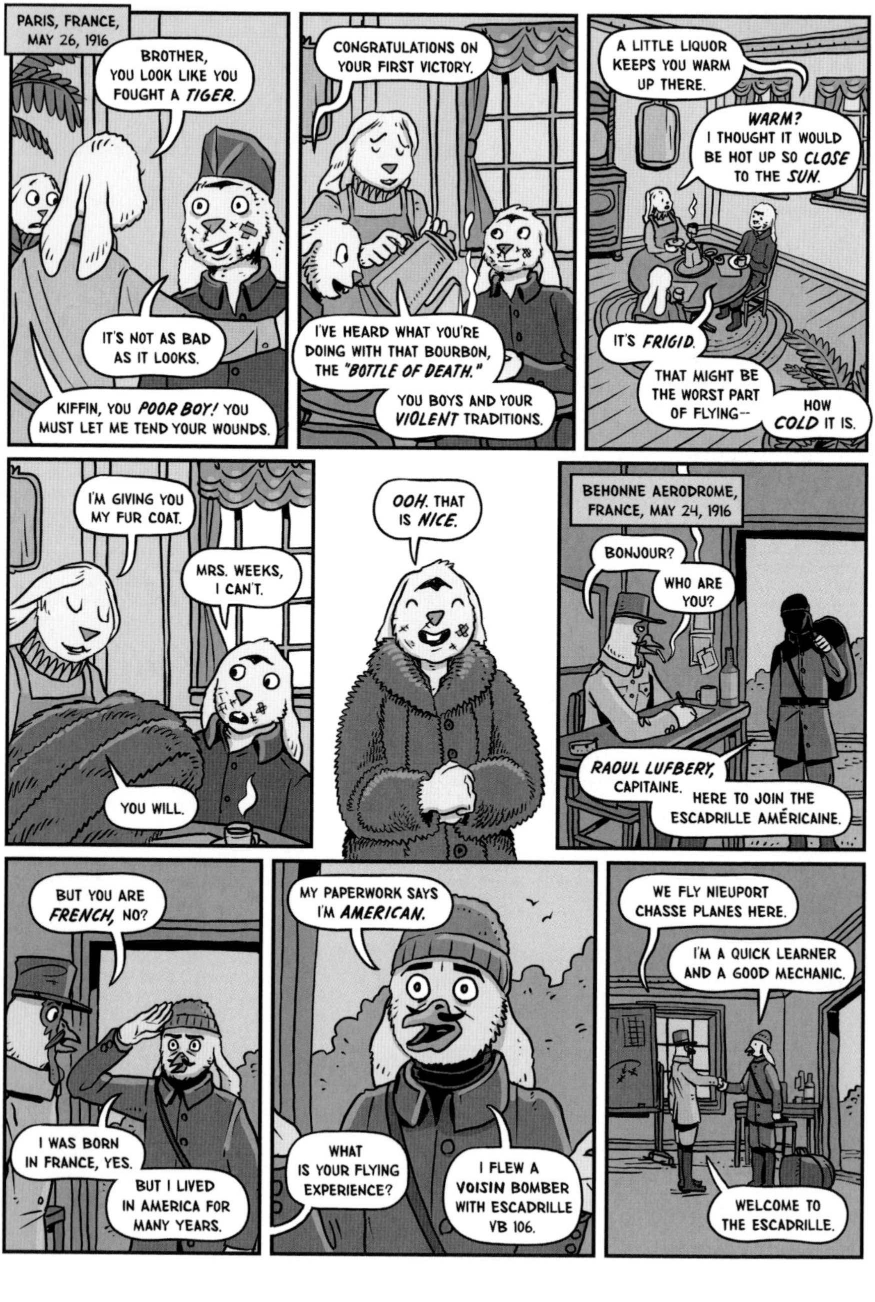
PARIS, FRANCE, MAY 26, 1916
BROTHER, YOU LOOK LIKE YOU FOUGHT A TIGER.
IT'S NOT AS BAD AS IT LOOKS.
KIFFIN, YOU POOR BOY! YOU MUST LET ME TEND YOUR WOUNDS.
CONGRATULATIONS ON YOUR FIRST VICTORY.
I'VE HEARD WHAT YOU'RE DOING WITH THAT BOURBON, THE "BOTTLE OF DEATH."
YOU BOYS AND YOUR VIOLENT TRADITIONS.
A LITTLE LIQUOR KEEPS YOU WARM UP THERE.
WARM? I THOUGHT IT WOULD BE HOT UP SO CLOSE TO THE SUN.
IT'S FRIGID.
THAT MIGHT BE THE WORST PART OF FLYING--
HOW COLD IT IS.
I'M GIVING YOU MY FUR COAT.
MRS. WEEKS, I CAN'T.
YOU WILL.
OOH. THAT IS NICE.
BEHONNE AERODROME, FRANCE, MAY 24, 1916
BONJOUR?
WHO ARE YOU?
RAOUL LUFBERY, CAPITAINE.
HERE TO JOIN THE ESCADRILLE AMÉRICAINE.
BUT YOU ARE FRENCH, NO?
I WAS BORN IN FRANCE, YES.
BUT I LIVED IN AMERICA FOR MANY YEARS.
MY PAPERWORK SAYS I'M AMERICAN.
WHAT IS YOUR FLYING EXPERIENCE?
I FLEW A VOISIN BOMBER WITH ESCADRILLE VB 106.
WE FLY NIEUPORT CHASSE PLANES HERE.
I'M A QUICK LEARNER AND A GOOD MECHANIC.
WELCOME TO THE ESCADRILLE.

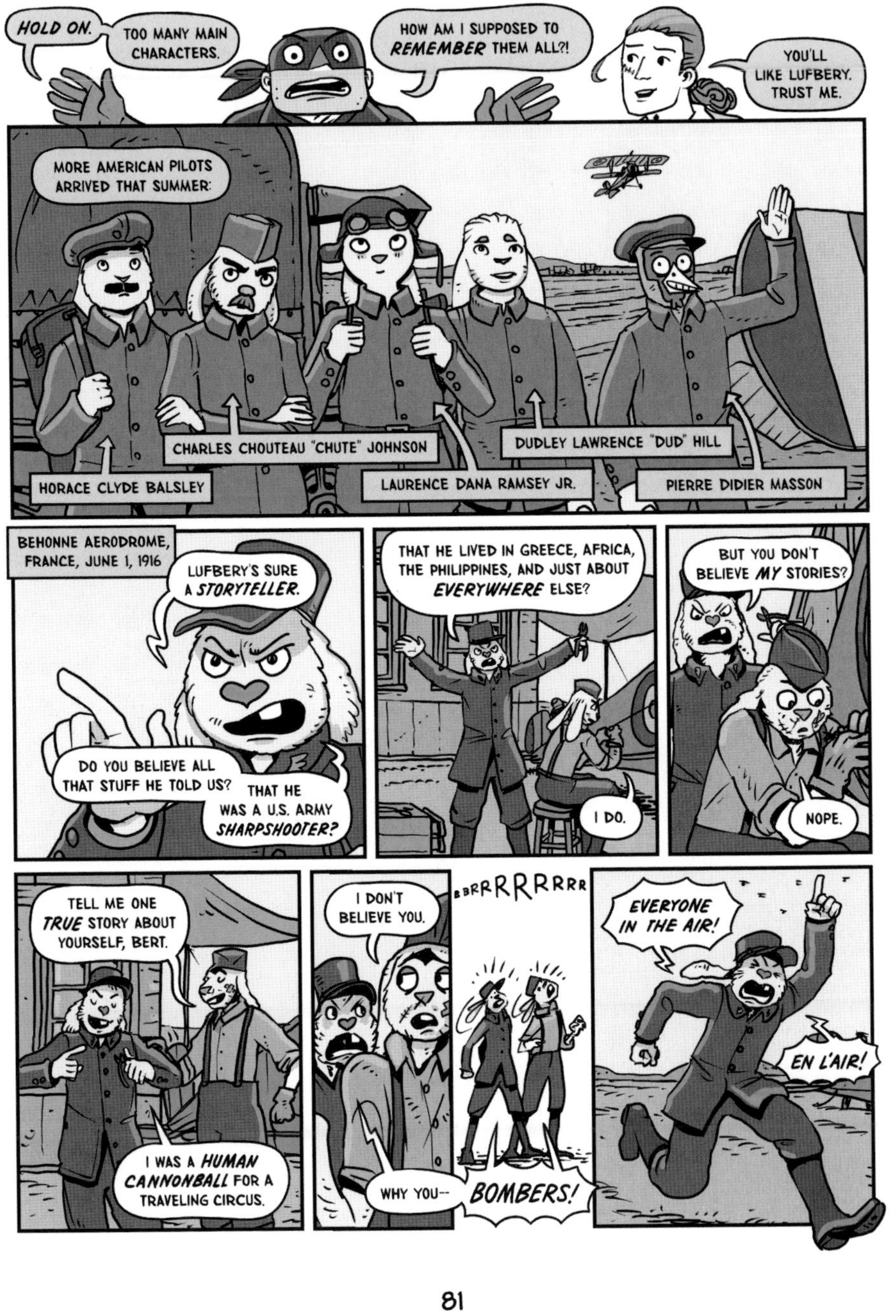
HOLD ON.
TOO MANY MAIN CHARACTERS.
HOW AM I SUPPOSED TO REMEMBER THEM ALL?!
YOU'LL LIKE LUFBERY. TRUST ME.
MORE AMERICAN PILOTS ARRIVED THAT SUMMER:
HORACE CLYDE BALSLEY
CHARLES CHOUTEAU "CHUTE" JOHNSON
LAURENCE DANA RAMSEY JR.
DUDLEY LAWRENCE "DUD" HILL
PIERRE DIDIER MASSON
BEHONNE AERODROME, FRANCE, JUNE 1, 1916
LUFBERY'S SURE A STORYTELLER.
DO YOU BELIEVE ALL THAT STUFF HE TOLD US?
THAT HE WAS A U.S. ARMY SHARPSHOOTER?
THAT HE LIVED IN GREECE, AFRICA, THE PHILIPPINES, AND JUST ABOUT EVERYWHERE ELSE?
I DO.
BUT YOU DON'T BELIEVE MY STORIES?
NOPE.
TELL ME ONE TRUE STORY ABOUT YOURSELF, BERT.
I WAS A HUMAN CANNONBALL FOR A TRAVELING CIRCUS.
I DON'T BELIEVE YOU.
WHY YOU--
BBRRRRRRRR
BOMBERS!
EVERYONE IN THE AIR!
EN L'AIR!

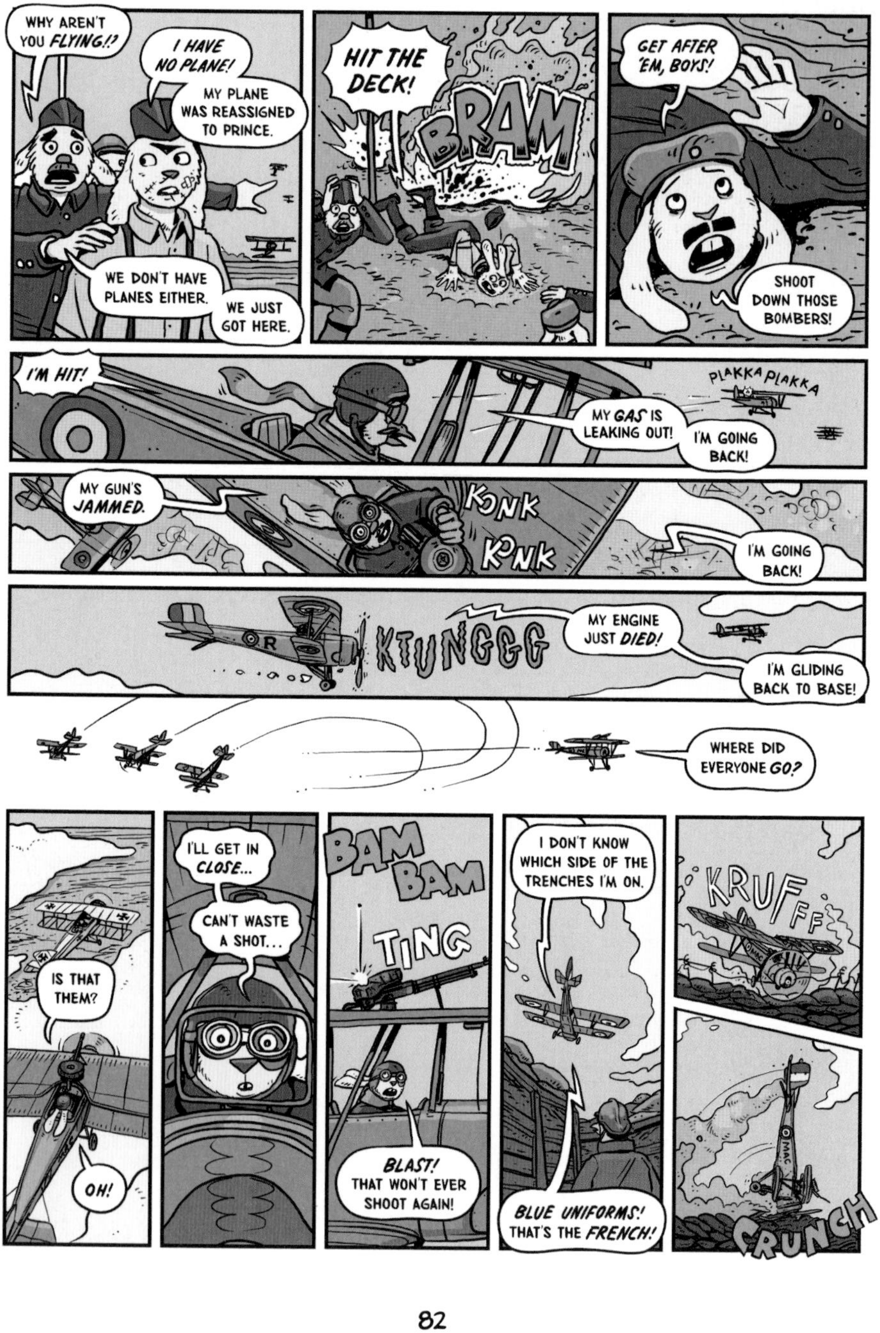
WHY AREN'T YOU FLYING!?
I HAVE NO PLANE!
MY PLANE WAS REASSIGNED TO PRINCE.
WE DON'T HAVE PLANES EITHER.
WE JUST GOT HERE.
HIT THE DECK!
BRAM
GET AFTER 'EM, BOYS!
SHOOT DOWN THOSE BOMBERS!
I'M HIT!
PLAKKA PLAKKA
MY GAS IS LEAKING OUT!
I'M GOING BACK!
MY GUN'S JAMMED.
KONK
KONK
I'M GOING BACK!
KTUNGGG
MY ENGINE JUST DIED!
I'M GLIDING BACK TO BASE!
WHERE DID EVERYONE GO?
IS THAT THEM?
OH!
I'LL GET IN CLOSE...
CAN'T WASTE A SHOT...
BAM
BAM
TING
BLAST! THAT WON'T EVER SHOOT AGAIN!
I DON'T KNOW WHICH SIDE OF THE TRENCHES I'M ON.
BLUE UNIFORMS! THAT'S THE FRENCH!
KRUFFF
CRUNCH

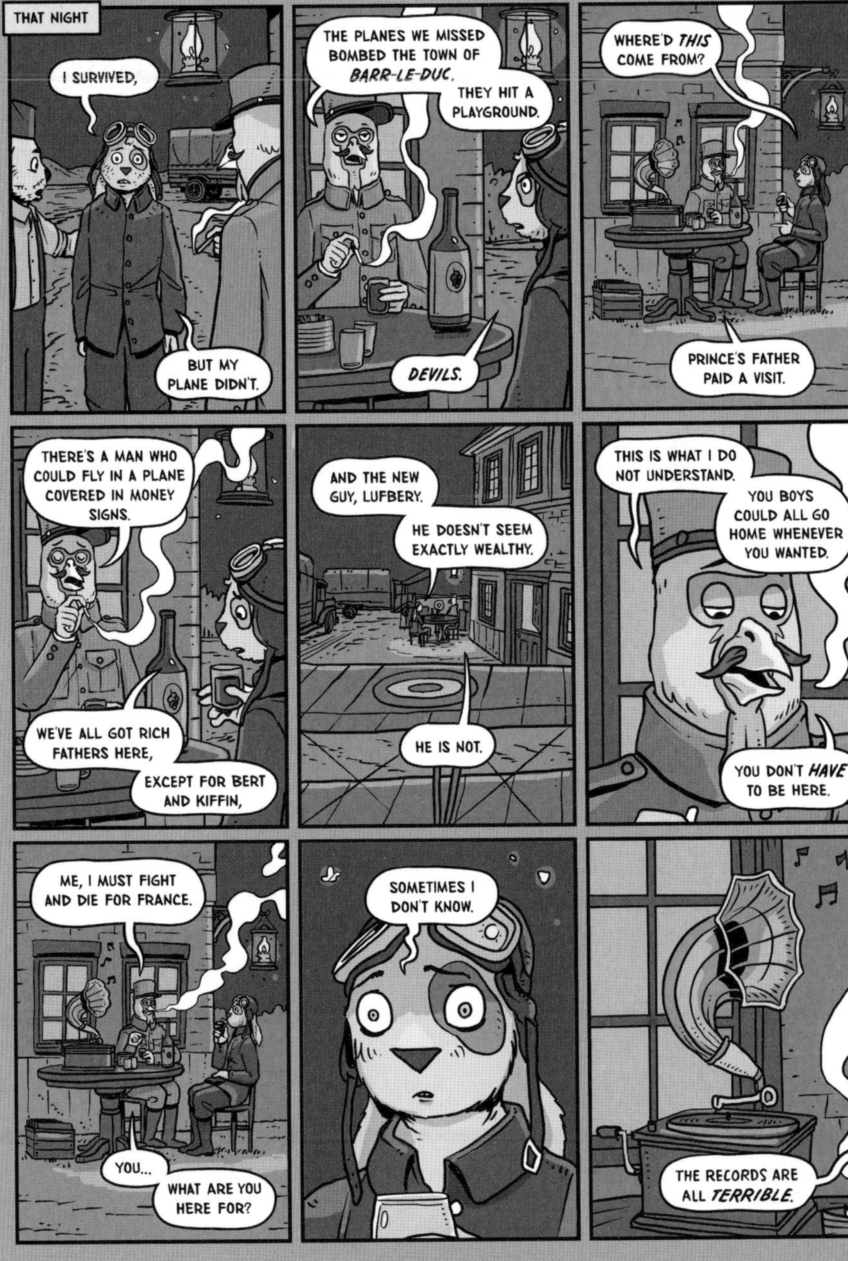
THAT NIGHT
I SURVIVED,
BUT MY PLANE DIDN'T.
THE PLANES WE MISSED BOMBED THE TOWN OF *BARR-LE-DUC*.
THEY HIT A PLAYGROUND.
DEVILS.
WHERE'D *THIS* COME FROM?
PRINCE'S FATHER PAID A VISIT.
THERE'S A MAN WHO COULD FLY IN A PLANE COVERED IN MONEY SIGNS.
WE'VE ALL GOT RICH FATHERS HERE,
EXCEPT FOR BERT AND KIFFIN,
AND THE NEW GUY, LUFBERY.
HE DOESN'T SEEM EXACTLY WEALTHY.
HE IS NOT.
THIS IS WHAT I DO NOT UNDERSTAND.
YOU BOYS COULD ALL GO HOME WHENEVER YOU WANTED.
YOU DON'T *HAVE* TO BE HERE.
ME, I MUST FIGHT AND DIE FOR FRANCE.
YOU...
WHAT ARE YOU HERE FOR?
SOMETIMES I DON'T KNOW.
THE RECORDS ARE ALL *TERRIBLE.*

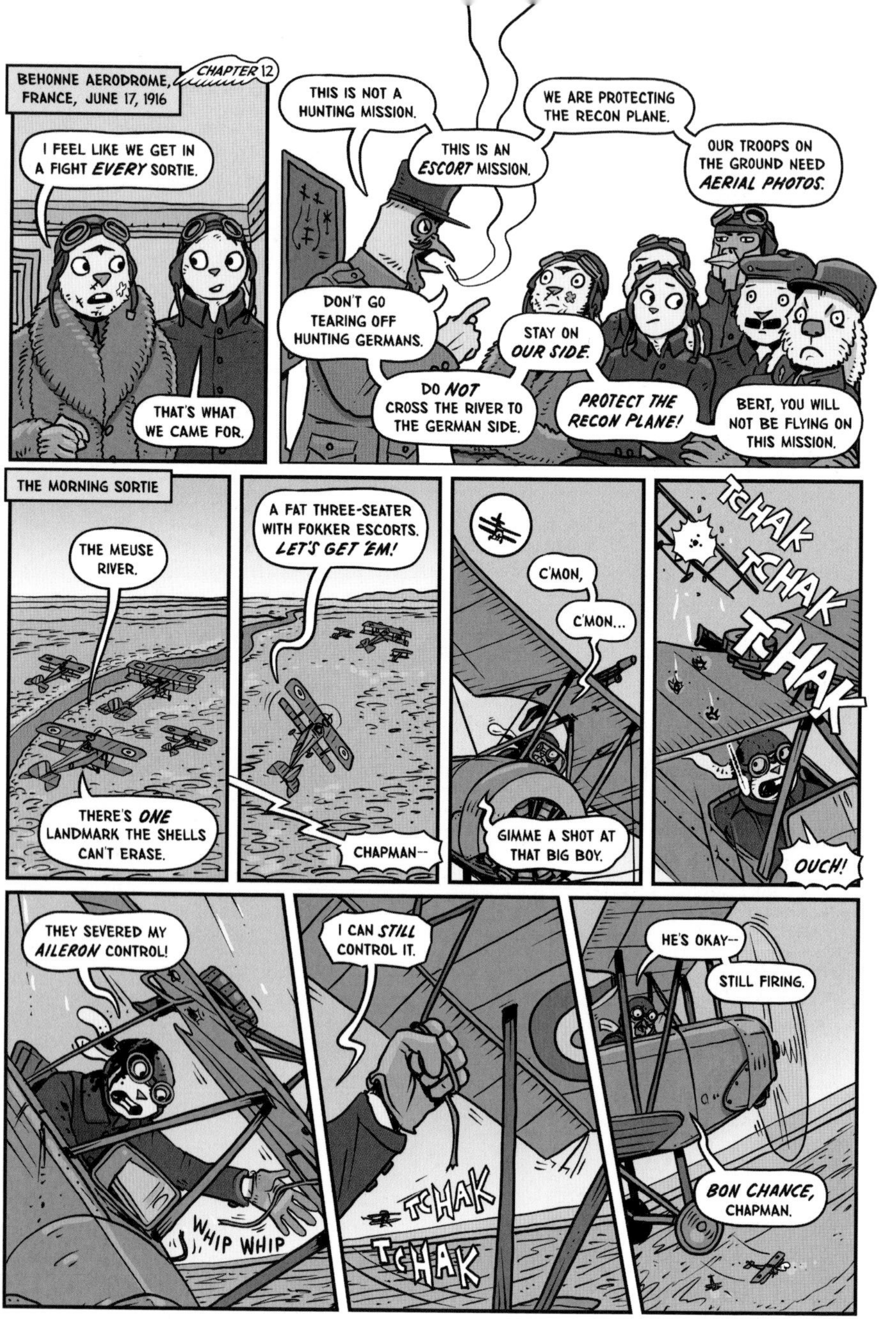

CHAPTER 12
BEHONNE AERODROME, FRANCE, JUNE 17, 1916
I FEEL LIKE WE GET IN A FIGHT *EVERY* SORTIE.
THAT'S WHAT WE CAME FOR.
THIS IS NOT A HUNTING MISSION.
THIS IS AN *ESCORT* MISSION.
WE ARE PROTECTING THE RECON PLANE.
OUR TROOPS ON THE GROUND NEED *AERIAL PHOTOS.*
DON'T GO TEARING OFF HUNTING GERMANS.
STAY ON *OUR SIDE.*
DO *NOT* CROSS THE RIVER TO THE GERMAN SIDE.
PROTECT THE RECON PLANE!
BERT, YOU WILL NOT BE FLYING ON THIS MISSION.
THE MORNING SORTIE
THE MEUSE RIVER.
THERE'S *ONE* LANDMARK THE SHELLS CAN'T ERASE.
A FAT THREE-SEATER WITH FOKKER ESCORTS. *LET'S GET 'EM!*
CHAPMAN--
C'MON,
C'MON...
GIMME A SHOT AT THAT BIG BOY.
TCHAK TCHAK TCHAK TCHAK
OUCH!
THEY SEVERED MY *AILERON* CONTROL!
WHIP WHIP
I CAN *STILL* CONTROL IT.
TCHAK
TCHAK
HE'S OKAY--
STILL FIRING.
BON CHANCE, CHAPMAN.

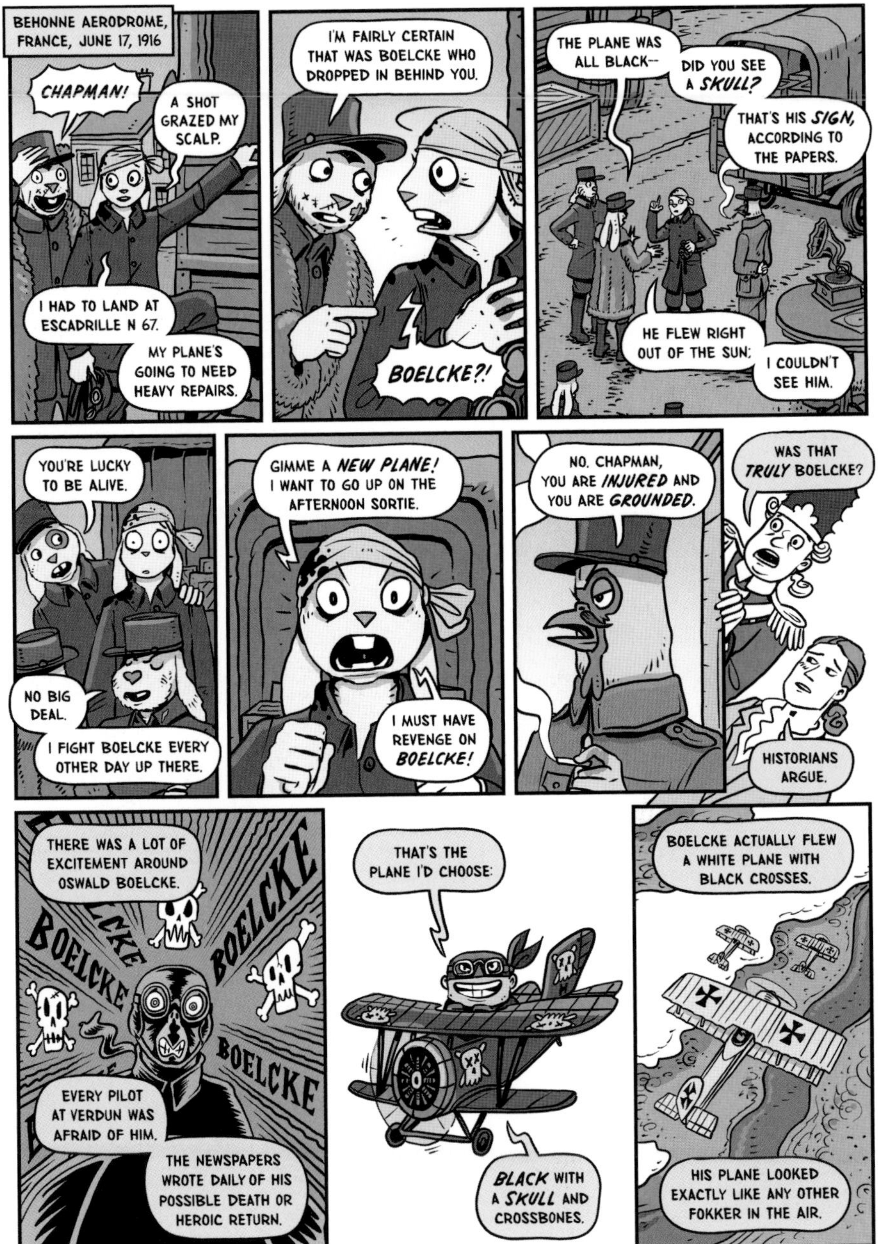
BEHONNE AERODROME, FRANCE, JUNE 17, 1916
CHAPMAN!
A SHOT GRAZED MY SCALP.
I HAD TO LAND AT ESCADRILLE N 67.
MY PLANE'S GOING TO NEED HEAVY REPAIRS.
I'M FAIRLY CERTAIN THAT WAS BOELCKE WHO DROPPED IN BEHIND YOU.
BOELCKE?!
THE PLANE WAS ALL BLACK--
DID YOU SEE A SKULL?
THAT'S HIS SIGN, ACCORDING TO THE PAPERS.
HE FLEW RIGHT OUT OF THE SUN;
I COULDN'T SEE HIM.
YOU'RE LUCKY TO BE ALIVE.
NO BIG DEAL.
I FIGHT BOELCKE EVERY OTHER DAY UP THERE.
GIMME A NEW PLANE! I WANT TO GO UP ON THE AFTERNOON SORTIE.
I MUST HAVE REVENGE ON BOELCKE!
NO. CHAPMAN, YOU ARE INJURED AND YOU ARE GROUNDED.
WAS THAT TRULY BOELCKE?
HISTORIANS ARGUE.
THERE WAS A LOT OF EXCITEMENT AROUND OSWALD BOELCKE.
BOELCKE
BOELCKE
BOELCKE
BOELCKE
EVERY PILOT AT VERDUN WAS AFRAID OF HIM.
THE NEWSPAPERS WROTE DAILY OF HIS POSSIBLE DEATH OR HEROIC RETURN.
THAT'S THE PLANE I'D CHOOSE:
BLACK WITH A SKULL AND CROSSBONES.
BOELCKE ACTUALLY FLEW A WHITE PLANE WITH BLACK CROSSES.
HIS PLANE LOOKED EXACTLY LIKE ANY OTHER FOKKER IN THE AIR.

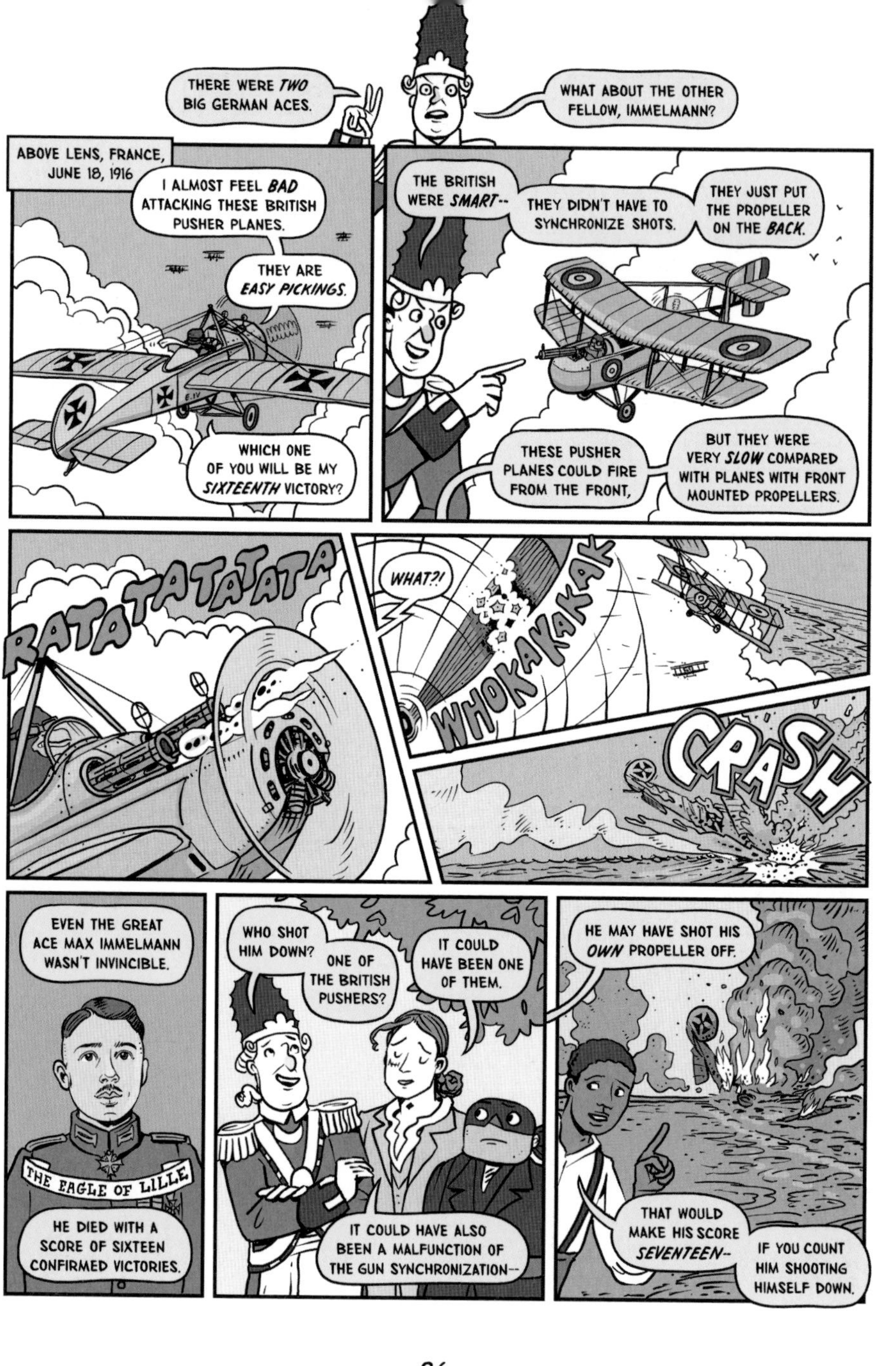

THERE WERE *TWO* BIG GERMAN ACES.
WHAT ABOUT THE OTHER FELLOW, IMMELMANN?
ABOVE LENS, FRANCE, JUNE 18, 1916
I ALMOST FEEL *BAD* ATTACKING THESE BRITISH PUSHER PLANES.
THEY ARE *EASY PICKINGS*.
WHICH ONE OF YOU WILL BE MY *SIXTEENTH* VICTORY?
THE BRITISH WERE *SMART*--
THEY DIDN'T HAVE TO SYNCHRONIZE SHOTS.
THEY JUST PUT THE PROPELLER ON THE *BACK*.
THESE PUSHER PLANES COULD FIRE FROM THE FRONT,
BUT THEY WERE VERY *SLOW* COMPARED WITH PLANES WITH FRONT MOUNTED PROPELLERS.
RATATATATATA
WHAT?!
WHOKAKAKAK
CRASH
EVEN THE GREAT ACE MAX IMMELMANN WASN'T INVINCIBLE.
THE EAGLE OF LILLE
HE DIED WITH A SCORE OF SIXTEEN CONFIRMED VICTORIES.
WHO SHOT HIM DOWN?
ONE OF THE BRITISH PUSHERS?
IT COULD HAVE BEEN ONE OF THEM.
IT COULD HAVE ALSO BEEN A MALFUNCTION OF THE GUN SYNCHRONIZATION--
HE MAY HAVE SHOT HIS *OWN* PROPELLER OFF.
THAT WOULD MAKE HIS SCORE *SEVENTEEN*--
IF YOU COUNT HIM SHOOTING HIMSELF DOWN.

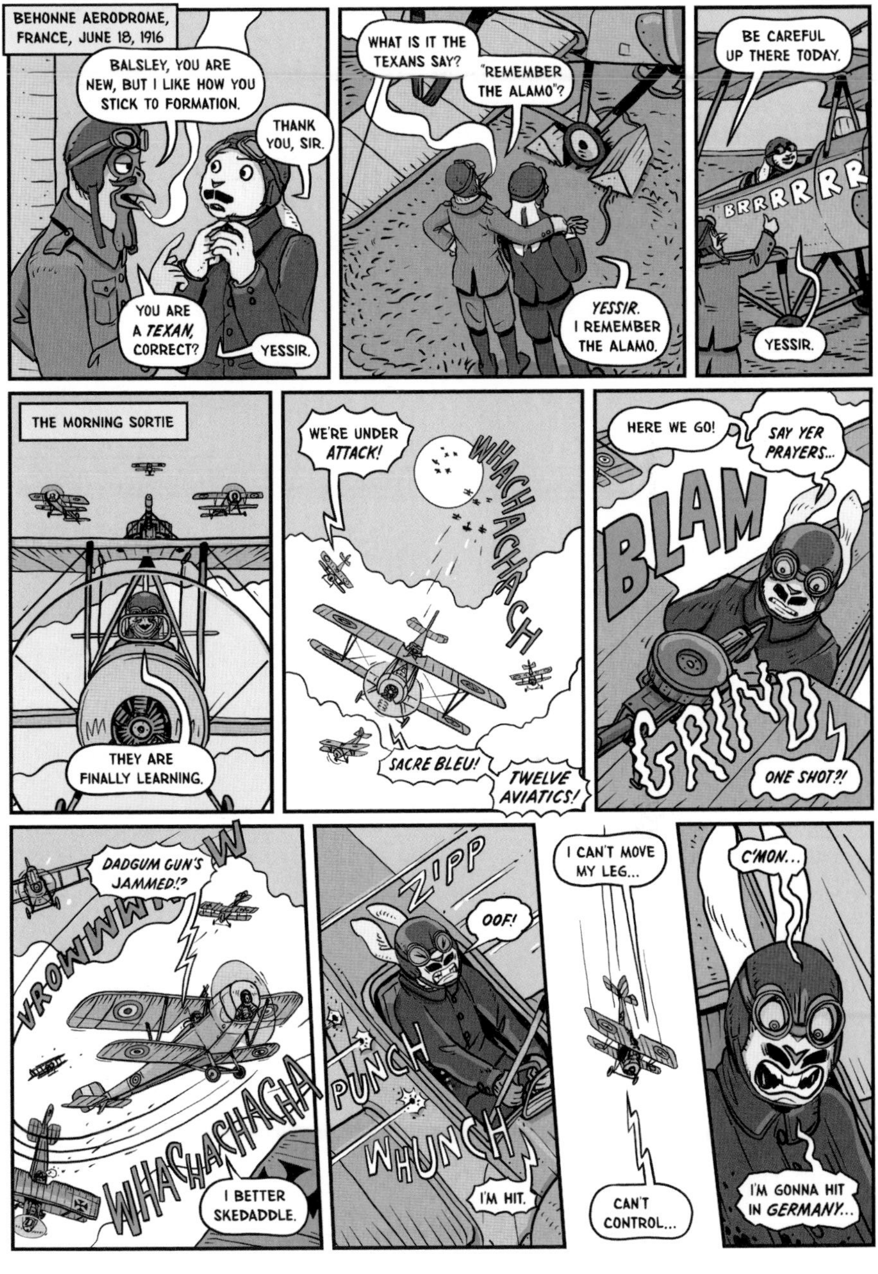
BEHONNE AERODROME, FRANCE, JUNE 18, 1916
BALSLEY, YOU ARE NEW, BUT I LIKE HOW YOU STICK TO FORMATION.
THANK YOU, SIR.
YOU ARE A *TEXAN,* CORRECT?
YESSIR.
WHAT IS IT THE TEXANS SAY?
"REMEMBER THE ALAMO"?
YESSIR. I REMEMBER THE ALAMO.
BE CAREFUL UP THERE TODAY.
BRRRRRR
YESSIR.
THE MORNING SORTIE
THEY ARE FINALLY LEARNING.
WE'RE UNDER *ATTACK!*
WHACHACHACH
SACRE BLEU!
TWELVE AVIATICS!
HERE WE GO!
SAY YER PRAYERS...
BLAM
GRIND
ONE SHOT?!
DADGUM GUN'S JAMMED!?
VROWWWWWW
WHACHACHACHA
I BETTER SKEDADDLE.
Z'IPP
OOF!
PUNCH
WHUNCH
I'M HIT.
I CAN'T MOVE MY LEG...
CAN'T CONTROL...
C'MON...
I'M GONNA HIT IN *GERMANY...*

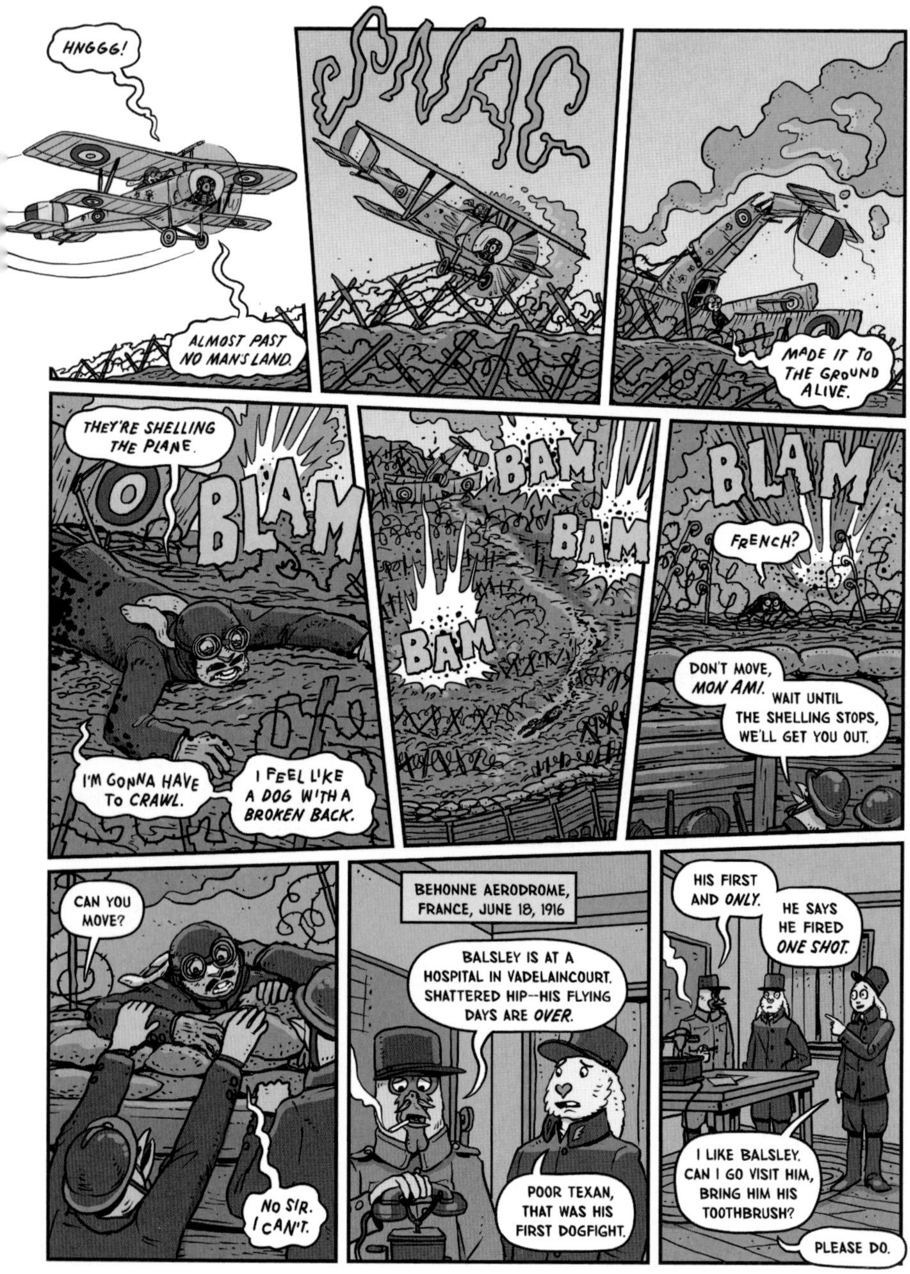

HNGGG!
ALMOST PAST NO MAN'S LAND.
SNAG
MADE IT TO THE GROUND ALIVE.
THEY'RE SHELLING THE PLANE.
BLAM
I'M GONNA HAVE TO CRAWL.
I FEEL LIKE A DOG WITH A BROKEN BACK.
BAM
BAM
BAM
BLAM
FRENCH?
DON'T MOVE, MON AMI. WAIT UNTIL THE SHELLING STOPS, WE'LL GET YOU OUT.
CAN YOU MOVE?
NO SIR. I CAN'T.
BEHONNE AERODROME, FRANCE, JUNE 18, 1916
BALSLEY IS AT A HOSPITAL IN VADELAINCOURT. SHATTERED HIP--HIS FLYING DAYS ARE OVER.
POOR TEXAN, THAT WAS HIS FIRST DOGFIGHT.
HIS FIRST AND ONLY.
HE SAYS HE FIRED ONE SHOT.
I LIKE BALSLEY. CAN I GO VISIT HIM, BRING HIM HIS TOOTHBRUSH?
PLEASE DO.

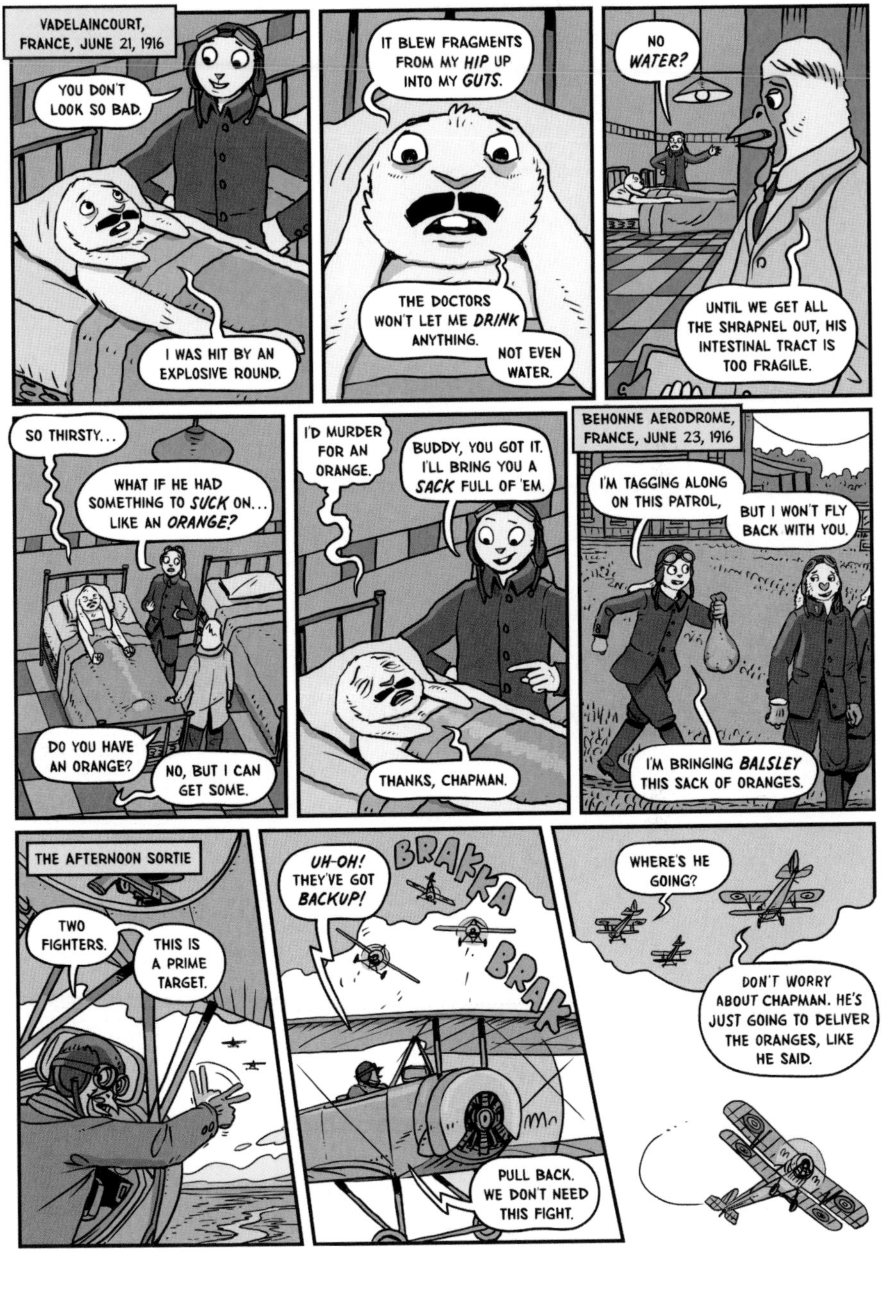
VADELAINCOURT, FRANCE, JUNE 21, 1916
YOU DON'T LOOK SO BAD.
I WAS HIT BY AN EXPLOSIVE ROUND.
IT BLEW FRAGMENTS FROM MY HIP UP INTO MY GUTS.
THE DOCTORS WON'T LET ME DRINK ANYTHING.
NOT EVEN WATER.
NO WATER?
UNTIL WE GET ALL THE SHRAPNEL OUT, HIS INTESTINAL TRACT IS TOO FRAGILE.
SO THIRSTY...
WHAT IF HE HAD SOMETHING TO SUCK ON... LIKE AN ORANGE?
DO YOU HAVE AN ORANGE?
NO, BUT I CAN GET SOME.
I'D MURDER FOR AN ORANGE.
BUDDY, YOU GOT IT. I'LL BRING YOU A SACK FULL OF 'EM.
THANKS, CHAPMAN.
BEHONNE AERODROME, FRANCE, JUNE 23, 1916
I'M TAGGING ALONG ON THIS PATROL,
BUT I WON'T FLY BACK WITH YOU.
I'M BRINGING BALSLEY THIS SACK OF ORANGES.
THE AFTERNOON SORTIE
TWO FIGHTERS.
THIS IS A PRIME TARGET.
UH-OH! THEY'VE GOT BACKUP!
BRAKKA BRAK
PULL BACK. WE DON'T NEED THIS FIGHT.
WHERE'S HE GOING?
DON'T WORRY ABOUT CHAPMAN. HE'S JUST GOING TO DELIVER THE ORANGES, LIKE HE SAID.

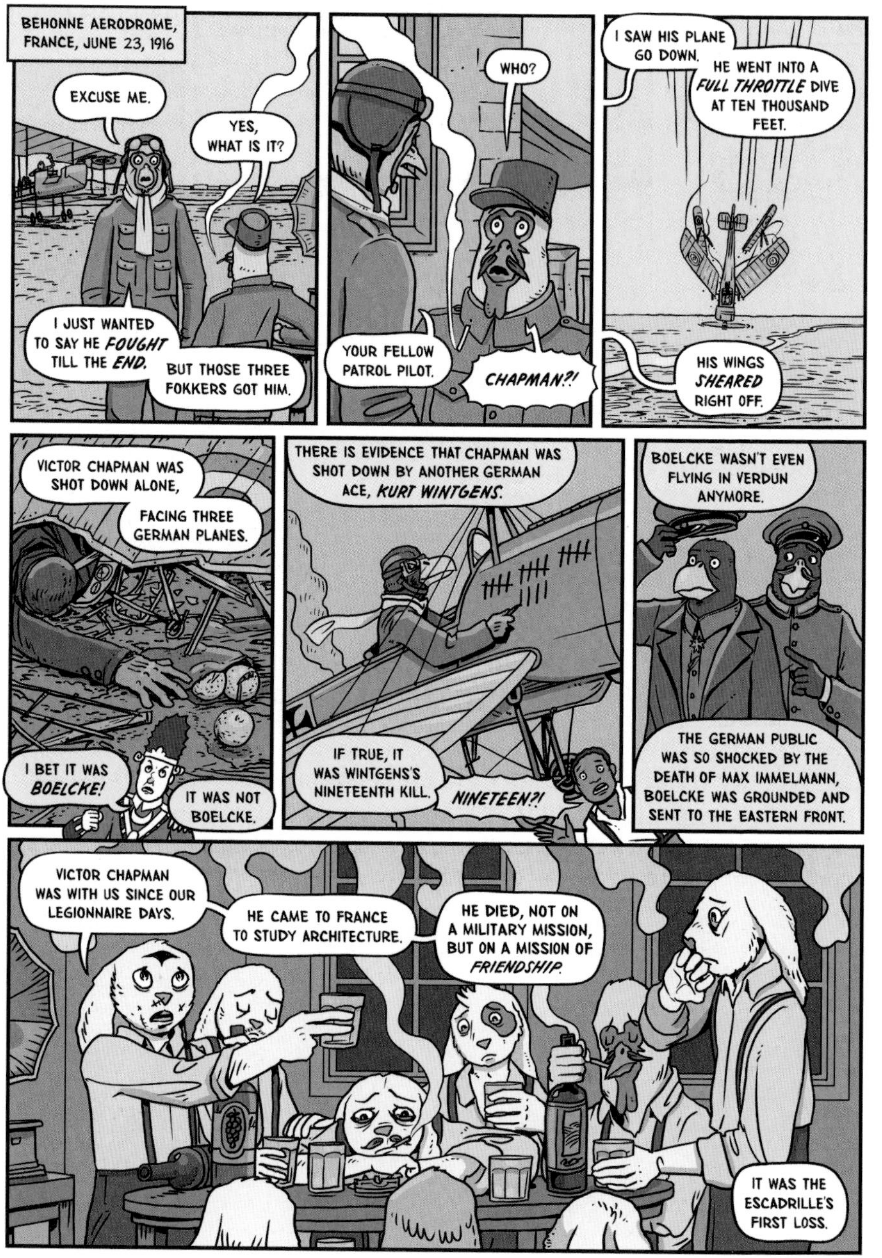

BEHONNE AERODROME, FRANCE, JUNE 23, 1916
EXCUSE ME.
YES, WHAT IS IT?
I JUST WANTED TO SAY HE FOUGHT TILL THE END.
BUT THOSE THREE FOKKERS GOT HIM.
WHO?
YOUR FELLOW PATROL PILOT.
CHAPMAN?!
I SAW HIS PLANE GO DOWN.
HE WENT INTO A FULL THROTTLE DIVE AT TEN THOUSAND FEET.
HIS WINGS SHEARED RIGHT OFF.
VICTOR CHAPMAN WAS SHOT DOWN ALONE,
FACING THREE GERMAN PLANES.
I BET IT WAS BOELCKE!
IT WAS NOT BOELCKE.
THERE IS EVIDENCE THAT CHAPMAN WAS SHOT DOWN BY ANOTHER GERMAN ACE, KURT WINTGENS.
IF TRUE, IT WAS WINTGENS'S NINETEENTH KILL.
NINETEEN?!
BOELCKE WASN'T EVEN FLYING IN VERDUN ANYMORE.
THE GERMAN PUBLIC WAS SO SHOCKED BY THE DEATH OF MAX IMMELMANN, BOELCKE WAS GROUNDED AND SENT TO THE EASTERN FRONT.
VICTOR CHAPMAN WAS WITH US SINCE OUR LEGIONNAIRE DAYS.
HE CAME TO FRANCE TO STUDY ARCHITECTURE.
HE DIED, NOT ON A MILITARY MISSION, BUT ON A MISSION OF FRIENDSHIP.
IT WAS THE ESCADRILLE'S FIRST LOSS.

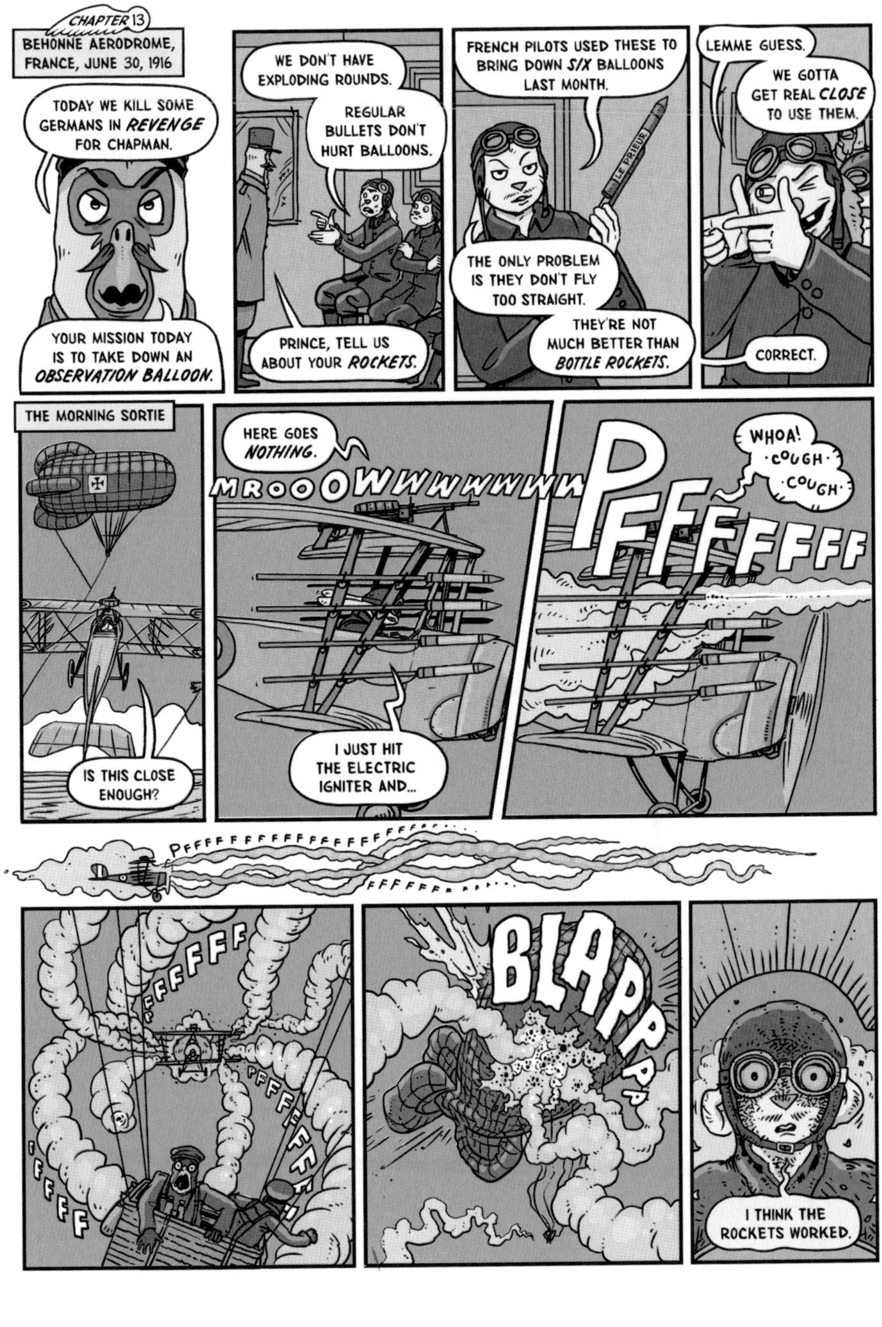
CHAPTER 13
BEHONNE AERODROME, FRANCE, JUNE 30, 1916
TODAY WE KILL SOME GERMANS IN REVENGE FOR CHAPMAN.
YOUR MISSION TODAY IS TO TAKE DOWN AN OBSERVATION BALLOON.
WE DON'T HAVE EXPLODING ROUNDS.
REGULAR BULLETS DON'T HURT BALLOONS.
PRINCE, TELL US ABOUT YOUR ROCKETS.
FRENCH PILOTS USED THESE TO BRING DOWN SIX BALLOONS LAST MONTH.
LE PRIEUR
THE ONLY PROBLEM IS THEY DON'T FLY TOO STRAIGHT.
THEY'RE NOT MUCH BETTER THAN BOTTLE ROCKETS.
LEMME GUESS.
WE GOTTA GET REAL CLOSE TO USE THEM.
CORRECT.
THE MORNING SORTIE
IS THIS CLOSE ENOUGH?
HERE GOES NOTHING.
MROOOOWWWWWWWW
I JUST HIT THE ELECTRIC IGNITER AND...
PFFFFFFFF
WHOA! COUGH COUGH
PFFFFFFFFFFFFFFFFF...
FFFFFF...
FFFFFF
PFFFFFF
FFFF
BLAPPP
I THINK THE ROCKETS WORKED.

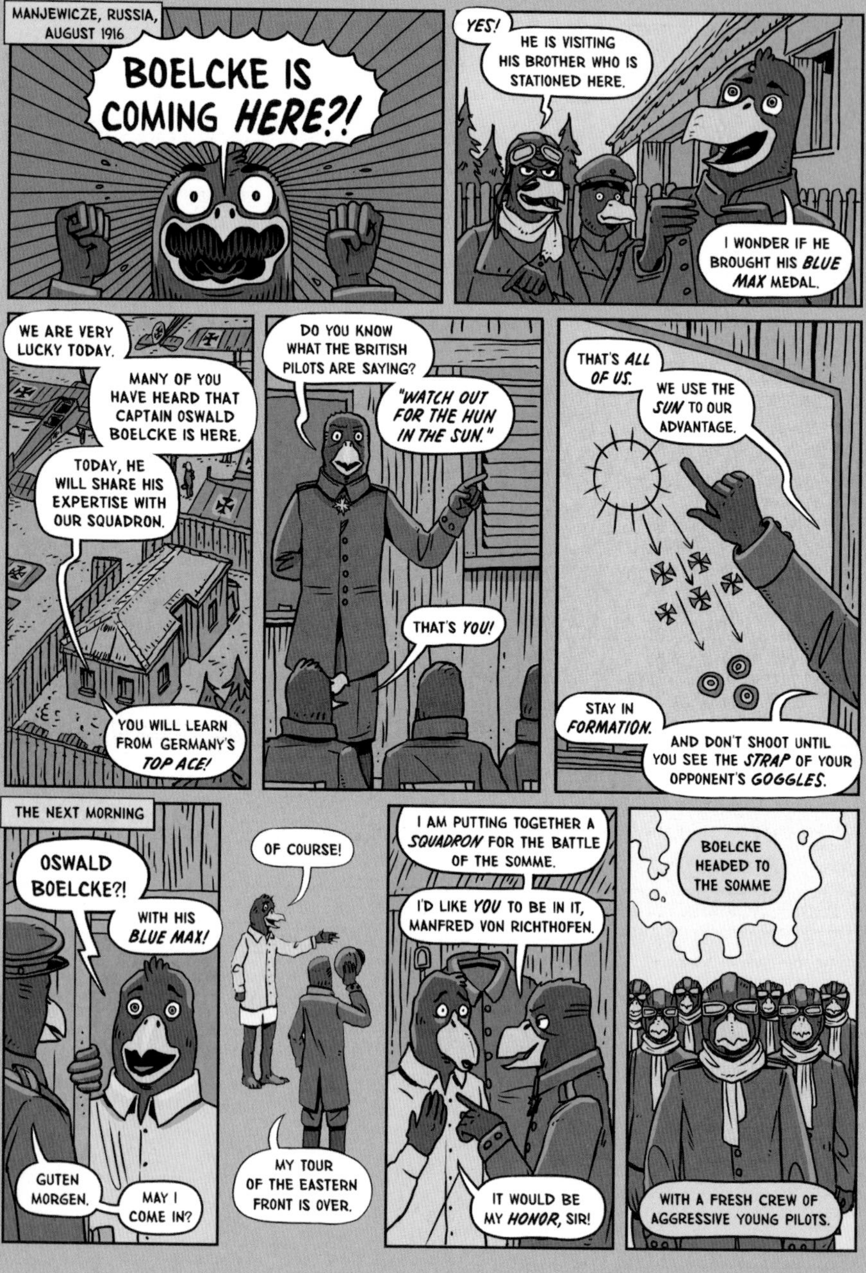
MANJEWICZE, RUSSIA, AUGUST 1916
BOELCKE IS COMING HERE?!
YES!
HE IS VISITING HIS BROTHER WHO IS STATIONED HERE.
I WONDER IF HE BROUGHT HIS BLUE MAX MEDAL.
WE ARE VERY LUCKY TODAY.
MANY OF YOU HAVE HEARD THAT CAPTAIN OSWALD BOELCKE IS HERE.
TODAY, HE WILL SHARE HIS EXPERTISE WITH OUR SQUADRON.
YOU WILL LEARN FROM GERMANY'S TOP ACE!
DO YOU KNOW WHAT THE BRITISH PILOTS ARE SAYING?
"WATCH OUT FOR THE HUN IN THE SUN."
THAT'S YOU!
THAT'S ALL OF US.
WE USE THE SUN TO OUR ADVANTAGE.
STAY IN FORMATION.
AND DON'T SHOOT UNTIL YOU SEE THE STRAP OF YOUR OPPONENT'S GOGGLES.
THE NEXT MORNING
OSWALD BOELCKE?!
WITH HIS BLUE MAX!
GUTEN MORGEN.
MAY I COME IN?
OF COURSE!
MY TOUR OF THE EASTERN FRONT IS OVER.
I AM PUTTING TOGETHER A SQUADRON FOR THE BATTLE OF THE SOMME.
I'D LIKE YOU TO BE IN IT, MANFRED VON RICHTHOFEN.
IT WOULD BE MY HONOR, SIR!
BOELCKE HEADED TO THE SOMME
WITH A FRESH CREW OF AGGRESSIVE YOUNG PILOTS.

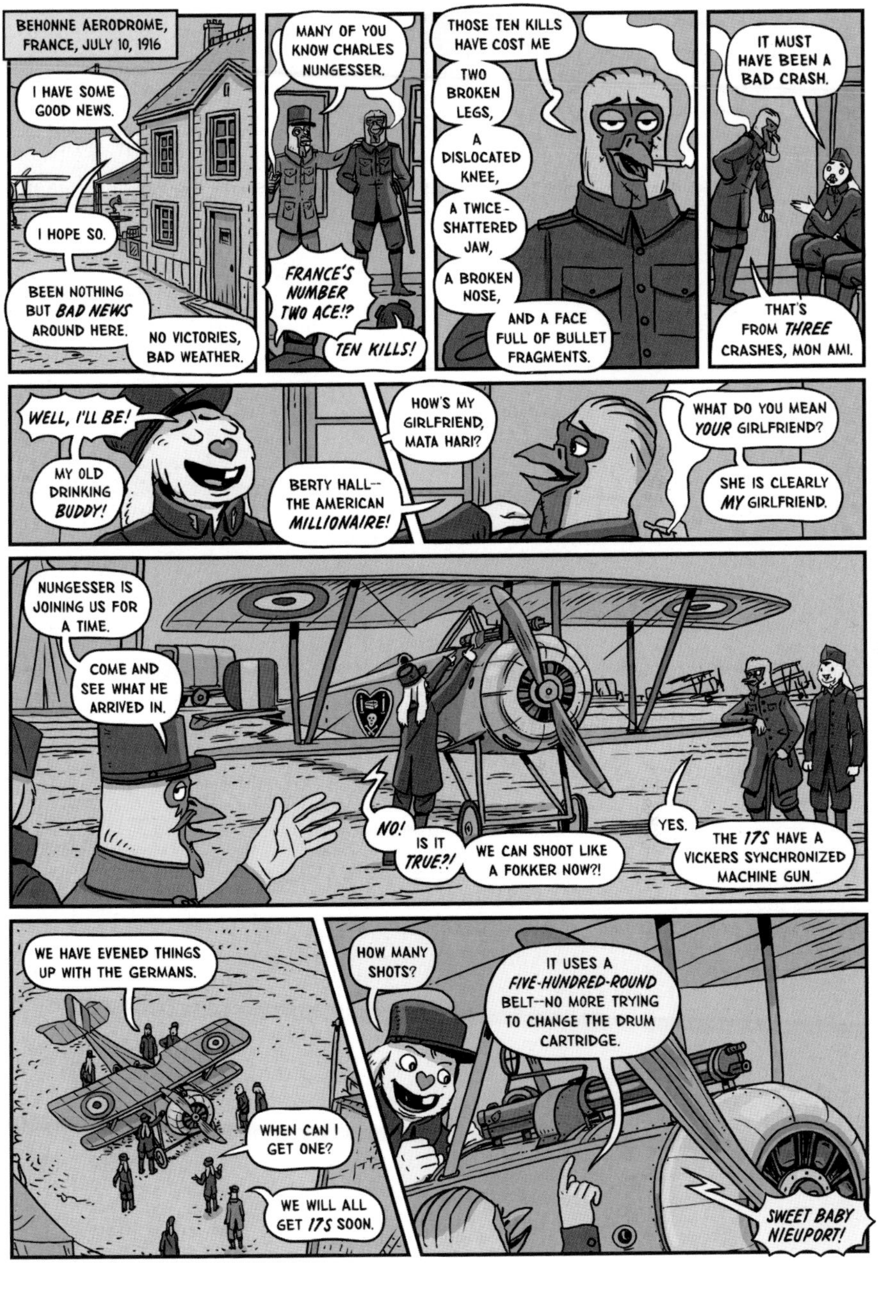
BEHONNE AERODROME, FRANCE, JULY 10, 1916
I HAVE SOME GOOD NEWS.
I HOPE SO.
BEEN NOTHING BUT *BAD NEWS* AROUND HERE.
NO VICTORIES, BAD WEATHER.
MANY OF YOU KNOW CHARLES NUNGESSER.
FRANCE'S NUMBER TWO ACE!?
TEN KILLS!
THOSE TEN KILLS HAVE COST ME
TWO BROKEN LEGS,
A DISLOCATED KNEE,
A TWICE-SHATTERED JAW,
A BROKEN NOSE,
AND A FACE FULL OF BULLET FRAGMENTS.
IT MUST HAVE BEEN A BAD CRASH.
THAT'S FROM *THREE* CRASHES, MON AMI.
WELL, I'LL BE!
MY OLD DRINKING *BUDDY!*
BERTY HALL-- THE AMERICAN *MILLIONAIRE!*
HOW'S MY GIRLFRIEND, MATA HARI?
WHAT DO YOU MEAN *YOUR* GIRLFRIEND?
SHE IS CLEARLY *MY* GIRLFRIEND.
NUNGESSER IS JOINING US FOR A TIME.
COME AND SEE WHAT HE ARRIVED IN.
NO!
IS IT *TRUE?!*
WE CAN SHOOT LIKE A FOKKER NOW?!
YES.
THE *17S* HAVE A VICKERS SYNCHRONIZED MACHINE GUN.
WE HAVE EVENED THINGS UP WITH THE GERMANS.
WHEN CAN I GET ONE?
WE WILL ALL GET *17S* SOON.
HOW MANY SHOTS?
IT USES A *FIVE-HUNDRED-ROUND* BELT--NO MORE TRYING TO CHANGE THE DRUM CARTRIDGE.
SWEET BABY NIEUPORT!

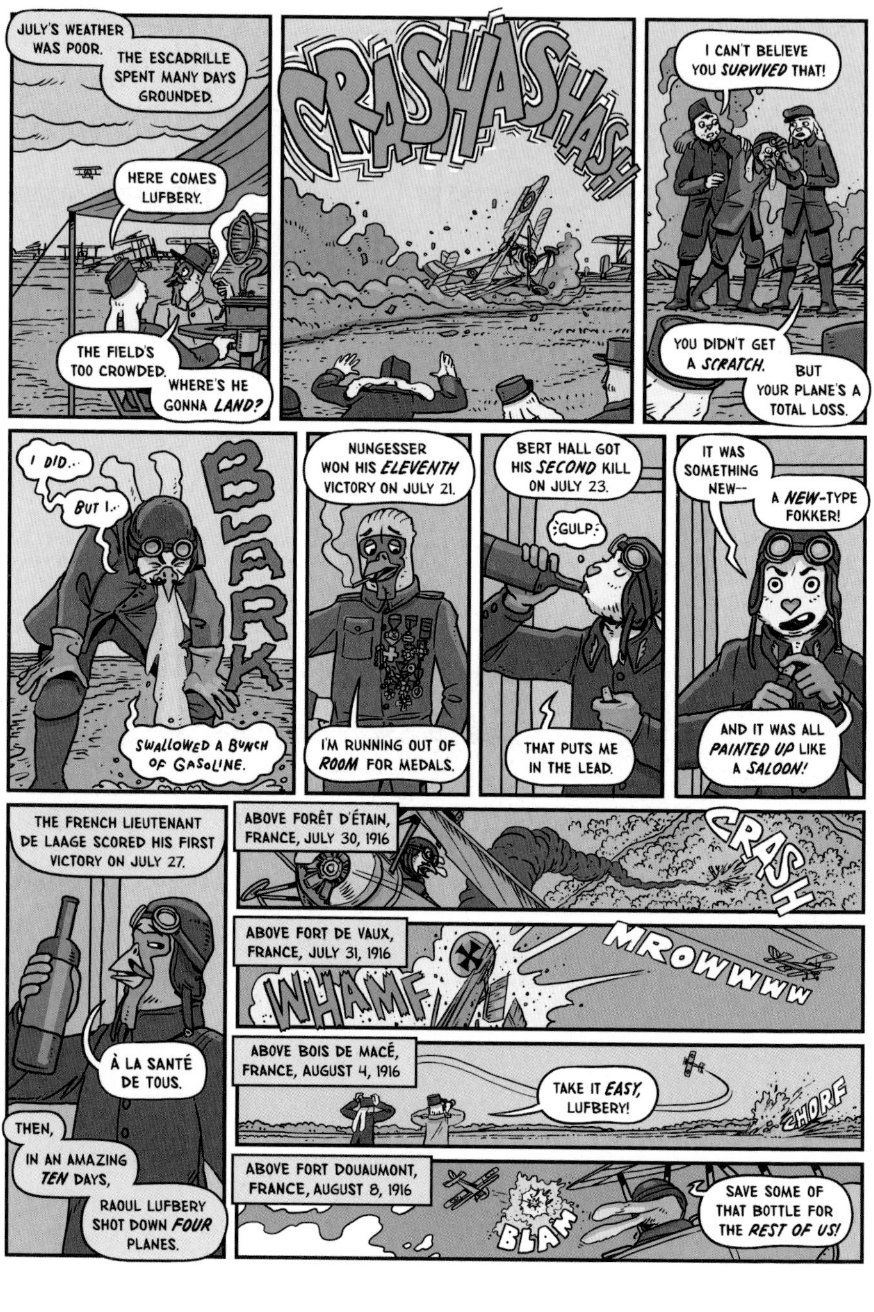

JULY'S WEATHER WAS POOR.
THE ESCADRILLE SPENT MANY DAYS GROUNDED.
HERE COMES LUFBERY.
THE FIELD'S TOO CROWDED.
WHERE'S HE GONNA LAND?
CRASHASHASH
I CAN'T BELIEVE YOU SURVIVED THAT!
YOU DIDN'T GET A SCRATCH.
BUT YOUR PLANE'S A TOTAL LOSS.
I DID...
BUT I...
BLARK
SWALLOWED A BUNCH OF GASOLINE.
NUNGESSER WON HIS ELEVENTH VICTORY ON JULY 21.
I'M RUNNING OUT OF ROOM FOR MEDALS.
BERT HALL GOT HIS SECOND KILL ON JULY 23.
GULP
THAT PUTS ME IN THE LEAD.
IT WAS SOMETHING NEW--
A NEW-TYPE FOKKER!
AND IT WAS ALL PAINTED UP LIKE A SALOON!
THE FRENCH LIEUTENANT DE LAAGE SCORED HIS FIRST VICTORY ON JULY 27.
À LA SANTÉ DE TOUS.
THEN,
IN AN AMAZING TEN DAYS,
RAOUL LUFBERY SHOT DOWN FOUR PLANES.
ABOVE FORÊT D'ÉTAIN, FRANCE, JULY 30, 1916
CRASH
ABOVE FORT DE VAUX, FRANCE, JULY 31, 1916
MROWWWWW
WHAMF
ABOVE BOIS DE MACÉ, FRANCE, AUGUST 4, 1916
TAKE IT EASY, LUFBERY!
CHORF
ABOVE FORT DOUAUMONT, FRANCE, AUGUST 8, 1916
BLAM
SAVE SOME OF THAT BOTTLE FOR THE REST OF US!

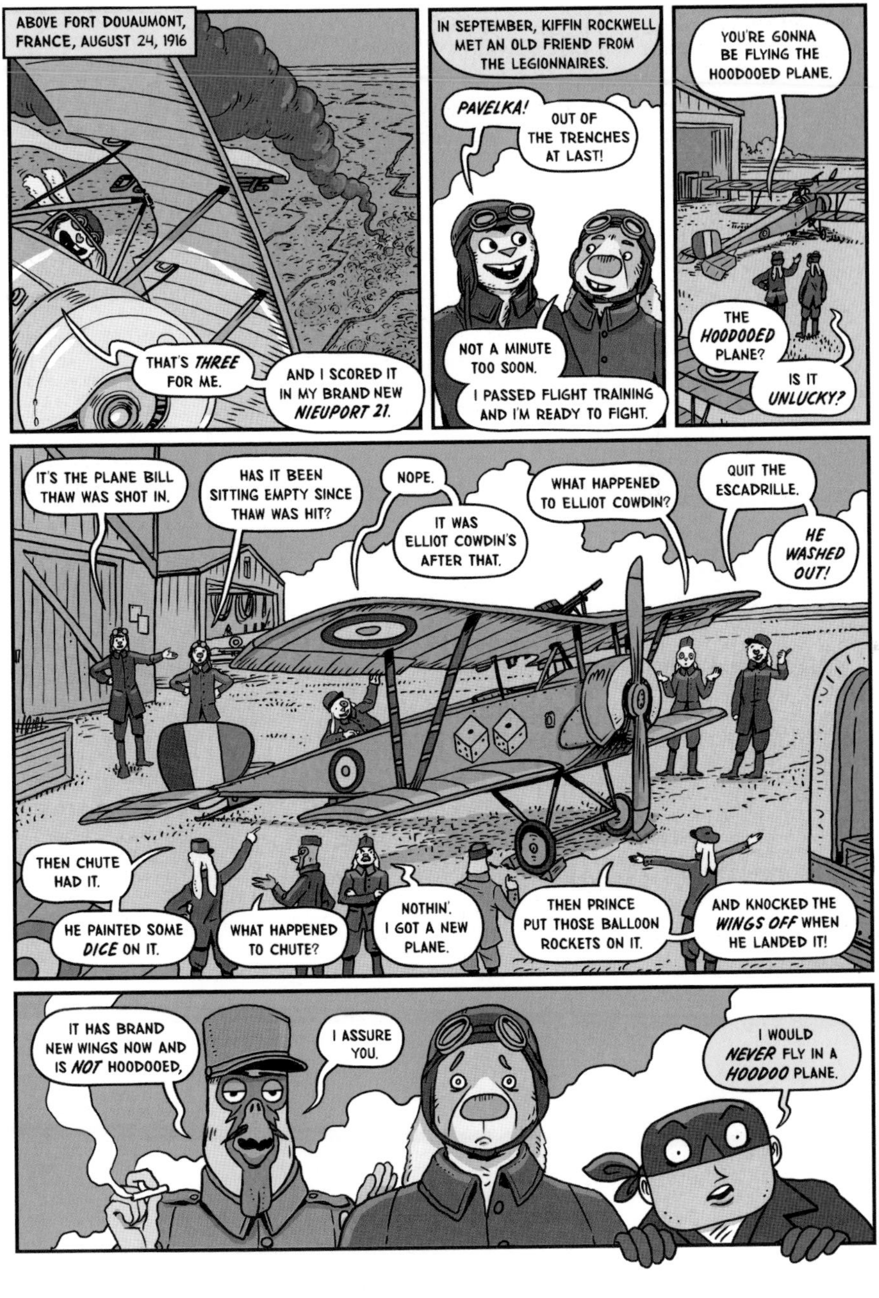
ABOVE FORT DOUAUMONT, FRANCE, AUGUST 24, 1916
THAT'S *THREE* FOR ME.
AND I SCORED IT IN MY BRAND NEW *NIEUPORT 21.*
IN SEPTEMBER, KIFFIN ROCKWELL MET AN OLD FRIEND FROM THE LEGIONNAIRES.
PAVELKA!
OUT OF THE TRENCHES AT LAST!
NOT A MINUTE TOO SOON.
I PASSED FLIGHT TRAINING AND I'M READY TO FIGHT.
YOU'RE GONNA BE FLYING THE HOODOOED PLANE.
THE *HOODOOED* PLANE?
IS IT *UNLUCKY?*
IT'S THE PLANE BILL THAW WAS SHOT IN.
HAS IT BEEN SITTING EMPTY SINCE THAW WAS HIT?
NOPE.
IT WAS ELLIOT COWDIN'S AFTER THAT.
WHAT HAPPENED TO ELLIOT COWDIN?
QUIT THE ESCADRILLE.
HE WASHED OUT!
THEN CHUTE HAD IT.
HE PAINTED SOME *DICE* ON IT.
WHAT HAPPENED TO CHUTE?
NOTHIN'. I GOT A NEW PLANE.
THEN PRINCE PUT THOSE BALLOON ROCKETS ON IT.
AND KNOCKED THE *WINGS OFF* WHEN HE LANDED IT!
IT HAS BRAND NEW WINGS NOW AND IS *NOT* HOODOOED,
I ASSURE YOU.
I WOULD *NEVER* FLY IN A *HOODOO* PLANE.

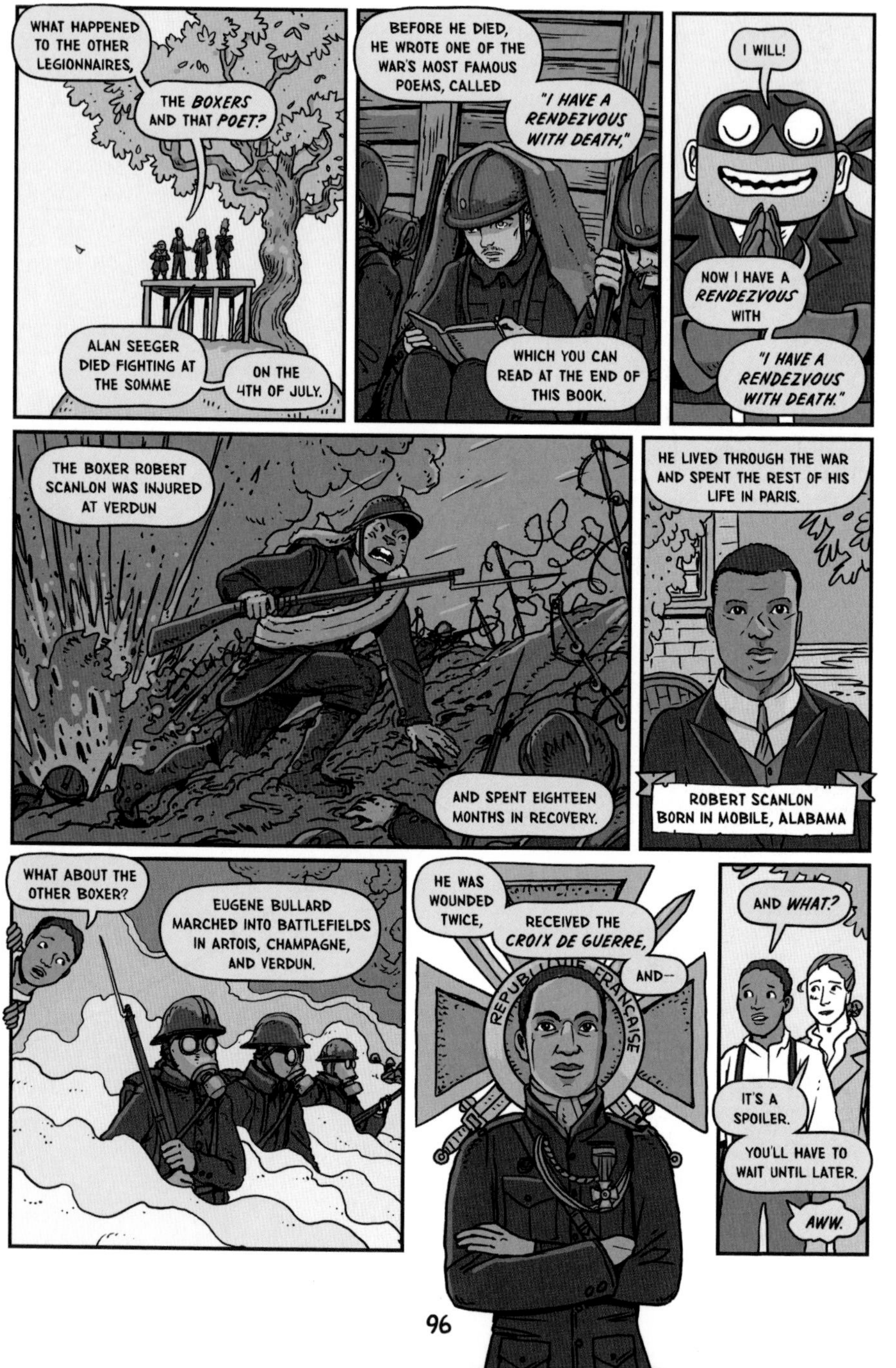
WHAT HAPPENED TO THE OTHER LEGIONNAIRES,
THE *BOXERS* AND THAT *POET?*
ALAN SEEGER DIED FIGHTING AT THE SOMME
ON THE 4TH OF JULY.
BEFORE HE DIED, HE WROTE ONE OF THE WAR'S MOST FAMOUS POEMS, CALLED
"I HAVE A RENDEZVOUS WITH DEATH,"
WHICH YOU CAN READ AT THE END OF THIS BOOK.
I WILL!
NOW I HAVE A *RENDEZVOUS* WITH
"I HAVE A RENDEZVOUS WITH DEATH."
THE BOXER ROBERT SCANLON WAS INJURED AT VERDUN
AND SPENT EIGHTEEN MONTHS IN RECOVERY.
HE LIVED THROUGH THE WAR AND SPENT THE REST OF HIS LIFE IN PARIS.
ROBERT SCANLON
BORN IN MOBILE, ALABAMA
WHAT ABOUT THE OTHER BOXER?
EUGENE BULLARD MARCHED INTO BATTLEFIELDS IN ARTOIS, CHAMPAGNE, AND VERDUN.
HE WAS WOUNDED TWICE,
RECEIVED THE *CROIX DE GUERRE,*
AND--
REPUBLIQUE FRANÇAISE
AND *WHAT?*
IT'S A SPOILER.
YOU'LL HAVE TO WAIT UNTIL LATER.
AWW.

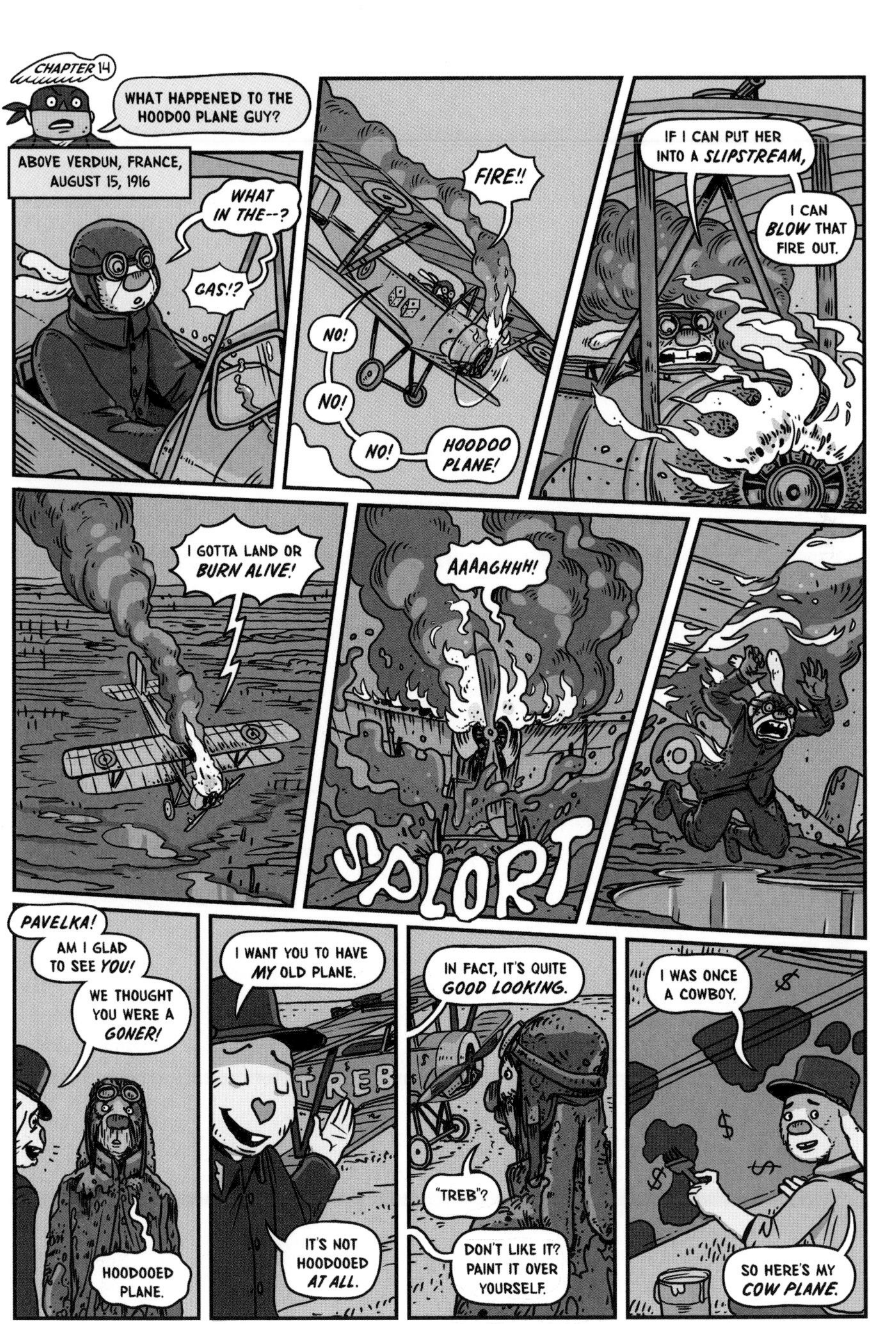
CHAPTER 14
WHAT HAPPENED TO THE HOODOO PLANE GUY?
ABOVE VERDUN, FRANCE, AUGUST 15, 1916
WHAT IN THE--?
GAS!?
FIRE!!
NO!
NO!
NO!
HOODOO PLANE!
IF I CAN PUT HER INTO A SLIPSTREAM,
I CAN BLOW THAT FIRE OUT.
I GOTTA LAND OR BURN ALIVE!
AAAAGHHH!
SPLORT
PAVELKA!
AM I GLAD TO SEE YOU!
WE THOUGHT YOU WERE A GONER!
HOODOOED PLANE.
I WANT YOU TO HAVE MY OLD PLANE.
TREB
IT'S NOT HOODOOED AT ALL.
IN FACT, IT'S QUITE GOOD LOOKING.
"TREB"?
DON'T LIKE IT? PAINT IT OVER YOURSELF.
I WAS ONCE A COWBOY.
SO HERE'S MY COW PLANE.

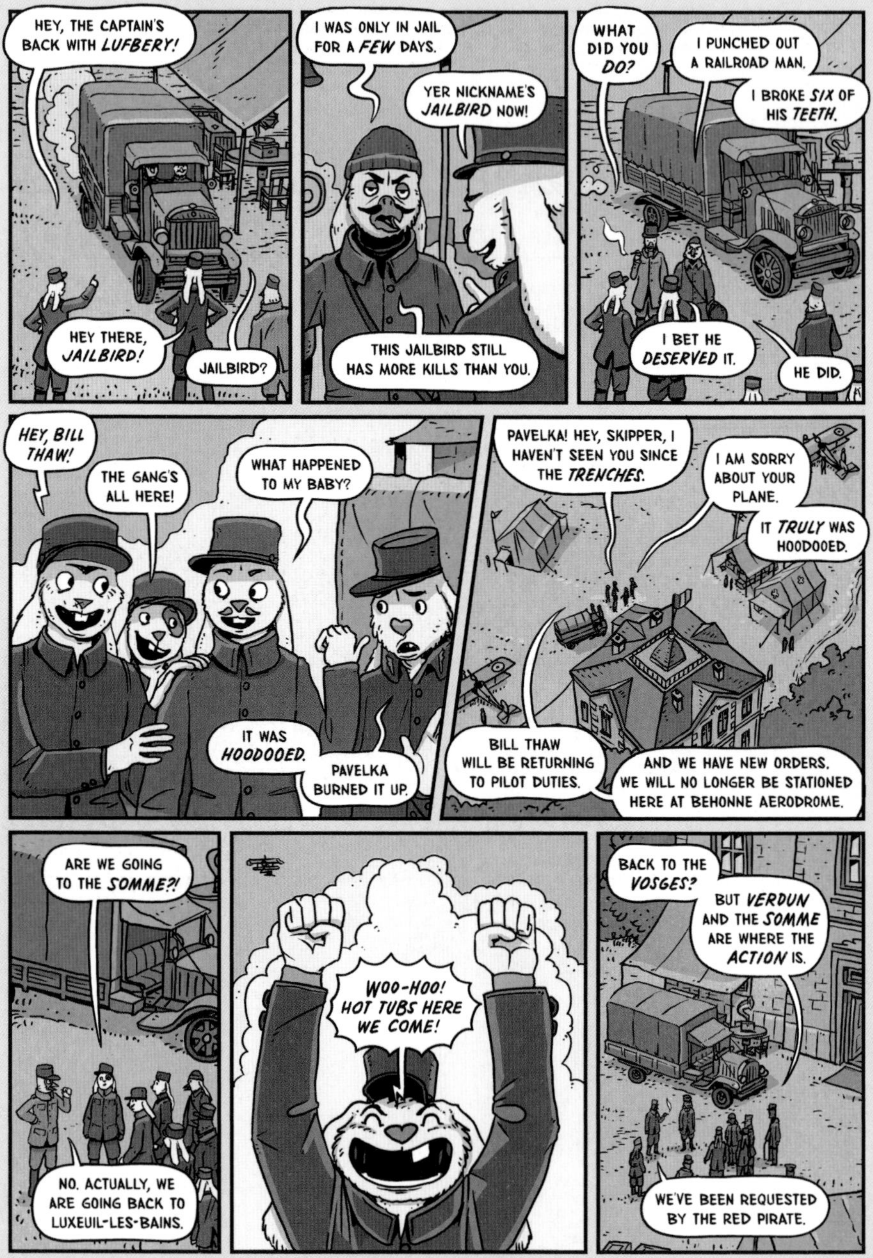

HEY, THE CAPTAIN'S BACK WITH LUFBERY!
HEY THERE, JAILBIRD!
JAILBIRD?
I WAS ONLY IN JAIL FOR A FEW DAYS.
YER NICKNAME'S JAILBIRD NOW!
THIS JAILBIRD STILL HAS MORE KILLS THAN YOU.
WHAT DID YOU DO?
I PUNCHED OUT A RAILROAD MAN.
I BROKE SIX OF HIS TEETH.
I BET HE DESERVED IT.
HE DID.
HEY, BILL THAW!
THE GANG'S ALL HERE!
WHAT HAPPENED TO MY BABY?
IT WAS HOODOOED.
PAVELKA BURNED IT UP.
PAVELKA! HEY, SKIPPER, I HAVEN'T SEEN YOU SINCE THE TRENCHES.
I AM SORRY ABOUT YOUR PLANE.
IT TRULY WAS HOODOOED.
BILL THAW WILL BE RETURNING TO PILOT DUTIES.
AND WE HAVE NEW ORDERS. WE WILL NO LONGER BE STATIONED HERE AT BEHONNE AERODROME.
ARE WE GOING TO THE SOMME?!
NO. ACTUALLY, WE ARE GOING BACK TO LUXEUIL-LES-BAINS.
WOO-HOO! HOT TUBS HERE WE COME!
BACK TO THE VOSGES?
BUT VERDUN AND THE SOMME ARE WHERE THE ACTION IS.
WE'VE BEEN REQUESTED BY THE RED PIRATE.

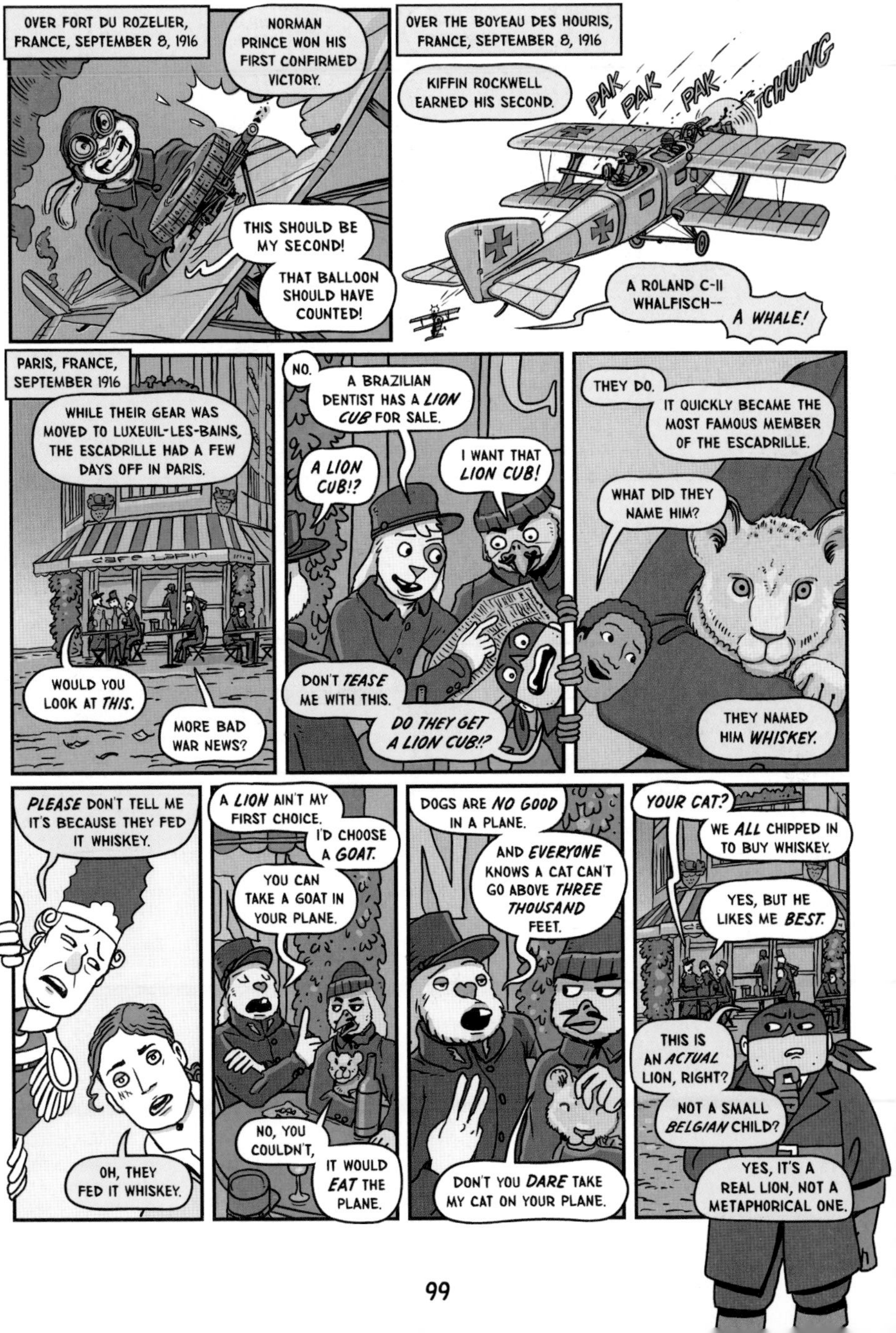
OVER FORT DU ROZELIER, FRANCE, SEPTEMBER 8, 1916
NORMAN PRINCE WON HIS FIRST CONFIRMED VICTORY.
THIS SHOULD BE MY SECOND!
THAT BALLOON SHOULD HAVE COUNTED!
OVER THE BOYEAU DES HOURIS, FRANCE, SEPTEMBER 8, 1916
KIFFIN ROCKWELL EARNED HIS SECOND.
PAK PAK PAK TCHUNG
A ROLAND C-II WHALFISCH--
A WHALE!
PARIS, FRANCE, SEPTEMBER 1916
WHILE THEIR GEAR WAS MOVED TO LUXEUIL-LES-BAINS, THE ESCADRILLE HAD A FEW DAYS OFF IN PARIS.
café Lapin
WOULD YOU LOOK AT THIS.
MORE BAD WAR NEWS?
NO.
A BRAZILIAN DENTIST HAS A LION CUB FOR SALE.
A LION CUB!?
I WANT THAT LION CUB!
DON'T TEASE ME WITH THIS.
DO THEY GET A LION CUB!?
THEY DO.
IT QUICKLY BECAME THE MOST FAMOUS MEMBER OF THE ESCADRILLE.
WHAT DID THEY NAME HIM?
THEY NAMED HIM WHISKEY.
PLEASE DON'T TELL ME IT'S BECAUSE THEY FED IT WHISKEY.
OH, THEY FED IT WHISKEY.
A LION AIN'T MY FIRST CHOICE.
I'D CHOOSE A GOAT.
YOU CAN TAKE A GOAT IN YOUR PLANE.
NO, YOU COULDN'T,
IT WOULD EAT THE PLANE.
DOGS ARE NO GOOD IN A PLANE.
AND EVERYONE KNOWS A CAT CAN'T GO ABOVE THREE THOUSAND FEET.
DON'T YOU DARE TAKE MY CAT ON YOUR PLANE.
YOUR CAT?
WE ALL CHIPPED IN TO BUY WHISKEY.
YES, BUT HE LIKES ME BEST.
THIS IS AN ACTUAL LION, RIGHT?
NOT A SMALL BELGIAN CHILD?
YES, IT'S A REAL LION, NOT A METAPHORICAL ONE.

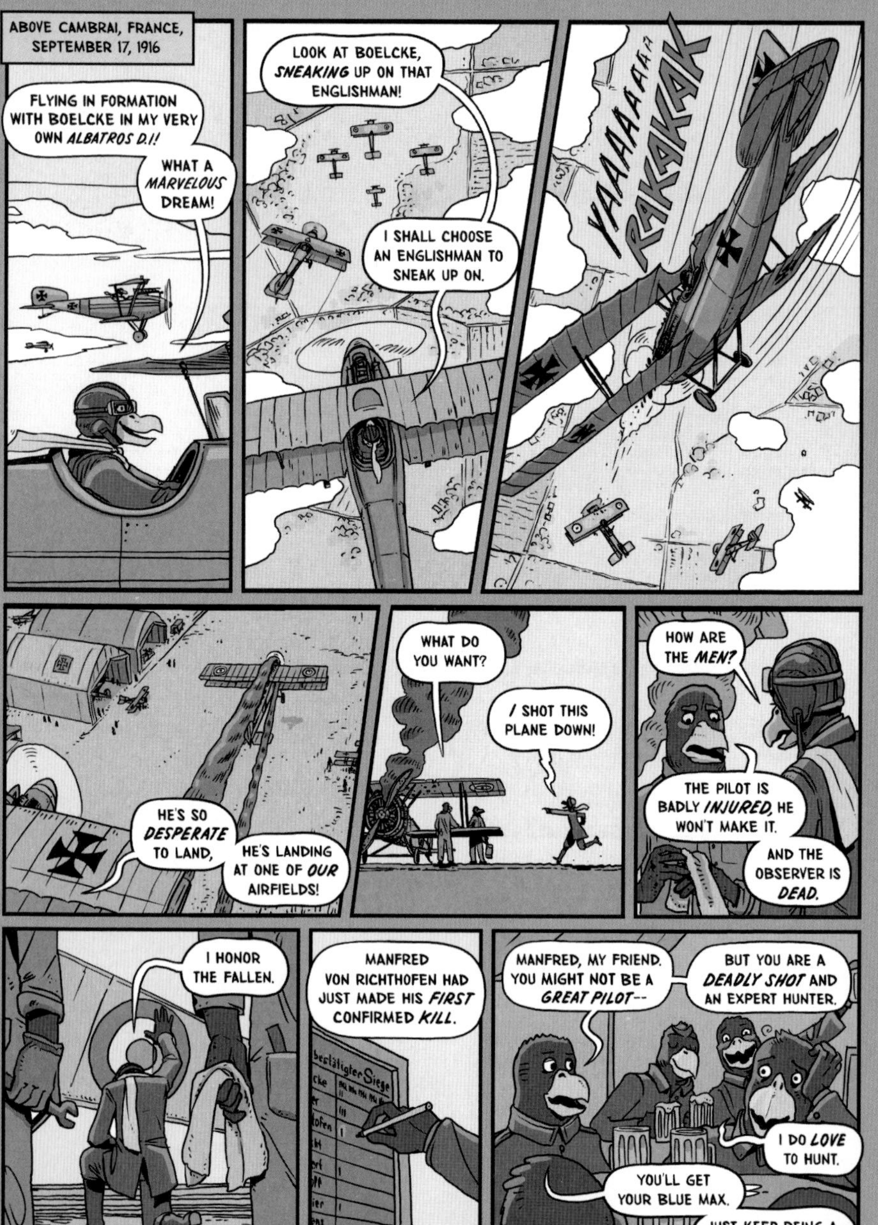
ABOVE CAMBRAI, FRANCE, SEPTEMBER 17, 1916
FLYING IN FORMATION WITH BOELCKE IN MY VERY OWN *ALBATROS D.I!*
WHAT A *MARVELOUS* DREAM!
LOOK AT BOELCKE, *SNEAKING* UP ON THAT ENGLISHMAN!
I SHALL CHOOSE AN ENGLISHMAN TO SNEAK UP ON.
YAAAAAAAA
RAKAKAK
HE'S SO *DESPERATE* TO LAND,
HE'S LANDING AT ONE OF *OUR* AIRFIELDS!
WHAT DO YOU WANT?
I SHOT THIS PLANE DOWN!
HOW ARE THE *MEN?*
THE PILOT IS BADLY *INJURED,* HE WON'T MAKE IT.
AND THE OBSERVER IS *DEAD.*
I HONOR THE FALLEN.
MANFRED VON RICHTHOFEN HAD JUST MADE HIS *FIRST* CONFIRMED *KILL.*
bestätigter Siege
MANFRED, MY FRIEND. YOU MIGHT NOT BE A *GREAT PILOT--*
BUT YOU ARE A *DEADLY SHOT* AND AN EXPERT HUNTER.
I DO *LOVE* TO HUNT.
YOU'LL GET YOUR BLUE MAX.
JUST KEEP BEING A *CAUTIOUS HUNTER.*

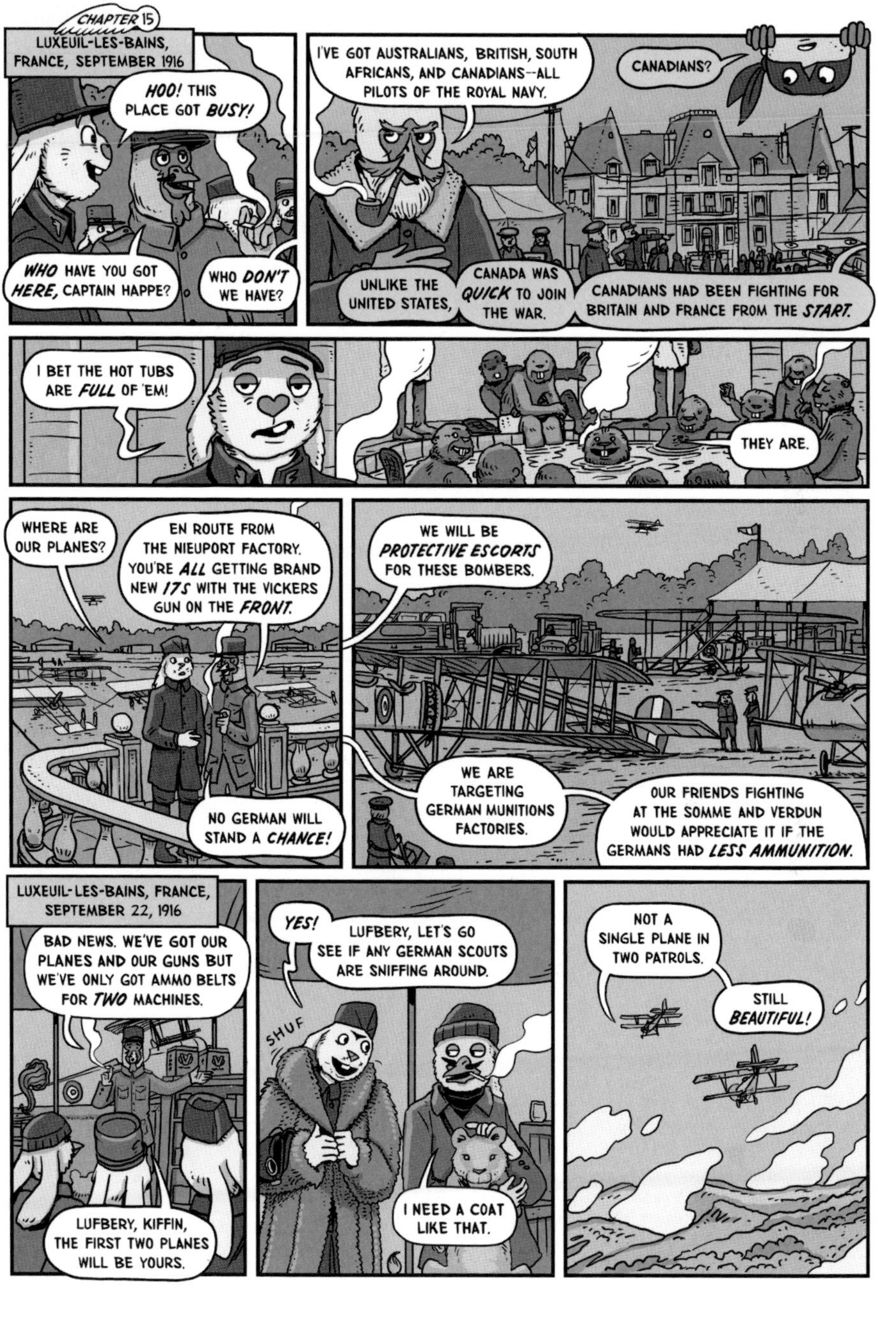
CHAPTER 15
LUXEUIL-LES-BAINS, FRANCE, SEPTEMBER 1916
HOO! THIS PLACE GOT BUSY!
WHO HAVE YOU GOT HERE, CAPTAIN HAPPE?
WHO DON'T WE HAVE?
I'VE GOT AUSTRALIANS, BRITISH, SOUTH AFRICANS, AND CANADIANS--ALL PILOTS OF THE ROYAL NAVY.
CANADIANS?
UNLIKE THE UNITED STATES,
CANADA WAS QUICK TO JOIN THE WAR.
CANADIANS HAD BEEN FIGHTING FOR BRITAIN AND FRANCE FROM THE START.
I BET THE HOT TUBS ARE FULL OF 'EM!
THEY ARE.
WHERE ARE OUR PLANES?
EN ROUTE FROM THE NIEUPORT FACTORY. YOU'RE ALL GETTING BRAND NEW 17S WITH THE VICKERS GUN ON THE FRONT.
NO GERMAN WILL STAND A CHANCE!
WE WILL BE PROTECTIVE ESCORTS FOR THESE BOMBERS.
WE ARE TARGETING GERMAN MUNITIONS FACTORIES.
OUR FRIENDS FIGHTING AT THE SOMME AND VERDUN WOULD APPRECIATE IT IF THE GERMANS HAD LESS AMMUNITION.
LUXEUIL-LES-BAINS, FRANCE, SEPTEMBER 22, 1916
BAD NEWS. WE'VE GOT OUR PLANES AND OUR GUNS BUT WE'VE ONLY GOT AMMO BELTS FOR TWO MACHINES.
LUFBERY, KIFFIN, THE FIRST TWO PLANES WILL BE YOURS.
YES!
LUFBERY, LET'S GO SEE IF ANY GERMAN SCOUTS ARE SNIFFING AROUND.
SHUF
I NEED A COAT LIKE THAT.
NOT A SINGLE PLANE IN TWO PATROLS.
STILL BEAUTIFUL!

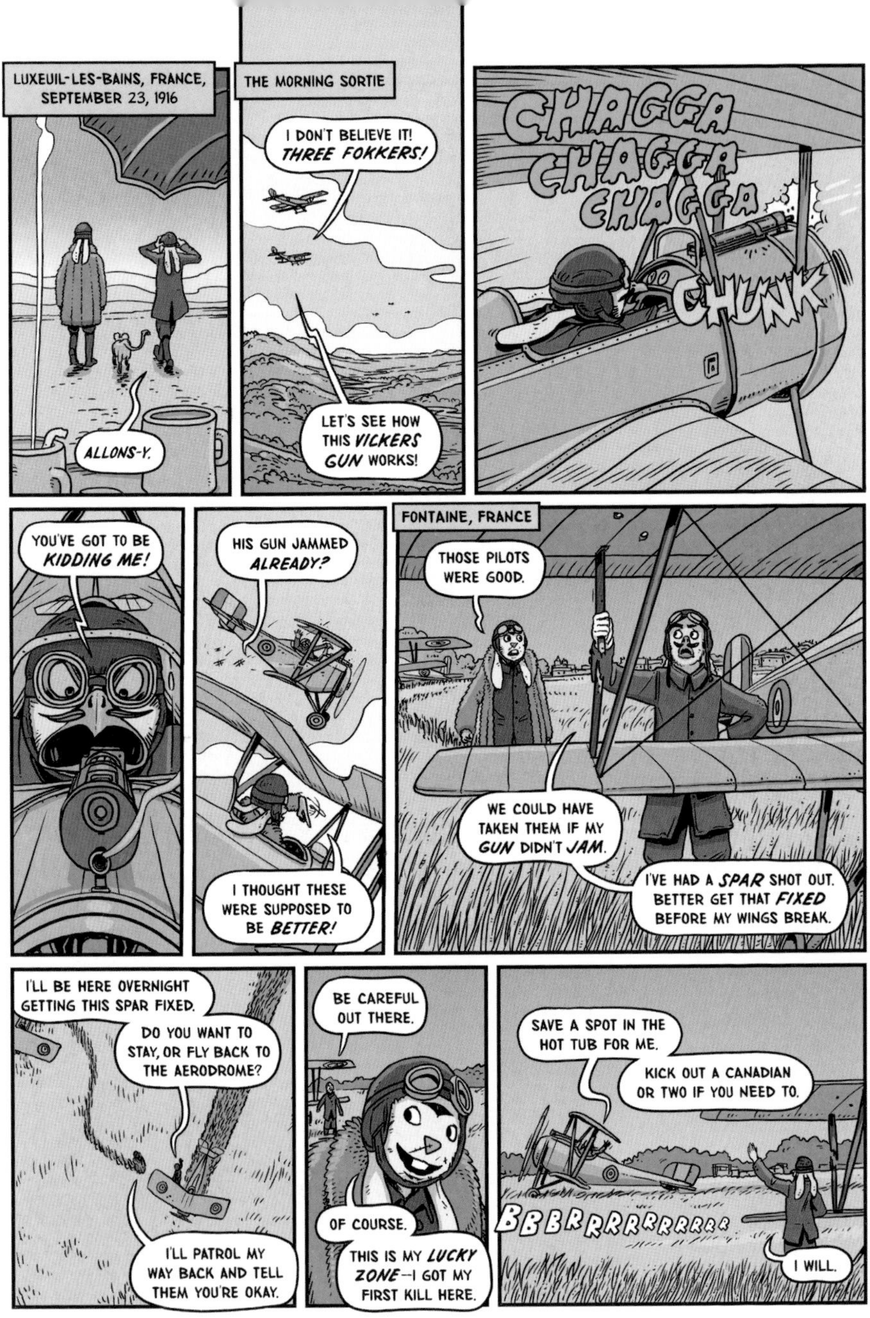
LUXEUIL-LES-BAINS, FRANCE, SEPTEMBER 23, 1916
ALLONS-Y.
THE MORNING SORTIE
I DON'T BELIEVE IT! THREE FOKKERS!
LET'S SEE HOW THIS VICKERS GUN WORKS!
CHAGGA CHAGGA CHAGGA
CHUNK
YOU'VE GOT TO BE KIDDING ME!
HIS GUN JAMMED ALREADY?
I THOUGHT THESE WERE SUPPOSED TO BE BETTER!
FONTAINE, FRANCE
THOSE PILOTS WERE GOOD.
WE COULD HAVE TAKEN THEM IF MY GUN DIDN'T JAM.
I'VE HAD A SPAR SHOT OUT. BETTER GET THAT FIXED BEFORE MY WINGS BREAK.
I'LL BE HERE OVERNIGHT GETTING THIS SPAR FIXED.
DO YOU WANT TO STAY, OR FLY BACK TO THE AERODROME?
I'LL PATROL MY WAY BACK AND TELL THEM YOU'RE OKAY.
BE CAREFUL OUT THERE.
OF COURSE.
THIS IS MY LUCKY ZONE--I GOT MY FIRST KILL HERE.
SAVE A SPOT IN THE HOT TUB FOR ME.
KICK OUT A CANADIAN OR TWO IF YOU NEED TO.
BBBRRRRRRRRRRR
I WILL.

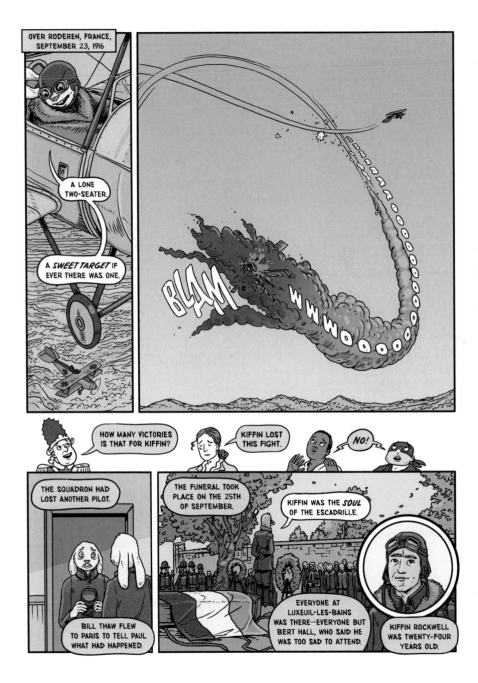

OVER RODEREN, FRANCE, SEPTEMBER 23, 1916

A LONE TWO-SEATER.

A *SWEET TARGET* IF EVER THERE WAS ONE.

BLAM

BRRRRRROOOOOOOO

WWWOOOOOOO

HOW MANY VICTORIES IS THAT FOR KIFFIN?

KIFFIN LOST THIS FIGHT.

NO!

THE SQUADRON HAD LOST ANOTHER PILOT.

BILL THAW FLEW TO PARIS TO TELL PAUL WHAT HAD HAPPENED.

THE FUNERAL TOOK PLACE ON THE 25TH OF SEPTEMBER.

KIFFIN WAS THE *SOUL* OF THE ESCADRILLE.

EVERYONE AT LUXEUIL-LES-BAINS WAS THERE—EVERYONE BUT BERT HALL, WHO SAID HE WAS TOO SAD TO ATTEND.

KIFFIN ROCKWELL WAS TWENTY-FOUR YEARS OLD.

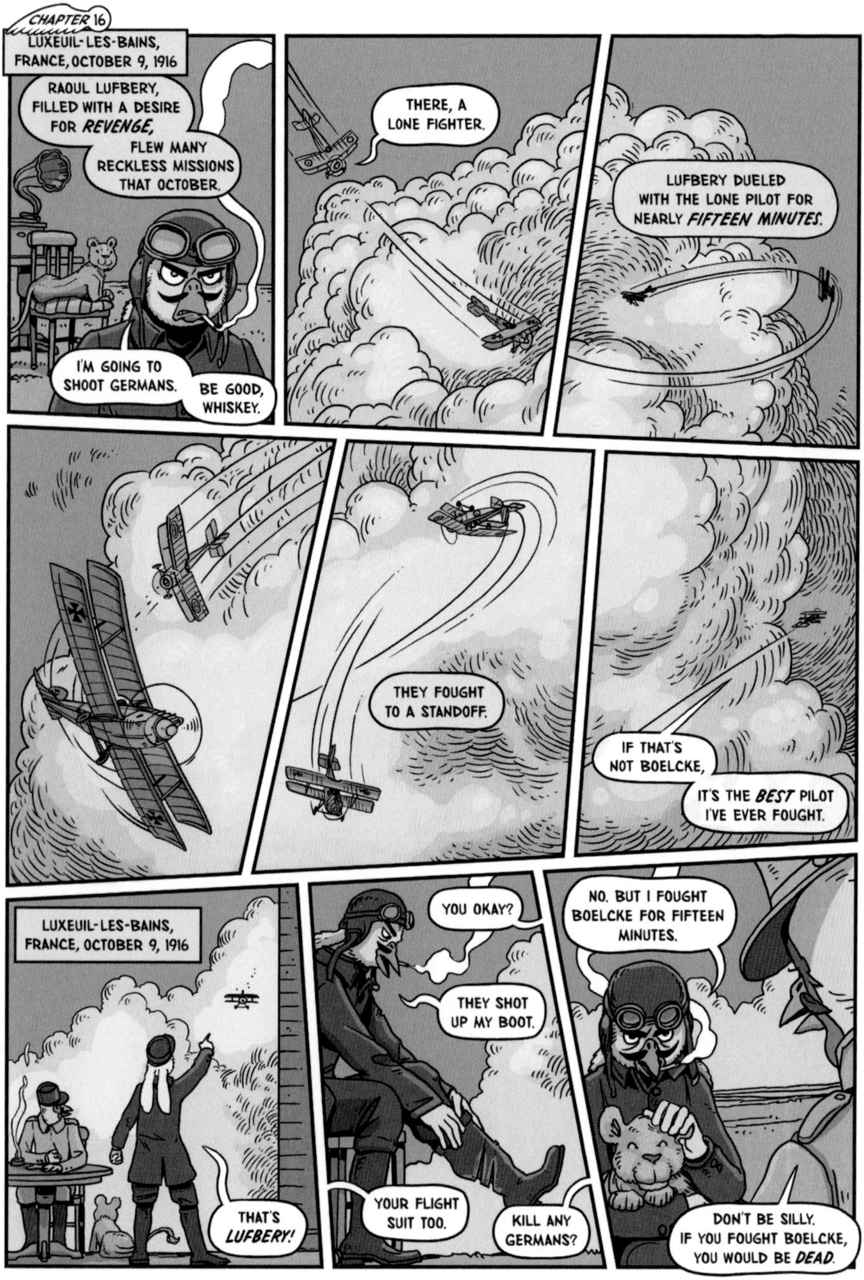
CHAPTER 16
LUXEUIL-LES-BAINS, FRANCE, OCTOBER 9, 1916
RAOUL LUFBERY, FILLED WITH A DESIRE FOR REVENGE,
FLEW MANY RECKLESS MISSIONS THAT OCTOBER.
I'M GOING TO SHOOT GERMANS.
BE GOOD, WHISKEY.
THERE, A LONE FIGHTER.
LUFBERY DUELED WITH THE LONE PILOT FOR NEARLY FIFTEEN MINUTES.
THEY FOUGHT TO A STANDOFF.
IF THAT'S NOT BOELCKE,
IT'S THE BEST PILOT I'VE EVER FOUGHT.
LUXEUIL-LES-BAINS, FRANCE, OCTOBER 9, 1916
THAT'S LUFBERY!
YOU OKAY?
THEY SHOT UP MY BOOT.
YOUR FLIGHT SUIT TOO.
KILL ANY GERMANS?
NO. BUT I FOUGHT BOELCKE FOR FIFTEEN MINUTES.
DON'T BE SILLY. IF YOU FOUGHT BOELCKE, YOU WOULD BE DEAD.

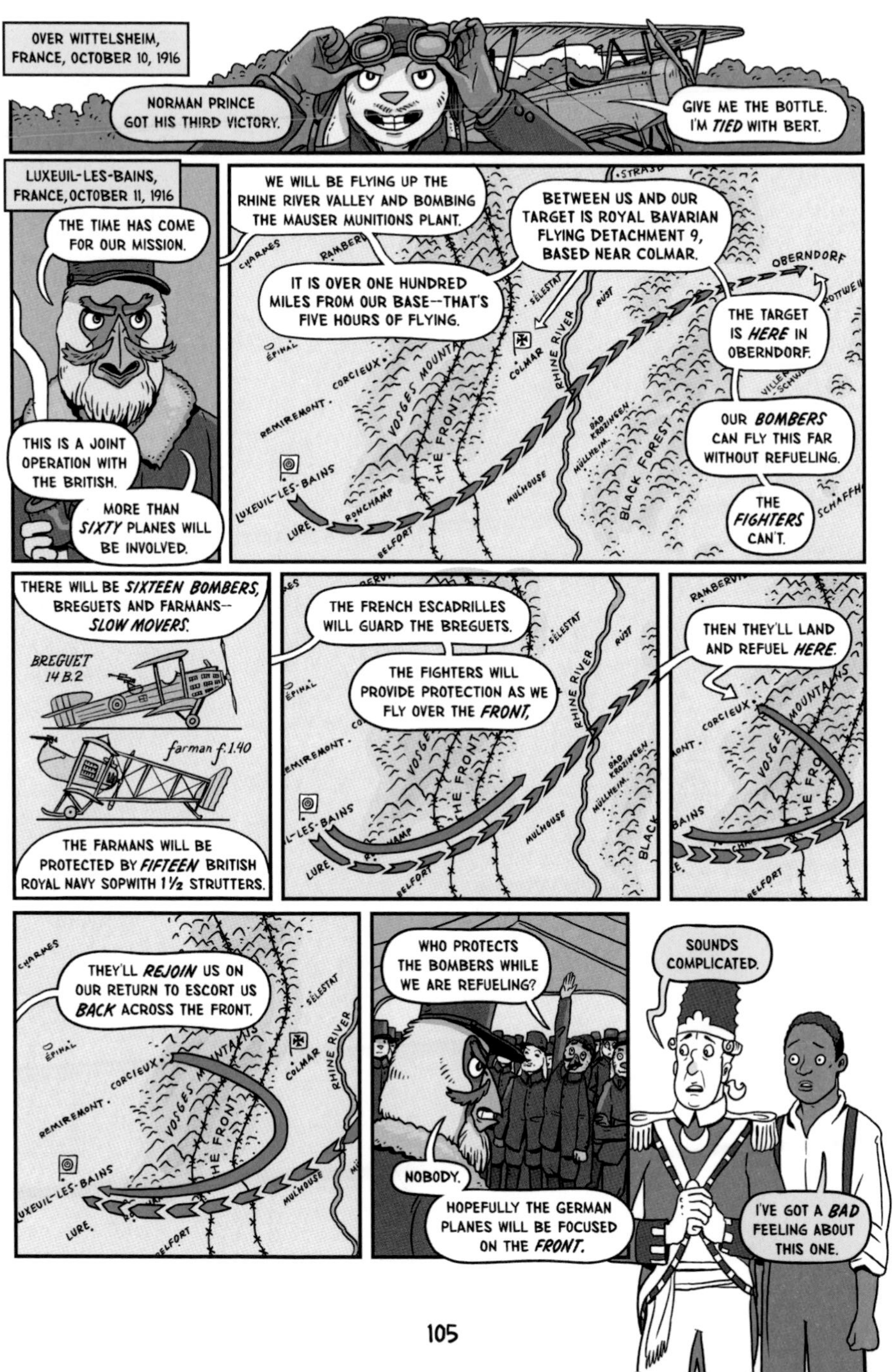
OVER WITTELSHEIM, FRANCE, OCTOBER 10, 1916
NORMAN PRINCE GOT HIS THIRD VICTORY.
GIVE ME THE BOTTLE. I'M *TIED* WITH BERT.
LUXEUIL-LES-BAINS, FRANCE, OCTOBER 11, 1916
THE TIME HAS COME FOR OUR MISSION.
WE WILL BE FLYING UP THE RHINE RIVER VALLEY AND BOMBING THE MAUSER MUNITIONS PLANT.
IT IS OVER ONE HUNDRED MILES FROM OUR BASE--THAT'S FIVE HOURS OF FLYING.
BETWEEN US AND OUR TARGET IS ROYAL BAVARIAN FLYING DETACHMENT 9, BASED NEAR COLMAR.
THE TARGET IS *HERE* IN OBERNDORF.
OUR *BOMBERS* CAN FLY THIS FAR WITHOUT REFUELING.
THE *FIGHTERS* CAN'T.
THIS IS A JOINT OPERATION WITH THE BRITISH.
MORE THAN *SIXTY* PLANES WILL BE INVOLVED.
CHARMES
RAMBERV
ÉPINAL
CORCIEUX
REMIREMONT
VOSGES MOUNTAINS
THE FRONT
COLMAR
SÉLESTAT
RÜST
RHINE RIVER
OBERNDORF
ROTTWEIL
BAD KROZINGEN
MÜLLHEIM
BLACK FOREST
MULHOUSE
LUXEUIL-LES-BAINS
RONCHAMP
LURE
BELFORT
SCHAFFH
THERE WILL BE *SIXTEEN BOMBERS*, BREGUETS AND FARMANS-- *SLOW MOVERS*.
BREGUET 14 B.2
farman f.1.40
THE FARMANS WILL BE PROTECTED BY *FIFTEEN* BRITISH ROYAL NAVY SOPWITH 1½ STRUTTERS.
THE FRENCH ESCADRILLES WILL GUARD THE BREGUETS.
THE FIGHTERS WILL PROVIDE PROTECTION AS WE FLY OVER THE *FRONT*,
THEN THEY'LL LAND AND REFUEL *HERE*.
THEY'LL *REJOIN* US ON OUR RETURN TO ESCORT US *BACK* ACROSS THE FRONT.
WHO PROTECTS THE BOMBERS WHILE WE ARE REFUELING?
NOBODY.
HOPEFULLY THE GERMAN PLANES WILL BE FOCUSED ON THE *FRONT*.
SOUNDS COMPLICATED.
I'VE GOT A *BAD* FEELING ABOUT THIS ONE.

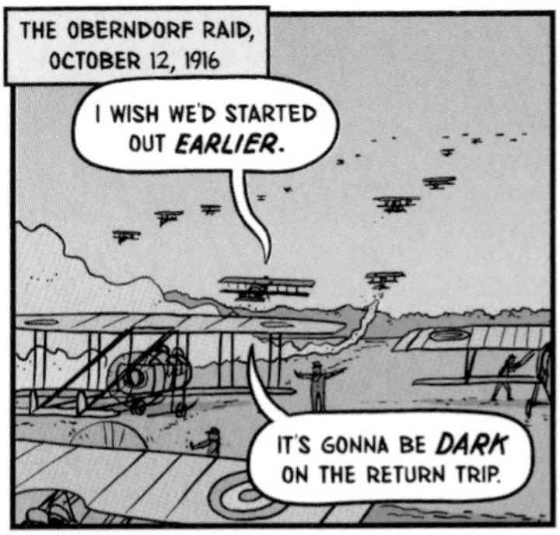
THE OBERNDORF RAID, OCTOBER 12, 1916
I WISH WE'D STARTED OUT EARLIER.
IT'S GONNA BE DARK ON THE RETURN TRIP.

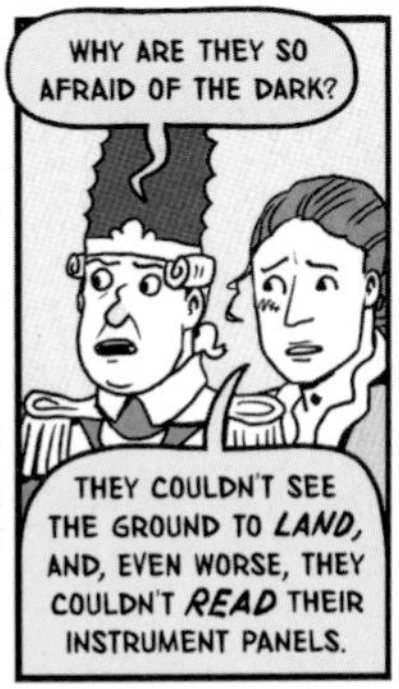
WHY ARE THEY SO AFRAID OF THE DARK?
THEY COULDN'T SEE THE GROUND TO LAND, AND, EVEN WORSE, THEY COULDN'T READ THEIR INSTRUMENT PANELS.

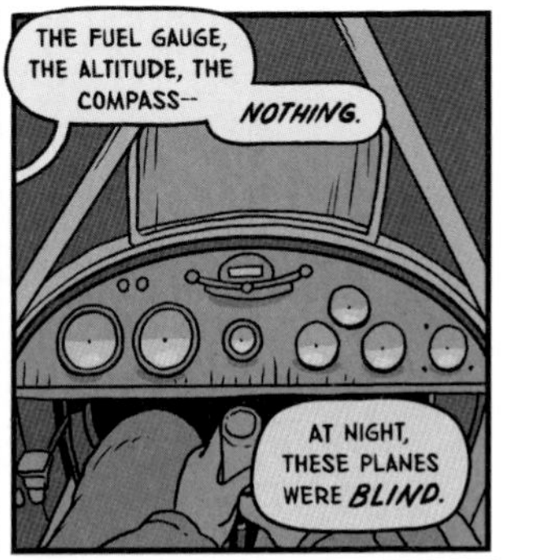
THE FUEL GAUGE, THE ALTITUDE, THE COMPASS--
NOTHING.
AT NIGHT, THESE PLANES WERE BLIND.

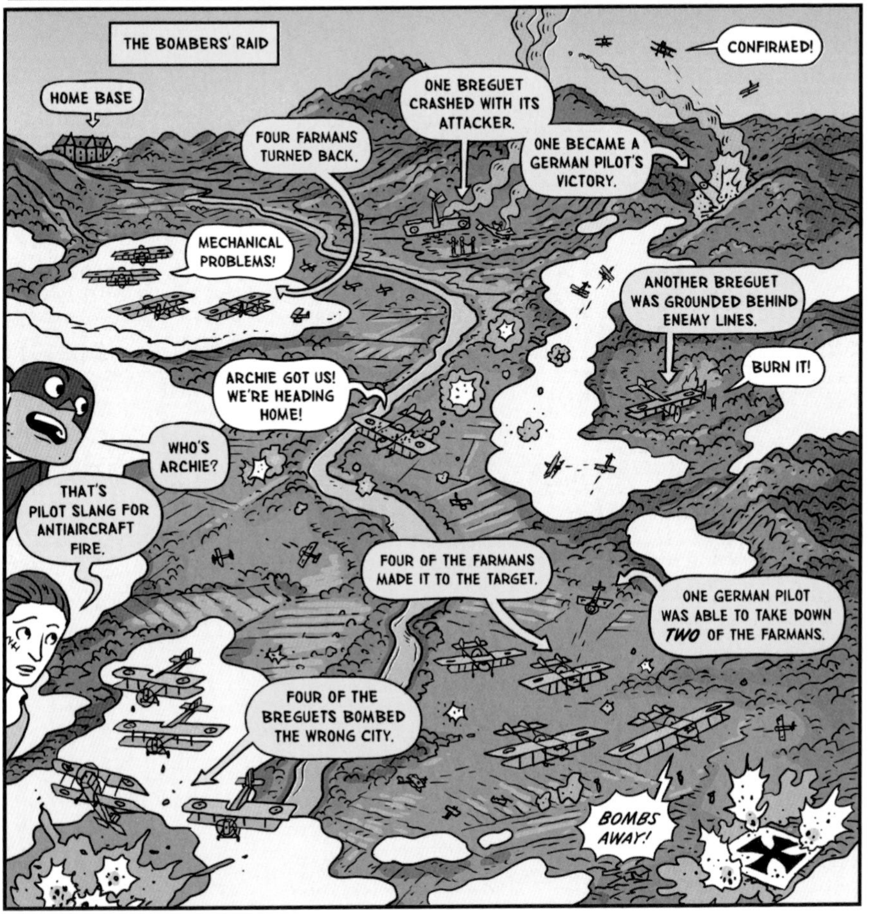
THE BOMBERS' RAID
CONFIRMED!
HOME BASE
ONE BREGUET CRASHED WITH ITS ATTACKER.
FOUR FARMANS TURNED BACK.
ONE BECAME A GERMAN PILOT'S VICTORY.
MECHANICAL PROBLEMS!
ANOTHER BREGUET WAS GROUNDED BEHIND ENEMY LINES.
BURN IT!
ARCHIE GOT US! WE'RE HEADING HOME!
WHO'S ARCHIE?
THAT'S PILOT SLANG FOR ANTIAIRCRAFT FIRE.
FOUR OF THE FARMANS MADE IT TO THE TARGET.
ONE GERMAN PILOT WAS ABLE TO TAKE DOWN TWO OF THE FARMANS.
FOUR OF THE BREGUETS BOMBED THE WRONG CITY.
BOMBS AWAY!

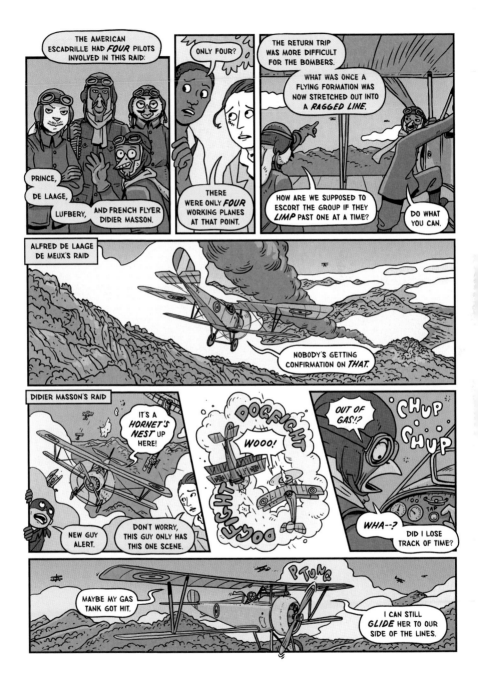

THE AMERICAN ESCADRILLE HAD *FOUR* PILOTS INVOLVED IN THIS RAID:

PRINCE,

DE LAAGE,

LUFBERY,

AND FRENCH FLYER DIDIER MASSON.

ONLY FOUR?

THERE WERE ONLY *FOUR* WORKING PLANES AT THAT POINT.

THE RETURN TRIP WAS MORE DIFFICULT FOR THE BOMBERS.

WHAT WAS ONCE A FLYING FORMATION WAS NOW STRETCHED OUT INTO A *RAGGED LINE*.

HOW ARE WE SUPPOSED TO ESCORT THE GROUP IF THEY *LIMP* PAST ONE AT A TIME?

DO WHAT YOU CAN.

ALFRED DE LAAGE DE MEUX'S RAID

NOBODY'S GETTING CONFIRMATION ON *THAT*.

DIDIER MASSON'S RAID

IT'S A *HORNET'S NEST* UP HERE!

NEW GUY ALERT.

DON'T WORRY, THIS GUY ONLY HAS THIS ONE SCENE.

DOGFIGHT

WOOO!

OUT OF GAS!?

CHUP CHUP

WHA--?

DID I LOSE TRACK OF TIME?

MAYBE MY GAS TANK GOT HIT.

PTUNG

I CAN STILL *GLIDE* HER TO OUR SIDE OF THE LINES.

107

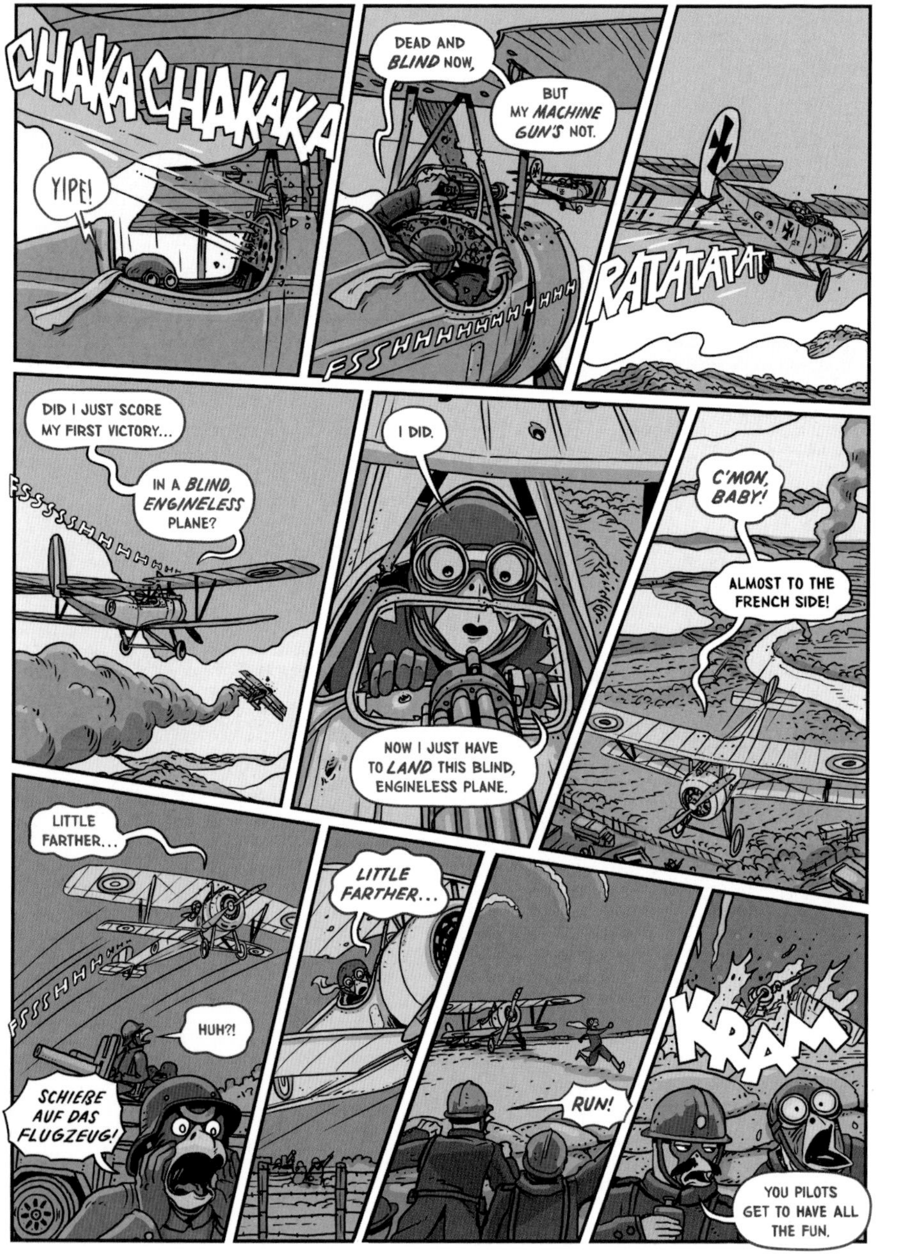
CHAKA CHAKAKAKA
YIPE!
DEAD AND BLIND NOW,
BUT MY MACHINE GUN'S NOT.
FSSHHHHHHHHHHHHH
RATATATATAT
DID I JUST SCORE MY FIRST VICTORY...
IN A BLIND, ENGINELESS PLANE?
FSSSSSSHHHHHH
I DID.
NOW I JUST HAVE TO LAND THIS BLIND, ENGINELESS PLANE.
C'MON, BABY!
ALMOST TO THE FRENCH SIDE!
LITTLE FARTHER...
FSSSHHHHHHH
HUH?!
SCHIEßE AUF DAS FLUGZEUG!
LITTLE FARTHER...
RUN!
KRAM
YOU PILOTS GET TO HAVE ALL THE FUN.

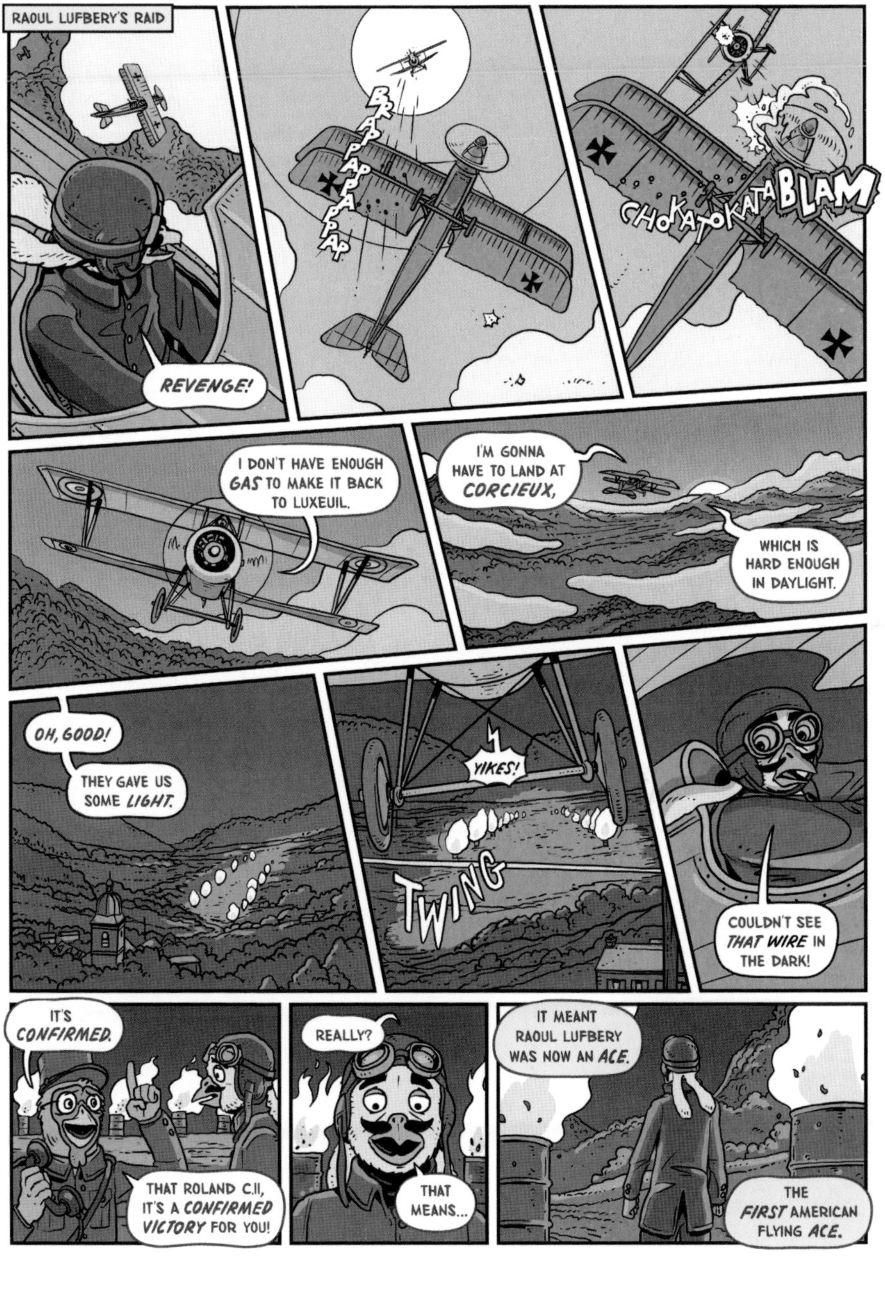
RAOUL LUFBERY'S RAID
REVENGE!
BRAPAPAPAPAPAP
CHOKATOKATABLAM
I DON'T HAVE ENOUGH GAS TO MAKE IT BACK TO LUXEUIL.
I'M GONNA HAVE TO LAND AT CORCIEUX,
WHICH IS HARD ENOUGH IN DAYLIGHT.
OH, GOOD!
THEY GAVE US SOME LIGHT.
YIKES!
TWING
COULDN'T SEE THAT WIRE IN THE DARK!
IT'S CONFIRMED.
THAT ROLAND C.II, IT'S A CONFIRMED VICTORY FOR YOU!
REALLY?
THAT MEANS...
IT MEANT RAOUL LUFBERY WAS NOW AN ACE.
THE FIRST AMERICAN FLYING ACE.

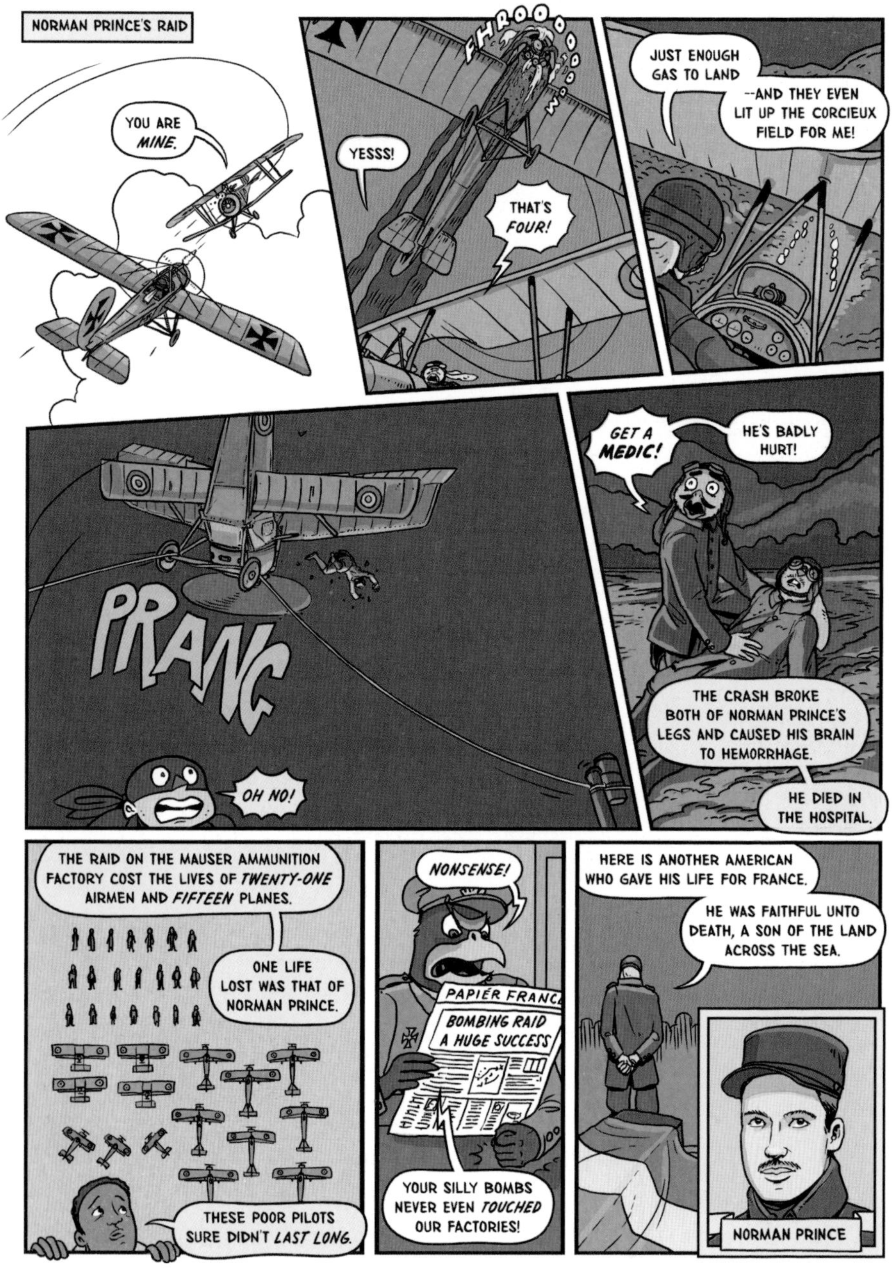
NORMAN PRINCE'S RAID
YOU ARE *MINE.*
FHROOOOOOOWOOM
YESSS!
THAT'S *FOUR!*
JUST ENOUGH GAS TO LAND
--AND THEY EVEN LIT UP THE CORCIEUX FIELD FOR ME!
PRANG
OH NO!
GET A *MEDIC!*
HE'S BADLY HURT!
THE CRASH BROKE BOTH OF NORMAN PRINCE'S LEGS AND CAUSED HIS BRAIN TO HEMORRHAGE.
HE DIED IN THE HOSPITAL.
THE RAID ON THE MAUSER AMMUNITION FACTORY COST THE LIVES OF *TWENTY-ONE* AIRMEN AND *FIFTEEN* PLANES.
ONE LIFE LOST WAS THAT OF NORMAN PRINCE.
THESE POOR PILOTS SURE DIDN'T *LAST LONG.*
NONSENSE!
PAPIER FRANC
BOMBING RAID A HUGE SUCCESS
YOUR SILLY BOMBS NEVER EVEN *TOUCHED* OUR FACTORIES!
HERE IS ANOTHER AMERICAN WHO GAVE HIS LIFE FOR FRANCE.
HE WAS FAITHFUL UNTO DEATH, A SON OF THE LAND ACROSS THE SEA.
NORMAN PRINCE

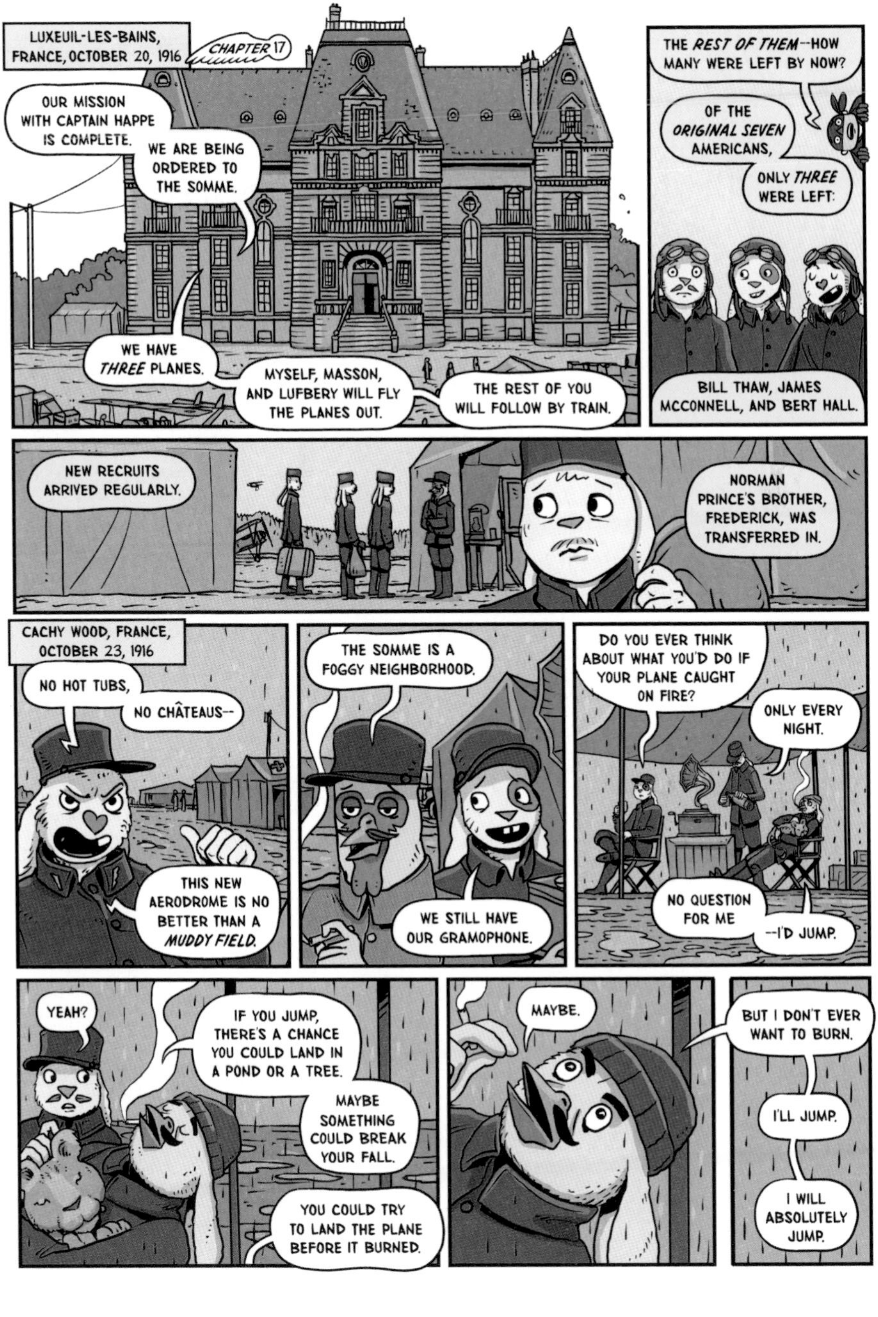

LUXEUIL-LES-BAINS, FRANCE, OCTOBER 20, 1916
CHAPTER 17
OUR MISSION WITH CAPTAIN HAPPE IS COMPLETE.
WE ARE BEING ORDERED TO THE SOMME.
WE HAVE *THREE* PLANES.
MYSELF, MASSON, AND LUFBERY WILL FLY THE PLANES OUT.
THE REST OF YOU WILL FOLLOW BY TRAIN.
THE *REST OF THEM*--HOW MANY WERE LEFT BY NOW?
OF THE *ORIGINAL SEVEN* AMERICANS,
ONLY *THREE* WERE LEFT:
BILL THAW, JAMES MCCONNELL, AND BERT HALL.
NEW RECRUITS ARRIVED REGULARLY.
NORMAN PRINCE'S BROTHER, FREDERICK, WAS TRANSFERRED IN.
CACHY WOOD, FRANCE, OCTOBER 23, 1916
NO HOT TUBS,
NO CHÂTEAUS--
THIS NEW AERODROME IS NO BETTER THAN A *MUDDY FIELD*.
THE SOMME IS A FOGGY NEIGHBORHOOD.
WE STILL HAVE OUR GRAMOPHONE.
DO YOU EVER THINK ABOUT WHAT YOU'D DO IF YOUR PLANE CAUGHT ON FIRE?
ONLY EVERY NIGHT.
NO QUESTION FOR ME
--I'D JUMP.
YEAH?
IF YOU JUMP, THERE'S A CHANCE YOU COULD LAND IN A POND OR A TREE.
MAYBE SOMETHING COULD BREAK YOUR FALL.
YOU COULD TRY TO LAND THE PLANE BEFORE IT BURNED.
MAYBE.
BUT I DON'T EVER WANT TO BURN.
I'LL JUMP.
I WILL ABSOLUTELY JUMP.

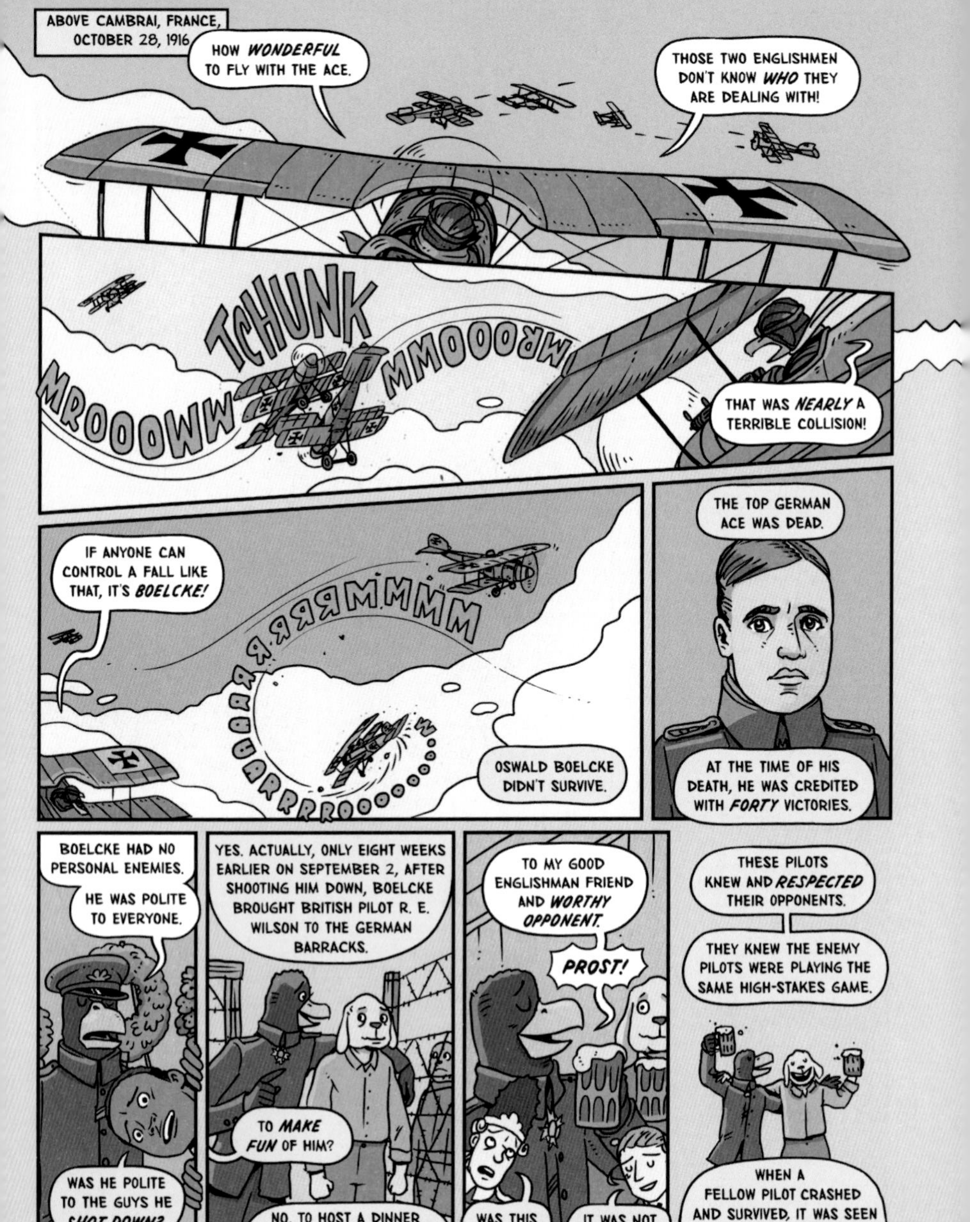
ABOVE CAMBRAI, FRANCE, OCTOBER 28, 1916
HOW WONDERFUL TO FLY WITH THE ACE.
THOSE TWO ENGLISHMEN DON'T KNOW WHO THEY ARE DEALING WITH!
MROOOWW
TCHUNK
MROOOWW
THAT WAS NEARLY A TERRIBLE COLLISION!
IF ANYONE CAN CONTROL A FALL LIKE THAT, IT'S BOELCKE!
MMMMRRRRRRUUARRRRROOOOOOOOOW
OSWALD BOELCKE DIDN'T SURVIVE.
THE TOP GERMAN ACE WAS DEAD.
AT THE TIME OF HIS DEATH, HE WAS CREDITED WITH FORTY VICTORIES.
BOELCKE HAD NO PERSONAL ENEMIES.
HE WAS POLITE TO EVERYONE.
WAS HE POLITE TO THE GUYS HE SHOT DOWN?
YES. ACTUALLY, ONLY EIGHT WEEKS EARLIER ON SEPTEMBER 2, AFTER SHOOTING HIM DOWN, BOELCKE BROUGHT BRITISH PILOT R. E. WILSON TO THE GERMAN BARRACKS.
TO MAKE FUN OF HIM?
NO, TO HOST A DINNER AND DRINK A TOAST TO HIM.
TO MY GOOD ENGLISHMAN FRIEND AND WORTHY OPPONENT.
PROST!
WAS THIS NORMAL?
IT WAS NOT UNCOMMON.
THESE PILOTS KNEW AND RESPECTED THEIR OPPONENTS.
THEY KNEW THE ENEMY PILOTS WERE PLAYING THE SAME HIGH-STAKES GAME.
WHEN A FELLOW PILOT CRASHED AND SURVIVED, IT WAS SEEN AS SOMETHING TO CELEBRATE.

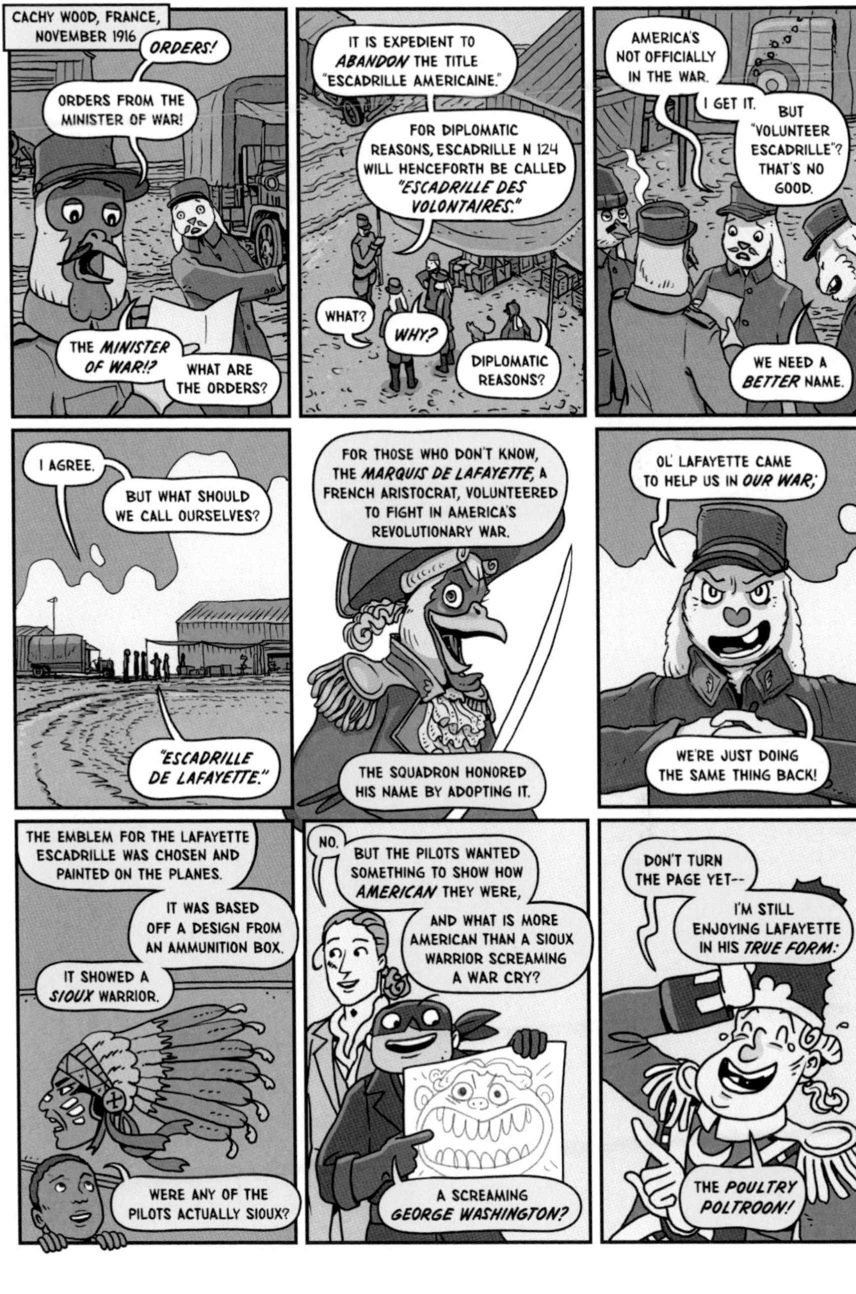

CACHY WOOD, FRANCE, NOVEMBER 1916
ORDERS!
ORDERS FROM THE MINISTER OF WAR!
THE MINISTER OF WAR!?
WHAT ARE THE ORDERS?
IT IS EXPEDIENT TO ABANDON THE TITLE "ESCADRILLE AMERICAINE."
FOR DIPLOMATIC REASONS, ESCADRILLE N 124 WILL HENCEFORTH BE CALLED "ESCADRILLE DES VOLONTAIRES."
WHAT?
WHY?
DIPLOMATIC REASONS?
AMERICA'S NOT OFFICIALLY IN THE WAR.
I GET IT.
BUT "VOLUNTEER ESCADRILLE"? THAT'S NO GOOD.
WE NEED A BETTER NAME.
I AGREE.
BUT WHAT SHOULD WE CALL OURSELVES?
"ESCADRILLE DE LAFAYETTE."
FOR THOSE WHO DON'T KNOW, THE MARQUIS DE LAFAYETTE, A FRENCH ARISTOCRAT, VOLUNTEERED TO FIGHT IN AMERICA'S REVOLUTIONARY WAR.
THE SQUADRON HONORED HIS NAME BY ADOPTING IT.
OL' LAFAYETTE CAME TO HELP US IN OUR WAR;
WE'RE JUST DOING THE SAME THING BACK!
THE EMBLEM FOR THE LAFAYETTE ESCADRILLE WAS CHOSEN AND PAINTED ON THE PLANES.
IT WAS BASED OFF A DESIGN FROM AN AMMUNITION BOX.
IT SHOWED A SIOUX WARRIOR.
WERE ANY OF THE PILOTS ACTUALLY SIOUX?
NO.
BUT THE PILOTS WANTED SOMETHING TO SHOW HOW AMERICAN THEY WERE,
AND WHAT IS MORE AMERICAN THAN A SIOUX WARRIOR SCREAMING A WAR CRY?
A SCREAMING GEORGE WASHINGTON?
DON'T TURN THE PAGE YET--
I'M STILL ENJOYING LAFAYETTE IN HIS TRUE FORM:
THE POULTRY POLTROON!

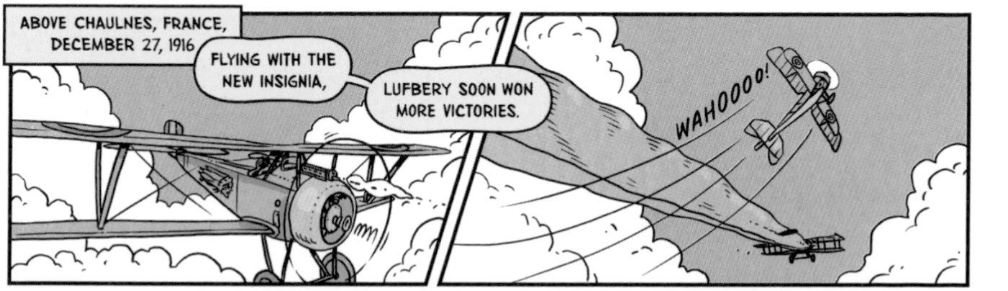
ABOVE CHAULNES, FRANCE, DECEMBER 27, 1916
FLYING WITH THE NEW INSIGNIA,
LUFBERY SOON WON MORE VICTORIES.
WAHOOOO!

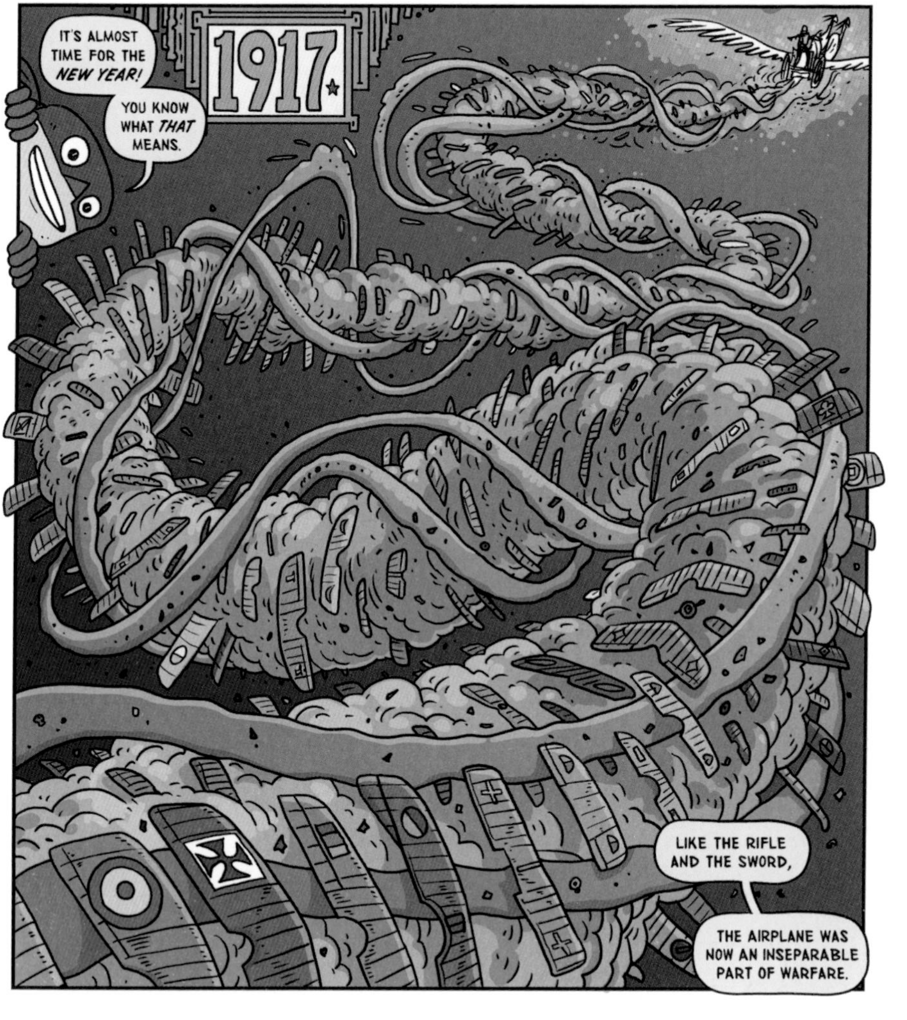
IT'S ALMOST TIME FOR THE NEW YEAR!
YOU KNOW WHAT THAT MEANS.
1917
LIKE THE RIFLE AND THE SWORD,
THE AIRPLANE WAS NOW AN INSEPARABLE PART OF WARFARE.

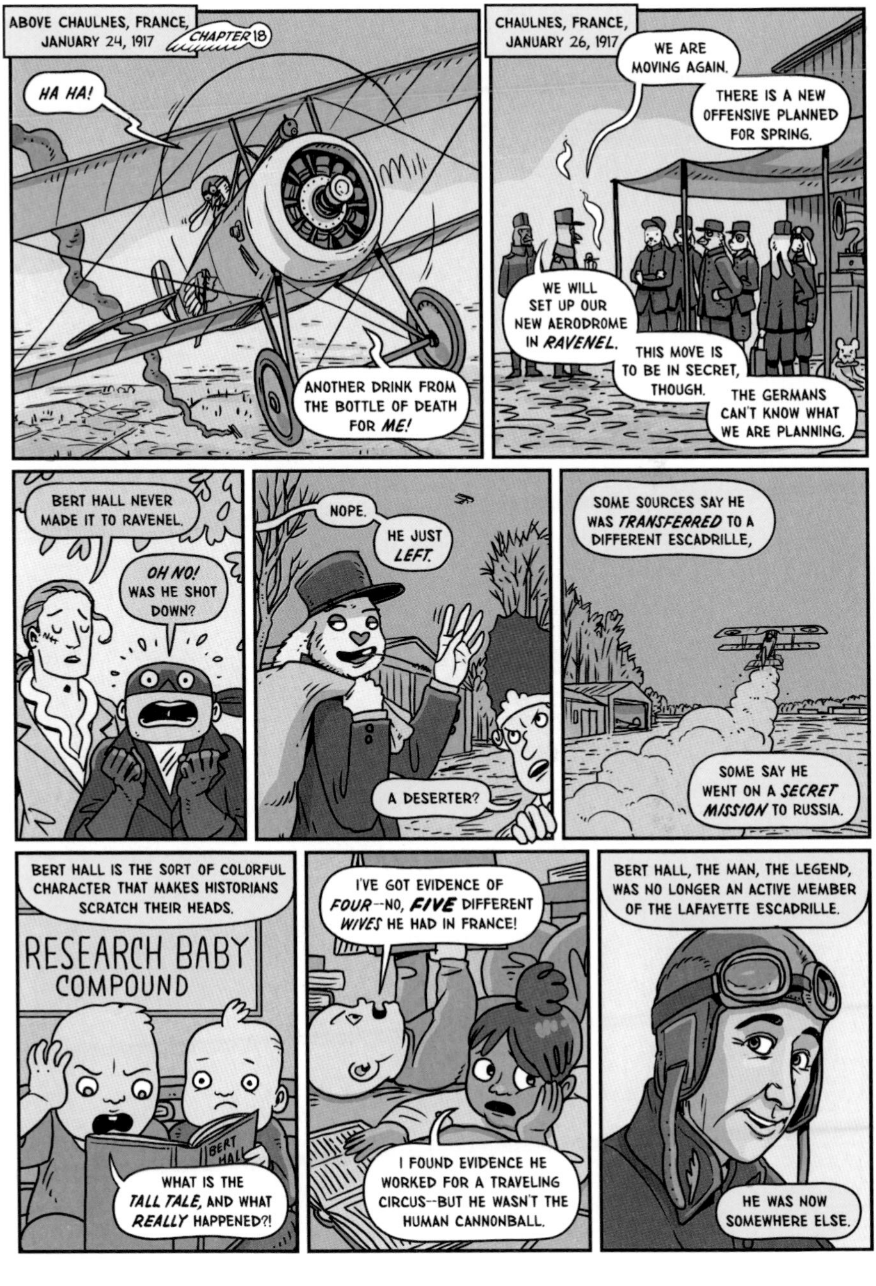

ABOVE CHAULNES, FRANCE, JANUARY 24, 1917
CHAPTER 18
HA HA!
ANOTHER DRINK FROM THE BOTTLE OF DEATH FOR *ME!*
CHAULNES, FRANCE, JANUARY 26, 1917
WE ARE MOVING AGAIN.
THERE IS A NEW OFFENSIVE PLANNED FOR SPRING.
WE WILL SET UP OUR NEW AERODROME IN *RAVENEL*.
THIS MOVE IS TO BE IN SECRET, THOUGH.
THE GERMANS CAN'T KNOW WHAT WE ARE PLANNING.
BERT HALL NEVER MADE IT TO RAVENEL.
OH NO! WAS HE SHOT DOWN?
NOPE.
HE JUST *LEFT.*
A DESERTER?
SOME SOURCES SAY HE WAS *TRANSFERRED* TO A DIFFERENT ESCADRILLE,
SOME SAY HE WENT ON A *SECRET MISSION* TO RUSSIA.
BERT HALL IS THE SORT OF COLORFUL CHARACTER THAT MAKES HISTORIANS SCRATCH THEIR HEADS.
RESEARCH BABY COMPOUND
BERT HALL
WHAT IS THE *TALL TALE,* AND WHAT *REALLY* HAPPENED?!
I'VE GOT EVIDENCE OF *FOUR*--NO, ***FIVE*** DIFFERENT *WIVES* HE HAD IN FRANCE!
I FOUND EVIDENCE HE WORKED FOR A TRAVELING CIRCUS--BUT HE WASN'T THE HUMAN CANNONBALL.
BERT HALL, THE MAN, THE LEGEND, WAS NO LONGER AN ACTIVE MEMBER OF THE LAFAYETTE ESCADRILLE.
HE WAS NOW SOMEWHERE ELSE.

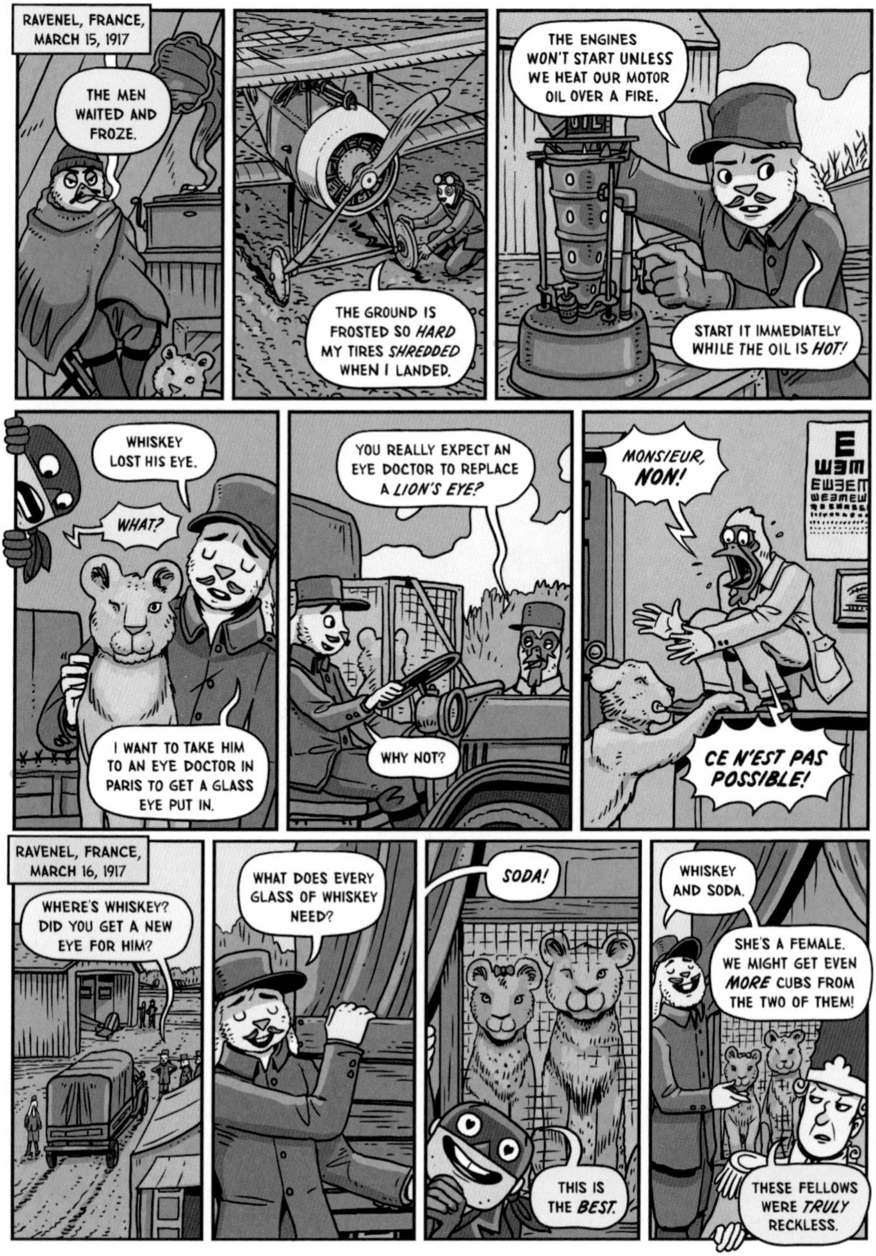
RAVENEL, FRANCE, MARCH 15, 1917
THE MEN WAITED AND FROZE.
THE GROUND IS FROSTED SO *HARD* MY TIRES *SHREDDED* WHEN I LANDED.
THE ENGINES WON'T START UNLESS WE HEAT OUR MOTOR OIL OVER A FIRE.
OIL
START IT IMMEDIATELY WHILE THE OIL IS *HOT!*
WHISKEY LOST HIS EYE.
WHAT?
I WANT TO TAKE HIM TO AN EYE DOCTOR IN PARIS TO GET A GLASS EYE PUT IN.
YOU REALLY EXPECT AN EYE DOCTOR TO REPLACE A *LION'S EYE?*
WHY NOT?
MONSIEUR, NON!
CE N'EST PAS POSSIBLE!
RAVENEL, FRANCE, MARCH 16, 1917
WHERE'S WHISKEY? DID YOU GET A NEW EYE FOR HIM?
WHAT DOES EVERY GLASS OF WHISKEY NEED?
SODA!
THIS IS THE *BEST.*
WHISKEY AND SODA.
SHE'S A FEMALE. WE MIGHT GET EVEN *MORE* CUBS FROM THE TWO OF THEM!
THESE FELLOWS WERE *TRULY* RECKLESS.

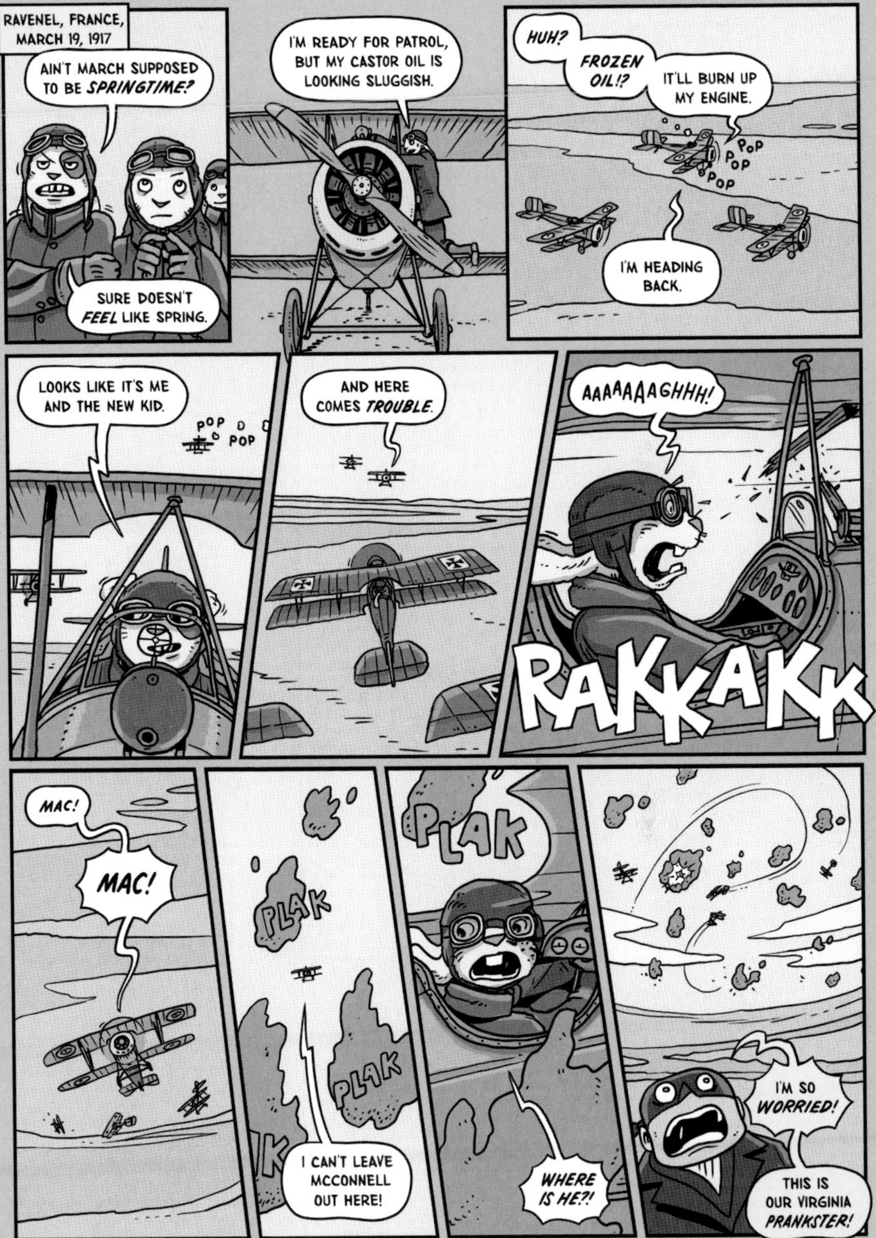
RAVENEL, FRANCE, MARCH 19, 1917
AIN'T MARCH SUPPOSED TO BE SPRINGTIME?
SURE DOESN'T FEEL LIKE SPRING.
I'M READY FOR PATROL, BUT MY CASTOR OIL IS LOOKING SLUGGISH.
HUH?
FROZEN OIL!?
IT'LL BURN UP MY ENGINE.
POP POP POP
I'M HEADING BACK.
LOOKS LIKE IT'S ME AND THE NEW KID.
POP POP
AND HERE COMES TROUBLE.
AAAAAAAGHHH!
RAKKAKK
MAC!
MAC!
PLAK
PLAK
I CAN'T LEAVE MCCONNELL OUT HERE!
PLAK
WHERE IS HE?!
I'M SO WORRIED!
THIS IS OUR VIRGINIA PRANKSTER!

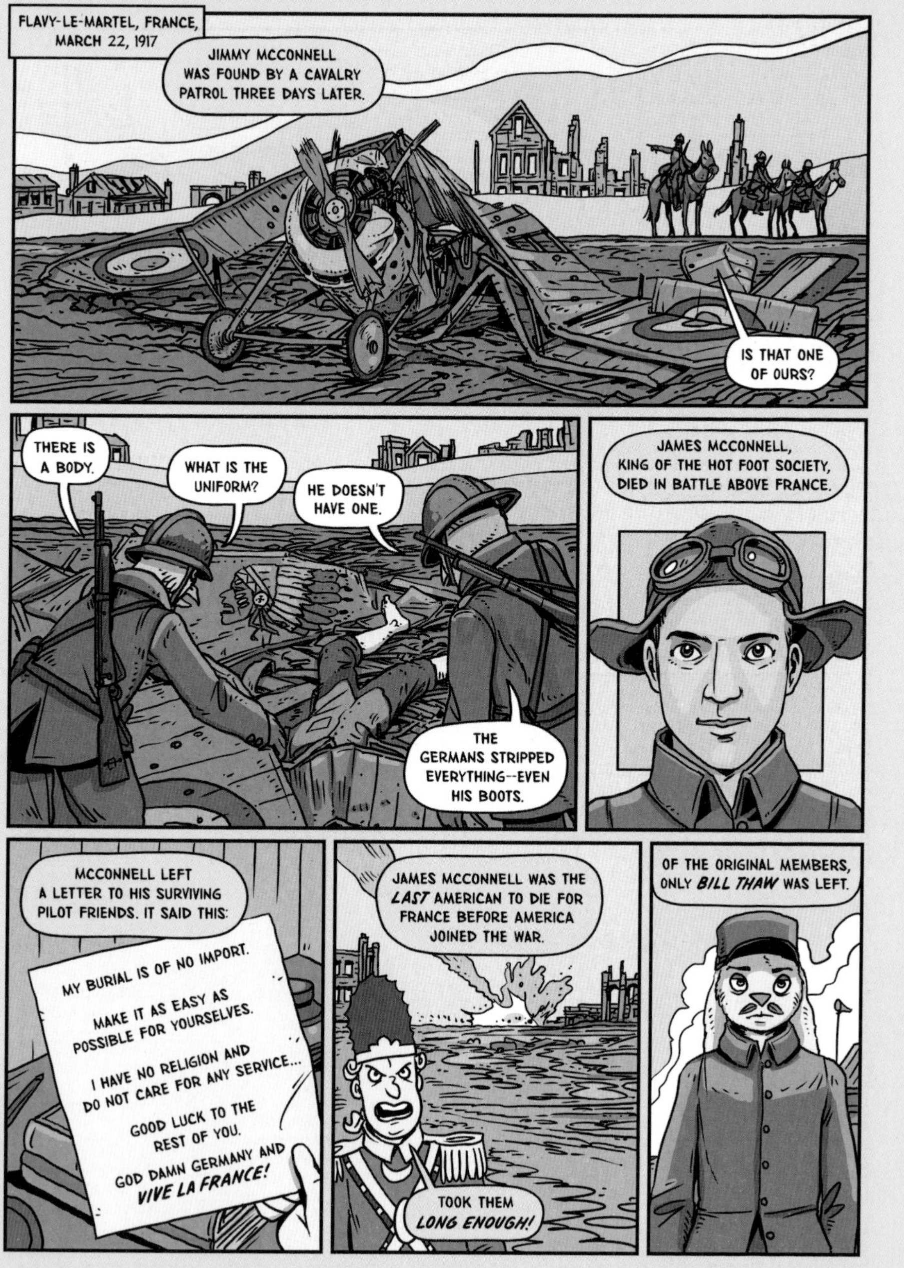
FLAVY-LE-MARTEL, FRANCE, MARCH 22, 1917
JIMMY MCCONNELL WAS FOUND BY A CAVALRY PATROL THREE DAYS LATER.
IS THAT ONE OF OURS?
THERE IS A BODY.
WHAT IS THE UNIFORM?
HE DOESN'T HAVE ONE.
THE GERMANS STRIPPED EVERYTHING--EVEN HIS BOOTS.
JAMES MCCONNELL, KING OF THE HOT FOOT SOCIETY, DIED IN BATTLE ABOVE FRANCE.
MCCONNELL LEFT A LETTER TO HIS SURVIVING PILOT FRIENDS. IT SAID THIS:
MY BURIAL IS OF NO IMPORT.
MAKE IT AS EASY AS POSSIBLE FOR YOURSELVES.
I HAVE NO RELIGION AND DO NOT CARE FOR ANY SERVICE...
GOOD LUCK TO THE REST OF YOU.
GOD DAMN GERMANY AND *VIVE LA FRANCE!*
JAMES MCCONNELL WAS THE *LAST* AMERICAN TO DIE FOR FRANCE BEFORE AMERICA JOINED THE WAR.
TOOK THEM *LONG ENOUGH!*
OF THE ORIGINAL MEMBERS, ONLY *BILL THAW* WAS LEFT.

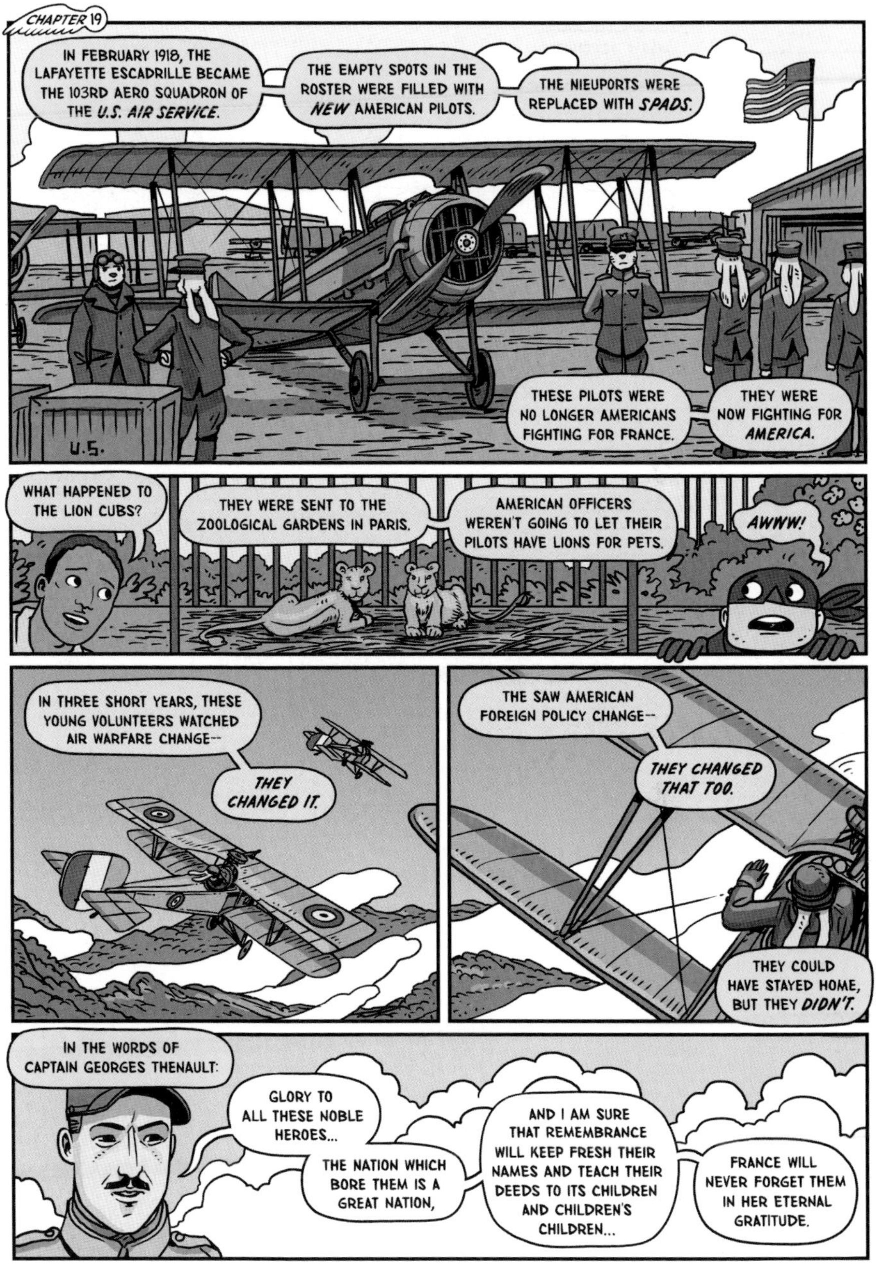

CHAPTER 19
IN FEBRUARY 1918, THE LAFAYETTE ESCADRILLE BECAME THE 103RD AERO SQUADRON OF THE U.S. AIR SERVICE.
THE EMPTY SPOTS IN THE ROSTER WERE FILLED WITH NEW AMERICAN PILOTS.
THE NIEUPORTS WERE REPLACED WITH SPADS.
U.S.
THESE PILOTS WERE NO LONGER AMERICANS FIGHTING FOR FRANCE.
THEY WERE NOW FIGHTING FOR AMERICA.
WHAT HAPPENED TO THE LION CUBS?
THEY WERE SENT TO THE ZOOLOGICAL GARDENS IN PARIS.
AMERICAN OFFICERS WEREN'T GOING TO LET THEIR PILOTS HAVE LIONS FOR PETS.
AWWW!
IN THREE SHORT YEARS, THESE YOUNG VOLUNTEERS WATCHED AIR WARFARE CHANGE--
THEY CHANGED IT.
THE SAW AMERICAN FOREIGN POLICY CHANGE--
THEY CHANGED THAT TOO.
THEY COULD HAVE STAYED HOME, BUT THEY DIDN'T.
IN THE WORDS OF CAPTAIN GEORGES THENAULT:
GLORY TO ALL THESE NOBLE HEROES...
THE NATION WHICH BORE THEM IS A GREAT NATION,
AND I AM SURE THAT REMEMBRANCE WILL KEEP FRESH THEIR NAMES AND TEACH THEIR DEEDS TO ITS CHILDREN AND CHILDREN'S CHILDREN...
FRANCE WILL NEVER FORGET THEM IN HER ETERNAL GRATITUDE.

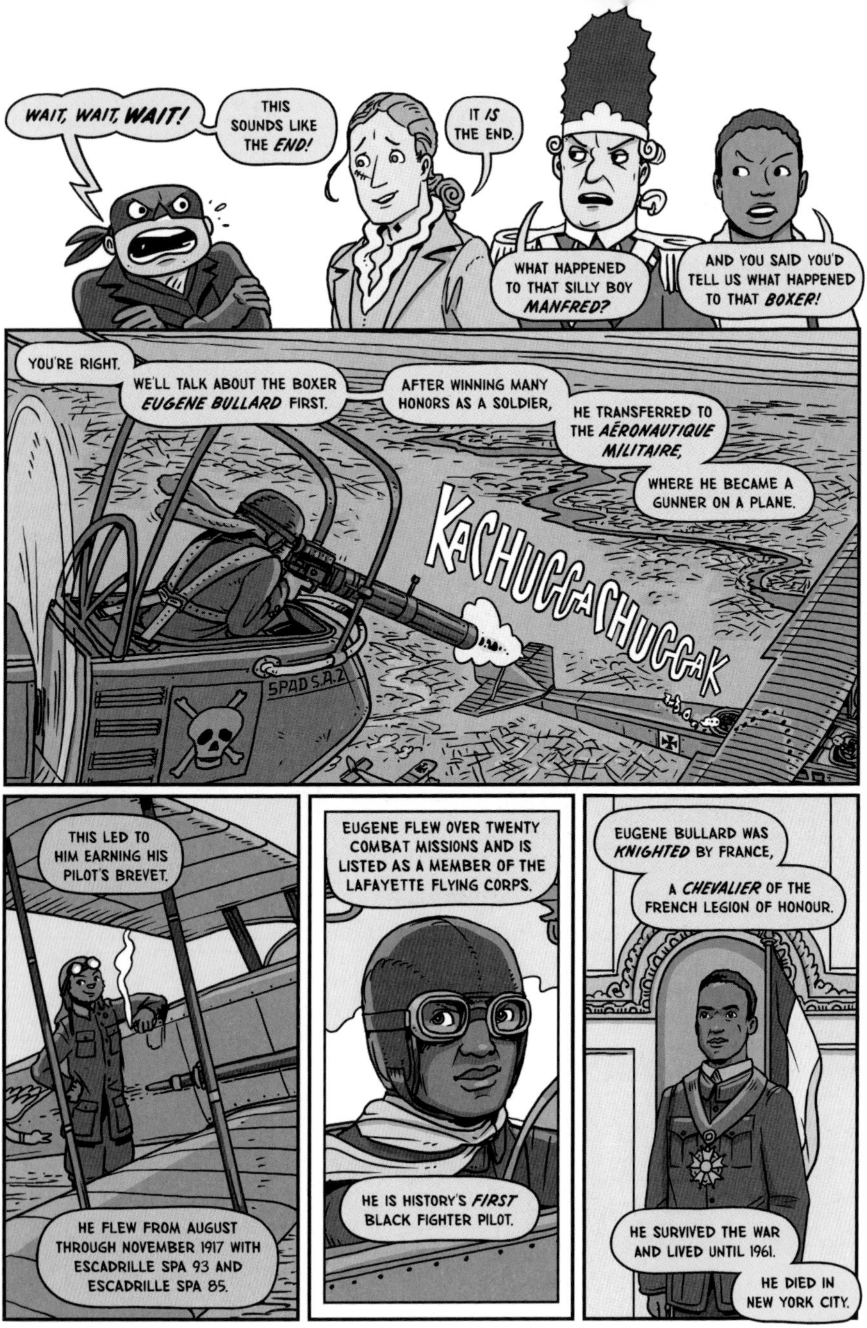
WAIT, WAIT, WAIT!
THIS SOUNDS LIKE THE END!
IT IS THE END.
WHAT HAPPENED TO THAT SILLY BOY MANFRED?
AND YOU SAID YOU'D TELL US WHAT HAPPENED TO THAT BOXER!
YOU'RE RIGHT.
WE'LL TALK ABOUT THE BOXER EUGENE BULLARD FIRST.
AFTER WINNING MANY HONORS AS A SOLDIER,
HE TRANSFERRED TO THE AÉRONAUTIQUE MILITAIRE,
WHERE HE BECAME A GUNNER ON A PLANE.
KACHUCCACHUCCACHUCCAK
SPAD S.A.2
THIS LED TO HIM EARNING HIS PILOT'S BREVET.
HE FLEW FROM AUGUST THROUGH NOVEMBER 1917 WITH ESCADRILLE SPA 93 AND ESCADRILLE SPA 85.
EUGENE FLEW OVER TWENTY COMBAT MISSIONS AND IS LISTED AS A MEMBER OF THE LAFAYETTE FLYING CORPS.
HE IS HISTORY'S FIRST BLACK FIGHTER PILOT.
EUGENE BULLARD WAS KNIGHTED BY FRANCE,
A CHEVALIER OF THE FRENCH LEGION OF HONOUR.
HE SURVIVED THE WAR AND LIVED UNTIL 1961.
HE DIED IN NEW YORK CITY.

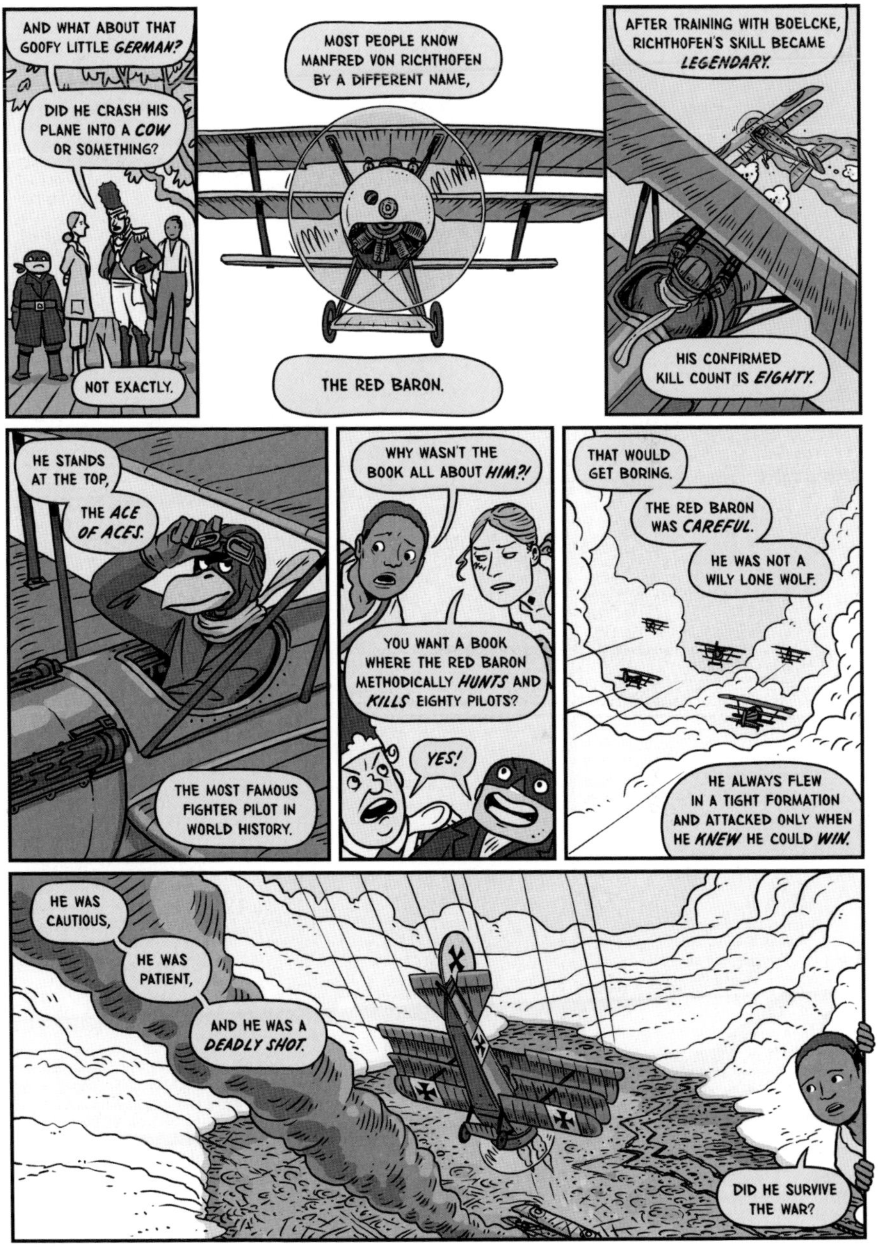

AND WHAT ABOUT THAT GOOFY LITTLE GERMAN?
DID HE CRASH HIS PLANE INTO A COW OR SOMETHING?
NOT EXACTLY.
MOST PEOPLE KNOW MANFRED VON RICHTHOFEN BY A DIFFERENT NAME,
THE RED BARON.
AFTER TRAINING WITH BOELCKE, RICHTHOFEN'S SKILL BECAME LEGENDARY.
HIS CONFIRMED KILL COUNT IS EIGHTY.
HE STANDS AT THE TOP,
THE ACE OF ACES.
THE MOST FAMOUS FIGHTER PILOT IN WORLD HISTORY.
WHY WASN'T THE BOOK ALL ABOUT HIM?!
YOU WANT A BOOK WHERE THE RED BARON METHODICALLY HUNTS AND KILLS EIGHTY PILOTS?
YES!
THAT WOULD GET BORING.
THE RED BARON WAS CAREFUL.
HE WAS NOT A WILY LONE WOLF.
HE ALWAYS FLEW IN A TIGHT FORMATION AND ATTACKED ONLY WHEN HE KNEW HE COULD WIN.
HE WAS CAUTIOUS,
HE WAS PATIENT,
AND HE WAS A DEADLY SHOT.
DID HE SURVIVE THE WAR?

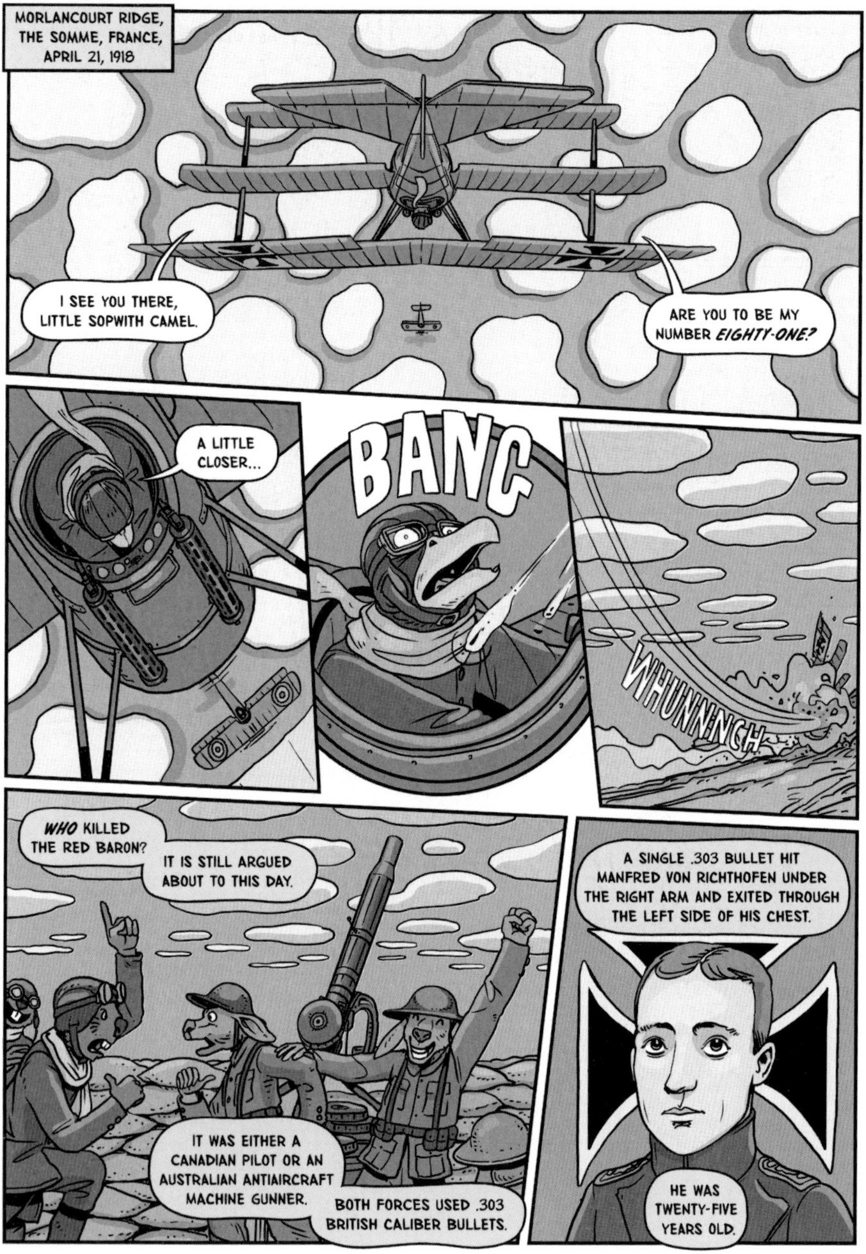
MORLANCOURT RIDGE, THE SOMME, FRANCE, APRIL 21, 1918
I SEE YOU THERE, LITTLE SOPWITH CAMEL.
ARE YOU TO BE MY NUMBER *EIGHTY-ONE?*
A LITTLE CLOSER...
BANG
WHUNNNCH
WHO KILLED THE RED BARON?
IT IS STILL ARGUED ABOUT TO THIS DAY.
IT WAS EITHER A CANADIAN PILOT OR AN AUSTRALIAN ANTIAIRCRAFT MACHINE GUNNER.
BOTH FORCES USED .303 BRITISH CALIBER BULLETS.
A SINGLE .303 BULLET HIT MANFRED VON RICHTHOFEN UNDER THE RIGHT ARM AND EXITED THROUGH THE LEFT SIDE OF HIS CHEST.
HE WAS TWENTY-FIVE YEARS OLD.

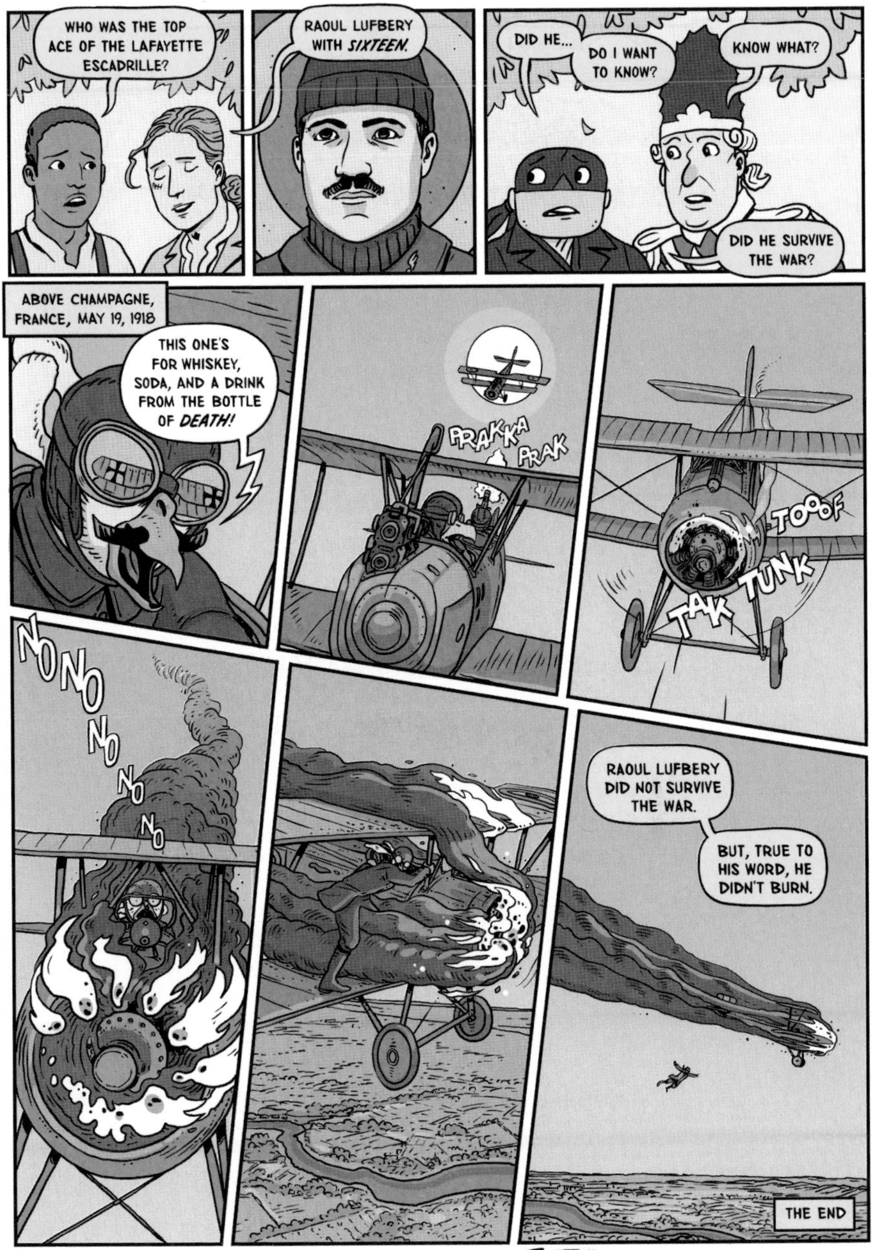
WHO WAS THE TOP ACE OF THE LAFAYETTE ESCADRILLE?
RAOUL LUFBERY WITH *SIXTEEN.*
DID HE...
DO I WANT TO KNOW?
KNOW WHAT?
DID HE SURVIVE THE WAR?
ABOVE CHAMPAGNE, FRANCE, MAY 19, 1918
THIS ONE'S FOR WHISKEY, SODA, AND A DRINK FROM THE BOTTLE OF *DEATH!*
PRAKKA PRAK
TOOOF
TUNK
TAK
NO NO NO NO NO NO NO
RAOUL LUFBERY DID NOT SURVIVE THE WAR.
BUT, TRUE TO HIS WORD, HE DIDN'T BURN.
THE END

I Have a Rendezvous with Death
By Alan Seeger

I have a rendezvous with Death
At some disputed barricade,
When Spring comes back with rustling shade
And apple-blossoms fill the air—
I have a rendezvous with Death
When Spring brings back blue days and fair.

It may be he shall take my hand
And lead me into his dark land
And close my eyes and quench my breath—
It may be I shall pass him still.
I have a rendezvous with Death
On some scarred slope of battered hill,
When Spring comes round again this year
And the first meadow-flowers appear.

God knows 'twere better to be deep
Pillowed in silk and scented down,
Where Love throbs out in blissful sleep,
Pulse nigh to pulse, and breath to breath,
Where hushed awakenings are dear ...
But I've a rendezvous with Death
At midnight in some flaming town,
When Spring trips north again this year,
And I to my pledged word am true,
I shall not fail that rendezvous.

WINGED AVIATOR

THIS SCULPTURE WAS INSPIRED BY
JAMES MCCONNELL. IT STANDS TODAY
AT THE UNIVERSITY OF VIRGINIA, WHERE
JAMES PLAYED HIS STATUE PRANK.

THE SCULPTOR IS
GUTZON BORGLUM, THE SAME
ARTIST WHO SCULPTED THE
FACES ON MOUNT RUSHMORE.

PHOTO BY NATHAN HALE

THE TOP ACES OF WORLD WAR ONE, 1914-1918 · *KIA--KILLED IN ACTION

CONFIRMED KILLS	NAME	NATIONALITY		CONFIRMED KILLS	NAME	NATIONALITY
80	MANFRED VON RICHTHOFEN	GERMAN EMPIRE KIA		36	JOSEPH STEWART TEMPLE FALL	CANADA
75	RENÉ FONCK	FRANCE		36	MAX RITTER VON MÜLLER	GERMAN EMPIRE KIA
72	BILLY BISHOP	CANADA		35	MAURICE BOYAU	FRANCE KIA
62	ERNST UDET	GERMAN EMPIRE		35	GODWIN VON BRUMOWSKI	AUSTRIA-HUNGARY
61	MICK MANNOCK	UNITED KINGDOM KIA		35	GUSTAV DÖRR	GERMAN EMPIRE
60	RAYMOND COLLISHAW	CANADA		35	OTTO KÖNNECKE	GERMAN EMPIRE
57	JAMES MCCUDDEN	UNITED KINGDOM KIA		35	FREDERICK MCCALL	CANADA
54	ANDREW BEAUCHAMP-PROCTOR	SOUTH AFRICA		35	EDUARD RITTER VON SCHLEICH	GERMAN EMPIRE
54	ERICH LOEWENHARDT	GERMAN EMPIRE KIA		35	EMIL THUY	GERMAN EMPIRE
54	DONALD MACLAREN	CANADA		35	JOSEF VELTJENS	GERMAN EMPIRE
53	GEORGES-MARIE GUYNEMER	FRANCE KIA		35	HENRY WINSLOW WOOLLETT	UNITED KINGDOM
50	WILLIAM GEORGE BARKER	CANADA		34	FRANCESCO BARACCA	ITALY KIA
48	JOSEF JACOBS	GERMAN EMPIRE		34	MICHEL COIFFARD	FRANCE KIA
48	WERNER VOSS	GERMAN EMPIRE KIA		33	HEINRICH BONGARTZ	GERMAN EMPIRE
47	ROBERT A. LITTLE	AUSTRALIA KIA		33	HEINRICH KROLL	GERMAN EMPIRE
47	GEORGE MCELROY	UNITED KINGDOM KIA		33	FRANK GRANGER QUIGLEY	CANADA KIA
45	FRITZ RUMEY	GERMAN EMPIRE KIA		33	KURT WOLFF	GERMAN EMPIRE KIA
44	ALBERT BALL	UNITED KINGDOM KIA		32	JULIUS ARIGI	AUSTRIA-HUNGARY
44	RUDOLF BERTHOLD	GERMAN EMPIRE		32	GEOFFREY HILTON BOWMAN	UNITED KINGDOM
44	BRUNO LOERZER	GERMAN EMPIRE		32	HERMANN FROMMHERZ	GERMAN EMPIRE
43	PAUL BÄUMER	GERMAN EMPIRE		32	SAMUEL KINKEAD	SOUTH AFRICA
43	TOM F. HAZELL	UNITED KINGDOM		32	THEODOR OSTERKAMP	GERMAN EMPIRE
43	CHARLES NUNGESSER	FRANCE		31	PAUL BILLIK	GERMAN EMPIRE
41	GEORGES MADON	FRANCE		31	ANDREW EDWARD MCKEEVER	CANADA
40	OSWALD BOELCKE	GERMAN EMPIRE KIA		31	GOTTHARD SACHSENBERG	GERMAN EMPIRE
40	FRANZ BÜCHNER	GERMAN EMPIRE		30	KARL ALLMENRÖDER	GERMAN EMPIRE KIA
40	PHILIP F. FULLARD	UNITED KINGDOM		30	CARL DEGELOW	GERMAN EMPIRE
40	LOTHAR VON RICHTHOFEN	GERMAN EMPIRE		30	JOSEF MAI	GERMAN EMPIRE
39	RODERIC DALLAS	AUSTRALIA KIA		30	ULRICH NECKEL	GERMAN EMPIRE
39	CHARLES GEORGE GASS	UNITED KINGDOM		30	KARL EMIL SCHÄFER	GERMAN EMPIRE KIA
39	JOHN INGLIS GILMOUR	UNITED KINGDOM		30	SAMUEL F. H. THOMPSON	UNITED KINGDOM KIA
39	HEINRICH GONTERMANN	GERMAN EMPIRE KIA		29	HARALD AUFFARTH	GERMAN EMPIRE
39	WILLIAM LANCELOT JORDAN	SOUTH AFRICA		29	CHARLES DAWSON BOOKER	UNITED KINGDOM KIA
39	CARL MENCKHOFF	GERMAN EMPIRE		29	PERCY JACK CLAYSON	UNITED KINGDOM
38	ALFRED ATKEY	CANADA		29	HARRY COBBY	AUSTRALIA
37	WILLIAM GORDON CLAXTON	CANADA		29	LEONARD HENRY ROCHFORD	UNITED KINGDOM
37	WILLY COPPENS	BELGIUM		28	WALTER BLUME	GERMAN EMPIRE
37	JAMES IRA THOMAS JONES	UNITED KINGDOM		28	LÉON BOURJADE	FRANCE
36	CARL BOLLE	GERMAN EMPIRE		28	WALTER VON BLOW-BOTHKAMP	GERMAN EMPIRE KIA
36	JULIUS BUCKLER	GERMAN EMPIRE		28	ALBERT DESBRISAY CARTER	CANADA KIA

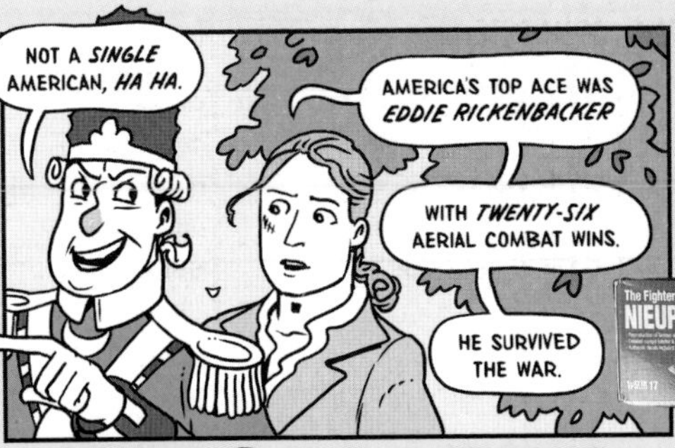
NOT A *SINGLE* AMERICAN, *HA HA.*
AMERICA'S TOP ACE WAS *EDDIE RICKENBACKER*
WITH *TWENTY-SIX* AERIAL COMBAT WINS.
HE SURVIVED THE WAR.

BIBLIOGRAPHY→

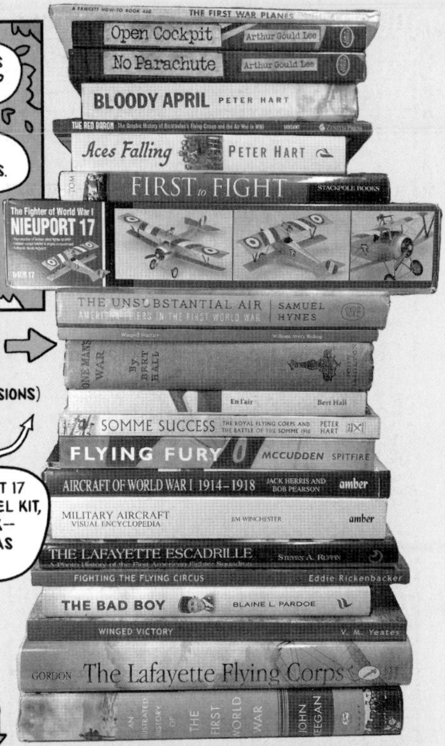
THE FIRST WAR PLANES
Open Cockpit
Arthur Gould Lee
No Parachute
Arthur Gould Lee
BLOODY APRIL
PETER HART
THE RED BARON
Aces Falling
PETER HART
FIRST to FIGHT
STACKPOLE BOOKS
The Fighter of World War I
NIEUPORT 17
THE UNSUBSTANTIAL AIR
AMERICAN FLIERS IN THE FIRST WORLD WAR
SAMUEL HYNES
Winged Warfare
William Avery Bishop
ONE MAN'S WAR
By BERT HALL
En l'air
Bert Hall
SOMME SUCCESS
THE ROYAL FLYING CORPS AND THE BATTLE OF THE SOMME 1916
PETER HART
FLYING FURY
MCCUDDEN
SPITFIRE
AIRCRAFT OF WORLD WAR I 1914–1918
JACK HERRIS AND BOB PEARSON
amber
MILITARY AIRCRAFT
VISUAL ENCYCLOPEDIA
JIM WINCHESTER
amber
THE LAFAYETTE ESCADRILLE
STEVEN A. RUFFIN
FIGHTING THE FLYING CIRCUS
Eddie Rickenbacker
THE BAD BOY
BLAINE L. PARDOE
WINGED VICTORY
V. M. Yeates
GORDON
The Lafayette Flying Corps
AN ILLUSTRATED HISTORY OF THE FIRST WORLD WAR
JOHN KEEGAN

MISSING FROM PHOTO: (LOST WHILE TRAVELING/DIGITAL VERSIONS)

THE RED BARON BY MANFRED VON RICHTOFEN, ORIGINALLY PUBLISHED IN 1918

THE STORY OF THE LAFAYETTE ESCADRILLE: TOLD BY ITS COMMANDER BY GEORGES THENAULT ORIGINALLY PUBLISHED IN 1921

I FLEW WITH THE LAFAYETTE ESCADRILLE BY EDWIN C. PARSONS ORIGINALLY PUBLISHED IN 1937

MARKED FOR DEATH: THE FIRST WAR IN THE AIR BY JAMES-HAMILTON PATERSON PEGASUS BOOKS, 2016

THE NIEUPORT 17 BOX IS A MODEL KIT, NOT A BOOK-- BUT JUST AS USEFUL!

author photo

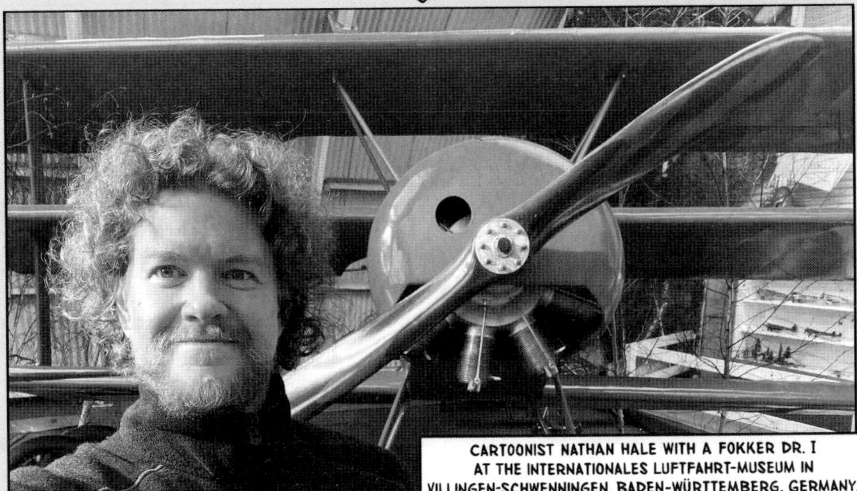

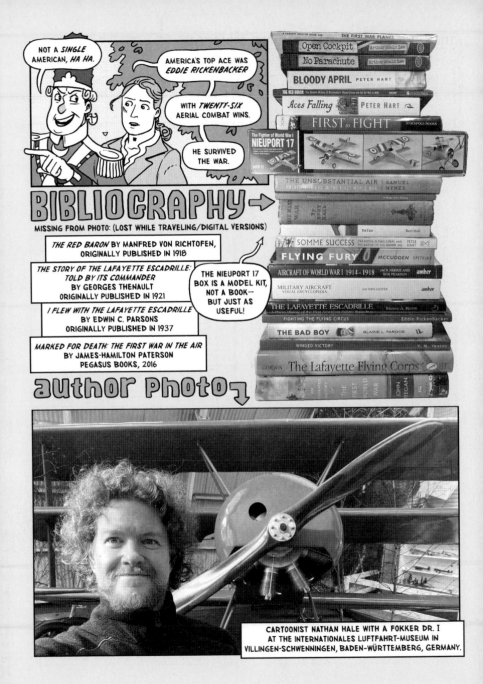

CARTOONIST NATHAN HALE WITH A FOKKER DR. I AT THE INTERNATIONALES LUFTFAHRT-MUSEUM IN VILLINGEN-SCHWENNINGEN, BADEN-WÜRTTEMBERG, GERMANY.

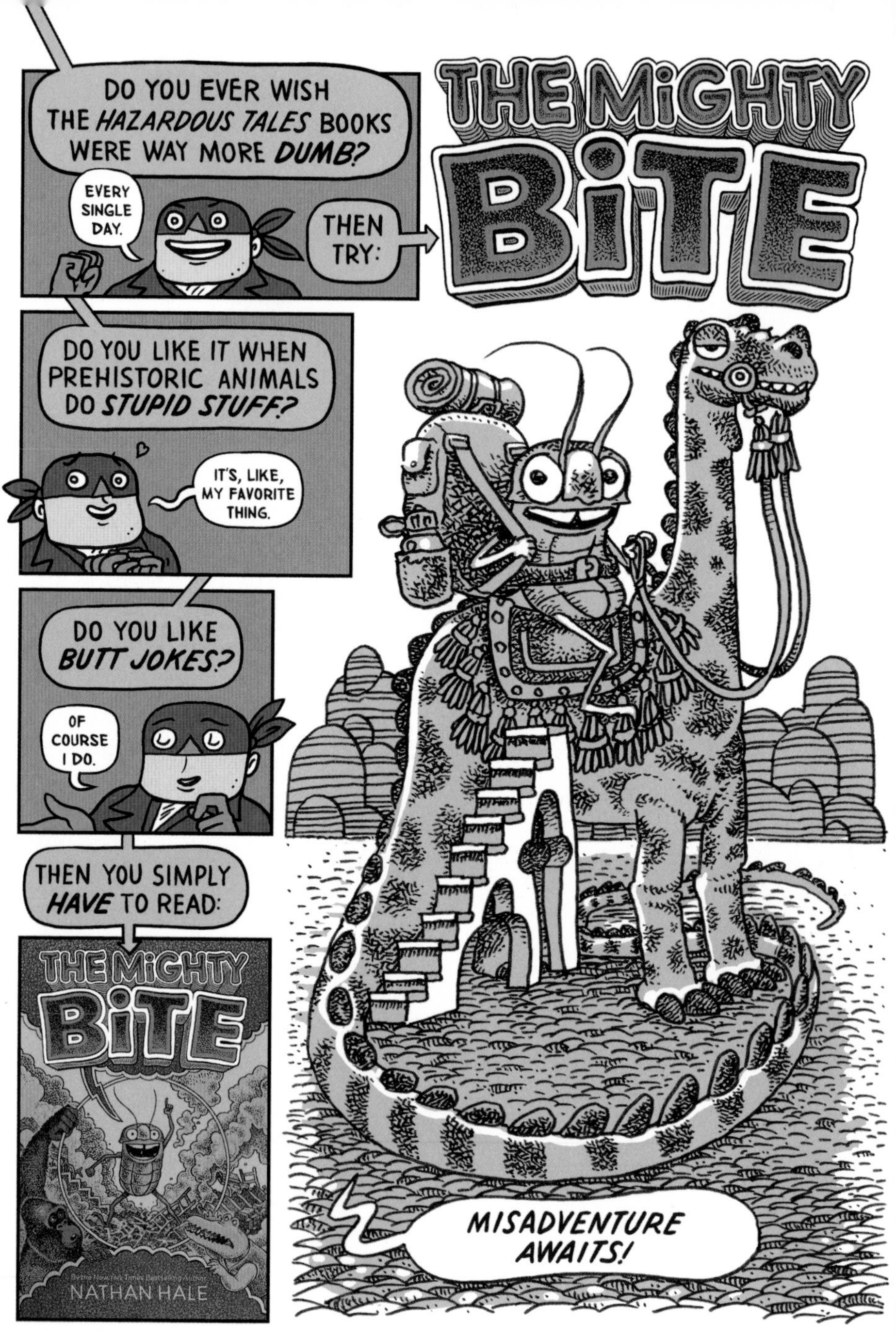
DO YOU EVER WISH THE *HAZARDOUS TALES* BOOKS WERE WAY MORE *DUMB?*
EVERY SINGLE DAY.
THEN TRY:
THE MiGHTY BiTE
DO YOU LIKE IT WHEN PREHISTORIC ANIMALS DO *STUPID STUFF?*
IT'S, LIKE, MY FAVORITE THING.
DO YOU LIKE *BUTT JOKES?*
OF COURSE I DO.
THEN YOU SIMPLY *HAVE* TO READ:
THE MiGHTY BiTE
NATHAN HALE
MISADVENTURE AWAITS!

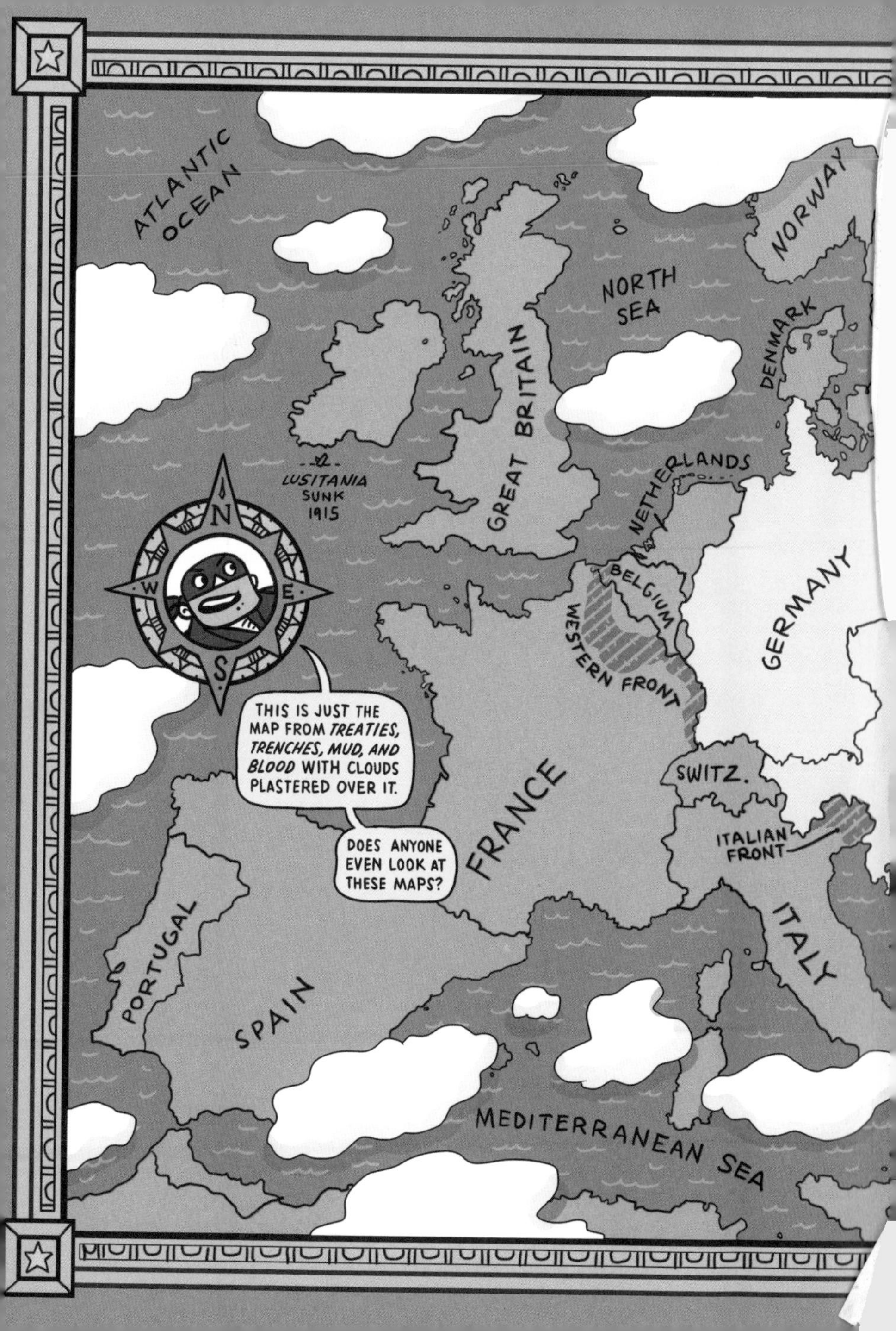
ATLANTIC OCEAN
NORWAY
NORTH SEA
DENMARK
GREAT BRITAIN
NETHERLANDS
LUSITANIA SUNK 1915
N
W
E
S
BELGIUM
WESTERN FRONT
GERMANY
THIS IS JUST THE MAP FROM *TREATIES, TRENCHES, MUD, AND BLOOD* WITH CLOUDS PLASTERED OVER IT.
DOES ANYONE EVEN LOOK AT THESE MAPS?
SWITZ.
FRANCE
ITALIAN FRONT
PORTUGAL
SPAIN
ITALY
MEDITERRANEAN SEA